A
SHERLOCK
HOLMES
HANDBOOK

A
SHERLOCK
HOLMES
HANDBOOK

CHRISTOPHER REDMOND

Simon & Pierre
Toronto, Canada

The writing of this manuscript and the publication of this book were made possible by support from several sources. We would like to acknowledge the generous assistance and ongoing support of **The Canada Council, The Book Publishing Industry Development Program** of the **Department of Communications, The Ontario Arts Council,** and **The Ontario Publishing Centre** of the **Ministry of Culture, Tourism and Recreation**.

Kirk Howard, President; Marian M. Wilson, Publisher

ISBN 0-88924-246-1
1 2 3 4 5 • 8 7 6 5 4
Simon & Pierre Publishing Co. Ltd., a subsidiary of Dundurn Press

Canadian Cataloguing in Publication Data

Redmond, Chris
    A Sherlock Holmes handbook

    Includes index.
    ISBN 0-88924-246-1
    1. Holmes, Sherlock (Fictitious character).
    2. Doyle, Arthur Conan, Sir, 1859-1930 - Characters -
    Sherlock Holmes. 3. England - Social life and
    customs - 19th century. 4. England - Social life and
    customs - 20th century. I. Title.

    PR4624.R44 1993   823'.8   C93-094437-2

Editor: Doris Cowan
Printed and bound in Canada by Best Gagné Book Manufacturers, Louiseville, Quebec, Canada

Order from Simon & Pierre Publishing Co. Ltd., care of

Dundurn Press Limited	**Dundurn Distribution**	**Dundurn Press Limited**
2181 Queen Street East	73 Lime Walk	1823 Maryland Avenue
Suite 301	Headington, Oxford	P.O. Box 1000
Toronto, Canada	England	Niagara Falls, N.Y.
M4E 1E5	0X3 7AD	U.S.A. 14302-1000

Contents

ILLUSTRATIONS

Introduction

Hardly a village library anywhere is without some volume of Sherlock Holmes. Hardly a cartoon or show business figure has never dressed up in "deerstalker" hat and magnifying glass to communicate instantly to a universal audience that here is the great detective, known to North American toddlers as "Sherlock Hemlock" and to late-night movie watchers as the hyperactive, overcoated Basil Rathbone. If the creator of Holmes, Arthur Conan Doyle, was once identified as "the best-known living Englishman", Sherlock Holmes has a claim to be the best-known Englishman who never — quite — lived.

Everyone who is literate knows Sherlock Holmes vaguely, and may some day wish to know more. A few enthusiasts already know far, far more, to the point that they exchange trivia at the regular meetings of Sherlock Holmes societies from Tokyo to Toronto. This book is intended for both kinds of people. For the enthusiasts, the Sherlockians, it may serve as a key to larger libraries, including their own shelves as well as to the largest imaginable library of Sherlockiana. It has been designed, too, as a ready reference for information currently scattered in often inaccessible places in the great Sherlockian literature. I hope it will stand beside the chief existing reference works for Sherlockians — Tracy's *Encyclopaedia Sherlockiana*, the DeWaal bibliographies, the Gibson and Green *Bibliography of Arthur Conan Doyle*, William D. Goodrich's *Good Old Index*, and the valuable though flawed *Annotated Sherlock Holmes*. For general readers, it may be of use as a companion to *The Complete Sherlock Holmes*, or to whichever smaller volume of Holmes stories may be at hand. By no means could I imagine including all knowledge about Sherlock Holmes in a single volume, but the essential facts are here, along with generalizations that provide a context for them, and a good many indications about what else has been said or written for those who want to know more. I welcome corrections, comments and suggestions.

I hope the style of these pages makes it clear that I take the stories of Sherlock Holmes seriously, but enjoy them at the same time. It would be a pity not to take them seriously, for they demonstrate such insight, and can teach us so much. It would be a disaster not to enjoy them as four generations have already done. As entertainment they generally speak for themselves, but perhaps this book will be a little help for those who hope to understand a little better the language in which Sherlock Holmes, and Arthur Conan Doyle, make themselves known.

In writing this book I have of course drawn on many sources. At my elbow I have kept the Canon itself, as well as the Goodrich *Index* and the Gibson and Green *Bibliography*. But rarely have I managed to write a paragraph without jumping up to consult some other volume: one of those standard reference works, or perhaps Steinbrunner and Michaels's *The Films of Sherlock Holmes*, Hugh Harrington's privately printed *Canonical Index*, *Bigelow on Holmes*, the indexes to the *Baker Street Journal*, and Bill Rabe's 1962 *Sherlockian Who's Who and What's What*. Practically every other volume on my shelves, I think, was needed at least once during the several months in which I drafted the pages that follow.

In the same way, many individuals have been of great help. Some were asked for information on specific points (and while I cannot provide an exhaustive list, I must certainly acknowledge Cameron Hollyer and Victoria Gill of the Metropolitan Toronto Reference Library). My good friend Barbara Rusch has encouraged me throughout the writing, and was of particular help as I planned, wrote and revised my chapter on the Victorian background. I take pleasure in acknowledging the help of Kate Karlson — once or twice she provided specific suggestions, but more generally she has, during my long friendship with her, contributed enormously to forming my view of the Sherlockian literature and the Sherlockian world, on which this book is based, and developing my knowledge of both. In the same way I am greatly indebted to my father, Donald A. Redmond, whose guidance and companionship have made my Sherlockian work possible. Further, he has read most of this book during its preparation and provided valuable suggestions.

My dear wife, Susan, resolutely resists becoming a Sherlockian (a policy that helps keep me in modest touch with the real world outside my study) but has provided affectionate moral support throughout the writing of these chapters. As I finish them, our Christopher is just reaching the stage of real literacy, with a special enthusiasm for *Nate the Great*. I look forward to the day when he may find this book a tool in truly discovering Sherlock Holmes.

CAR
May 1993

Chapter I

The Canon

The stories of Sherlock Holmes, known as "the Canon" in allusion to a term used by Bible scholars, were written by Arthur Conan Doyle over a period of some forty years, from 1887 to 1927. They include four novels and five volumes of short stories, for a total of sixty tales. According to a report by Charles E. Lauterbach in 1960, the Canon contains a total of 660,382 words.

The sixty stories, and the collections in which they appear, are considered here in "Canonical" order, the order in which they are usually published in collected editions. It corresponds closely, but not exactly, to the order in which they were first published.

A Study in Scarlet

The novel which began Doyle's writings about Sherlock Holmes was published at the end of 1887 as the principal contents of *Beeton's Christmas Annual* for that year, a paperback published by Ward Lock and Co., London. Few copies remain, and *Beeton's* has become the best-known treasure for which Sherlockian collectors long; a copy sold in 1991 for $57,000 and one was offered in 1992 at $125,000. Two facsimile editions have been produced, one in 1960 jointly by the Baker Street Irregulars and the Sherlock Holmes Society of London, one in 1987 by British publisher J. M. Gibson. *A Study in Scarlet* was subsequently published in a trade edition by Ward Lock (1888); the first American edition came from J. B. Lippincott Co. in 1890. Several magazine appearances are also recorded.

Detective stories not having been fully invented in 1887, it is hardly surprising that this first Sherlock Holmes novel does not follow what have come to be the conventions. Indeed, in an early chapter Holmes must virtually explain to Dr. Watson what it is that he does. Watson, as the narrator, devotes the first two chapters to introducing himself and the hero, whom he meets in a memorable scene in the pathology laboratory at "Bart's" (St. Bartholomew's Hospital, London). Only in Chapter III (of fourteen chapters, divided between two Parts) does a murder engage their attention.

The murder is virtually solved by Chapter VII of Part I, which is intriguingly subtitled "Being a Reprint from the Reminiscences of John H. Watson, M.D., Late of the Army Medical Department". The scene changes in Part II, "The Country of the Saints", which is narrated in third person rather than first. The action now takes place on the "great alkali plain" of western America, a region unknown to geography, and in the Mormon settlement at Salt Lake City, Utah. A sweet young romance is interrupted by the lecherous demands of the Mormon establishment, leading to events more characteristic of a western than of a detective tale. There is much about horses, ravines, rifles, and the purity of womanhood. The vicious and colourful behaviour attributed to the Mormons in these chapters is less than historically accurate, as Jack Tracy has concisely shown in *Conan Doyle and the Latter-Day Saints* (1979), but provides splendid motivation for the murder which is finally explained in the last chapter of the book.

The crude dramatics of both Parts echo Doyle's other early novels rather than the more sophisticated Holmes stories he would write later. Similarly, the prominence of the love interest and frontier adventure detract, in a modern reader's mind, from what fails to be a pure detective story, although they will have striking echoes in *The Valley of Fear*, written almost thirty years later. But the introduction of the principal characters (and their delineation in such passages as the famous "Sherlock Holmes — His Limits") are entirely convincing. Watson is shown as a respectable doctor, Holmes as a brilliant, unsystematic, easily bored young man, Lestrade of Scotland Yard as a self-important plodder. And such details as the comic constable John Rance and the moment when Holmes is taken in by an "old woman" show Doyle already in full command of his medium.

The Sign of the Four

J. B. Stoddart of *Lippincott's Magazine*, preparing to launch a British edition of his Philadelphia-based publication, took the young Doyle out for dinner August 30, 1889, along with another young author, Oscar Wilde. Both were commissioned to write novels for *Lippincott's*. Wilde's eventual product was *The Picture of Dorian Gray*, and Doyle's was *The Sign of the Four*, which appeared in British and American editions of the magazine in February 1890. Shortly afterwards it was issued in book form (no. 266 in the "Lippincott's Magazine Series") and that October in an edition from the firm of Spencer Blackett, classified by at least some bibliographers as the true first edition. There were also several newspaper serializations once the three-month exclusive rights purchased by J. B. Lippincott & Co. in England had expired.

In the United States, where Lippincott had rights in perpetuity, offprints from the magazine were also published, but the first identifiable American book edition was also the first in a long string of piracies (that is, unauthorized publications): a volume issued in March 1891 by P. F. Collier. Copyright protection in the United States did not extend (until July 1, 1891) to the works of foreign authors, and it quickly became open season on *The Sign of the Four*. Donald Redmond's 1990 book *Sherlock Holmes Among the Pirates: Copyright and Conan Doyle in America 1890-1930* is largely a study of how this one book was published and republished. He writes: "From 1890 at least until 1924 *The Sign of the Four* was never out of print. From 1894 until the eve of the First World War five to ten different versions were on sale simultaneously."

Because the piratical publishers worked fast and cheap, errors and verbal variations crept into their texts, some of which have survived into modern editions. The most famous, a reference to "crows" (rather than "crowds") at the Lyceum Theatre, inspired Newton Williams, an early student of textual variations, to dub his work "the great crow hunt". Such variation even extends to the title of this novel, which was *The Sign of the Four* in *Lippincott's*, but lost a definite article to become *The Sign of Four* in the Spencer Blackett edition and the Collier piracy (apparently typeset from the Spencer Blackett text). The four-word title is more widely used today. Green and Gibson assert in their *Bibliography of A. Conan Doyle* (1983) that "the author originally used the longer title though preferred the shorter one."

Under either title it is a splendid novel, vastly more mature than its predecessor. Presenting Sherlock Holmes for a return appearance, though still clearly not foreseeing that he had created an industry, Doyle crafted a tightly knit plot that can be recognized as a detective story in modern terms. But the love interest, linking Dr. Watson with the client in the case, Mary Morstan, is still conspicuous, alternating with detective work: Holmes and adventure yield the stage to Watson and love five times through the book's eleven chapters. Miss Morstan makes an early impression on Watson, he moons over her, he sees her become more and more responsive to his attentions, and at the end of the narrative he reveals to Holmes that he has proposed marriage and she has accepted. So neat is the tying-up of loose ends, after so brief a courtship, that one recognizes the author's intent to write Watson out of Holmes's life, ending their companionship and ruling out any future adventures.

The story is again set in London, with rich scenes set in its foggy streets and in a huge, mysterious suburban house, Pondicherry Lodge. The case begins not with a murder but with a puzzle brought to Holmes by Miss Morstan: she has been receiving valuable pearls from an anonymous source, and now a mysterious message has arrived. Holmes finds the explanation only after a murder does take place and requires solution, to say nothing of a fine scene in which he and a borrowed dog, Toby, follow a literal scent through London. An even finer chase scene takes place along the Thames, through glinting sunlight and evening fog. Explanations follow, but the inevitable flashback (to India in the time of the 1854 Mutiny, an era that would appear again in "The Crooked Man") is confined to a single chapter. Characters are excitingly drawn (Bartholomew Sholto is usually acknowledged to be a portrait of Wilde), and despite many improbabilities and fumbled details — the action shifts inexplicably from June to September within hours — the book can be said to deserve its immediate success and its continuing popularity.

The Adventures of Sherlock Holmes

The title "The Adventures of Sherlock Holmes" is popularly and loosely used for any part of the Holmes saga; it was the title of the second film starring Basil Rathbone as Holmes, and it has provided such distortions as *The Misadventures of Sherlock Holmes* (an early collection of parodies), The Adventuresses of Sherlock Holmes (a society of female enthusiasts), and *The Sexual Adventures of Sherlock Holmes*. But strictly it is the title only of one book, the first of five cumulations of the original short stories.

These twelve stories appeared in twelve consecutive issues of the *Strand* magazine, July 1891 through June 1892, helping to establish the new magazine's reputation for first-class fiction. (They were also published in the American edition of the *Strand*, a month later in each case, and syndicated in American and British newspapers.) They also created a new genre: a series of stories involving the same character, each of which could (unlike the episodes of a serial) stand alone. When the sequence began, Sherlock Holmes was almost unknown; a year later he was the popular rage, and his creator was recognized as a successful author.

In October 1892, a collected volume of the *Adventures* was published by George Newnes, Ltd., the proprietors of the *Strand*, priced at six shillings (about $24 in today's money). The first edition, 10,000 copies, was sold out by early in 1893, and succeeding editions have been in print ever since in both Britain and the United States (where the first edition is that of Harper & Brothers, 1892).

The Adventures of Sherlock Holmes include some of the best-known and, by general acclaim, the best of the Holmes tales, in particular "The Speckled Band" and "The Red-Headed League". By the time of "The Boscombe Valley Mystery", which is the fourth in the series, Doyle had established most of his bag of conventional tricks. That tale offers everything from the police-baiting (in which Holmes mocks professional incompetence) to the obligatory moment at which Holmes crawls about the scene of the crime with his magnifying-glass. The formula "The Adventure of", which begins the titles of more than half the stories, was used for the first time in the seventh of the series, "The Blue Carbuncle" — it had taken Doyle that long to recognize that he was writing to a genre. ("The Adventure of" is often omitted by commentators.) The slowness of that recognition explains both the frequent cross-references between these early stories (each one mentions some that had gone before, as the author reinforced the connections in the readers' minds) and the peculiarities of the first story of all, "A Scandal in Bohemia", which is so little like a "typical" Holmes adventure.

A Scandal in Bohemia. First published in the *Strand* in July 1891, this tale involves romance as much as detection. Its structure indeed suggests opera, appropriately as the heroine, Irene Adler, is an operatic contralto, entangled with a flamboyantly improbable king. Scholarship about the story has concentrated in determining the intended identity of "the king of Bohemia", and on the logistics of Ms. Adler's blackmail attempt. The chief influence of the story, however, has been the fancy that Holmes meant something erotic or even spiritual by the label "The Woman" he applied to her.

The Red-Headed League. This tale, first published in the *Strand* for August 1891, is a classic of detection (in it Holmes makes his celebrated remark about the importance of trouser-knees) and bank robbery. For grotesquerie, on which Holmes prides himself and on which Doyle so often relied for his literary effects, it would be difficult to beat the story's picture of Fleet Street choked with red-headed men of all tinctures. A striking reinterpretation of the tale is that of Samuel Rosenberg in *Naked is the Best Disguise* (1974), who identifies its motif of tunnelling, and its effeminate hero, as signs of a homosexual subtext.

A Case of Identity. First published in the *Strand* for September 1891, this tale is nearly as insipid as its near-sighted heroine, Mary Sutherland, who however becomes the first of the "damsels in distress" whom Holmes rescues in so many of his cases. One might describe "A Case of Identity" as being Poe's deceptively simple "Purloined Letter" in a setting of middle-class tedium. It remains almost the only one of the original stories which has never been adapted for radio, television, or film.

The Boscombe Valley Mystery. The fourth of the original tales, first published in the *Strand* for October 1891, may plausibly claim to be the perfect Sherlock Holmes story, offering everything readers have come to love, from a railway journey to a scene in which Holmes throws himself into the mud to look at clues through his lens. Once the mystery is solved and the innocent man cleared, to the discomfiture of Lestrade, Holmes arranges for the guilty man to go free, in view of extenuating circumstances. This tale is one of several in which an Australian background plays a part.

The Five Orange Pips. They are the sign of the Ku Klux Klan, whose American villainies (a favourite theme throughout the Canon) lie behind the violence in this tale, first published in the *Strand* for November 1891. The story also offers a particularly rich list of unpublished cases, and a revealing scene in which Holmes berates himself for failing to save a threatened client's life. Finally, it includes that splendid atmospheric line, "The wind cried and sobbed like a child in the chimney."

The Man with the Twisted Lip. Given to the world in the *Strand* for December 1891, this tale begins with a Watsonian domestic scene (the famous passage in which the doctor's wife calls him James rather than John) and moves on to an opium den before its main plot begins to appear. The story, one of double life and deception (and one in which Doyle gives full play to his fascination with deformed faces), is about a middle-class journalist who enters the dirty and unrespectable world of begging. Ugly economic truths come unusually clear to the reader as Holmes works out what is going on. Also featured in this tale are feminine beauty (in the form of Mrs. Neville St. Clair) and couture.

The Adventure of the Blue Carbuncle. Christopher Morley called this tale "a Christmas story without slush"; it was first published, presumably just before Christmas, in the *Strand* for January 1892. The tale has to do with a holiday goose, which in pre-refrigeration days must be eaten promptly and which proves to contain a stolen jewel. The comic Henry Baker is only an incident, and the actual thief is of no account. What matters in the story is its seasonal framework, from the "compliments" brought by Watson to Holmes on "the second morning after Christmas" to Holmes's pardoning of the thief at the end because it is "the season of forgiveness".

The Adventure of the Speckled Band. Best known and probably most often dramatized of the short stories, this tale brings Holmes to the assistance of a damsel in distress. Her sister has already died in mysterious circumstances in a lonely country house, and now she too is threatened. The climax comes after one of those late-night vigils in the dark, when Holmes conquers an improbable snake, a "swamp adder". (Much has been written by Sherlockians about its species and the likelihood that it could drink milk and respond to a whistle.) The flavour of exotic India adds grotesquerie to the English countryside as it subtracts realism from the story, which was first published in the *Strand* for February 1892.

The Adventure of the Engineer's Thumb. Doyle becomes luxuriously gruesome in this tale, beginning it in Watson's consulting-room as he (incompetently) treats an amputation. Then the patient — Victor Hatherley, whose profession of engineer was just the new thing for a smart, practical young man in the 1890's — tells the story of how he lost his thumb to a meat cleaver, and Holmes identifies the crime and the criminal for whom the attack on Hatherley was a mere incident. The story was first published in the *Strand* for March 1892.

The Adventure of the Noble Bachelor. One can hear an echo of Doyle's early social and romance tales in this story, which first appeared in the *Strand* for April 1892. The title is a novelty, for there is no acknowledged bachelor in the story. At its centre is a society wedding; in the background, events no less romantic that took place in the American west. Holmes, seeming not to share the Victorian impression of America as uncouth, speaks of the future "quartering of the Union Jack with the Stars and Stripes" as the hope for civilization. The story includes such other beloved details as Holmes's snub of a nobleman who suggests that the detective has not worked at such a social level before ("No, I am descending") and the arrival of "ancient and cobwebby bottles" to accompany a catered supper at 221B Baker Street.

The Adventure of the Beryl Coronet. Unusual for being set amid snow, this tale — which first appeared in the *Strand* for May 1892 — is one of several jewel-theft adventures in the early Canon. It also has a spicy sexual subplot, and brings Holmes into indirect contact with one of those mysterious quasi-royal personages who also figure in several of the tales. How plausible it is for any such personage to pawn state property (with a most respectable banker) for private advantage, and how plausible it is for a corner to break off such a coronet with an audible crack, it may be best for the reader not to enquire.

The Adventure of the Copper Beeches. This second of the "damsel in distress" tales, published in the *Strand* for June 1892, presents the first of the "four Violets", women — more or less distressed — who share that given name and appear in Holmes's cases. Violet Hunter, the governess puzzled about a household where she is compelled to cut off her beautiful red hair, is in fact a strikingly strong and interesting woman, whom writers have sometimes imagined as a possible mate for Holmes. The story is an admirable venture into the Gothic genre, with its isolated house, intimations of madness in the attic, feminine fear and final bloodshed.

The Memoirs of Sherlock Holmes

A second series of twelve "adventures of Sherlock Holmes", as they were first called, appeared in the *Strand* beginning in December 1892 and continuing through December 1893. Again, the American edition of the *Strand* carried them a month later, and they also appeared shortly afterwards in *Harper's Weekly* (except for "The Final Problem", which was published in *McClure's* as well as in the *Strand*).

As soon as the series was complete, it was published in book form as *The Memoirs of Sherlock Holmes*. The first American edition, from Harper & Brothers, contains all twelve of the 1892-1893 stories, but the first British edition, from George Newnes, Ltd., omits "The Cardboard Box", which was then dropped from all subsequent book editions of *The Memoirs*, including a "second issue" from Harper in September 1894.

The Adventure of Silver Blaze. Set against the irresistibly colourful background of horse-racing, and provided with some of the most dramatic dialogue anywhere in the Canon, this story is a favourite and has been dramatized often. It provides the "dog in the night-time" incident, which in non-Sherlockian contexts is the most frequently quoted of Holmes's sayings, and for Sherlockians it provides the vexing mathematical puzzle of the train whose speed Holmes could calculate to the nearest one-half mile per hour, as well as many interesting anomalies in the details of racing colours and regulations. Further, in the original publication, it provides the most popular of all Sidney Paget illustrations, showing Holmes and Watson in their railway carriage, in classic poses. The story, first published in the *Strand* for December 1892, and reprinted in *Harper's Weekly* for February 25, 1993, has a surprise ending of a kind that could hardly be improved upon.

The Adventure of the Cardboard Box. First published in the *Strand* for January 1893, and *Harper's Weekly* for January 14 of that year, this story involves fine detective work and a very satisfactory outcome. It also involves a double murder (the severing of the victims' ears, a mutilation of the kind Doyle used again and again in his writings, is particularly grotesque) and one motivated by sexual jealousy. Presumably for such reasons, Doyle chose to suppress the story soon after its publication, not to restore it for twenty-three years. He told an acquaintance in 1903 that "a tale involving sex was out of place in a collection designed for boys." Later he called it "sensational" and (which it is not) "weak". It may well be that his real reason for suppressing the story was its grimness; unlike most detective stories, it has nothing like a happy ending.

The Adventure of the Yellow Face. This tale, first published in the *Strand* for February 1893 and *Harper's Weekly* for February 11, 1893, is one of the less popular of the early stories, perhaps because Holmes's attempts at detection in it are utterly unsuccessful. The background references to the American South are less convincing than those in "The Five Orange Pips", and what it says about relations between the races makes many readers uncomfortable. The story's greatest strength is probably its picture of life in London's outer suburbs.

The Adventure of the Stock-Broker's Clerk. The *Strand* in March 1893 and *Harper's Weekly* for March 11, 1893, presented this tale of a clever robbery and a man who impersonates his own brother. It uses a theme that had already appeared in "The Red-Headed League" — distracting an innocent man with highly paid busy-work to allow thieves to have a clear shot at their booty. Perhaps because much of the action takes place in unelegant Birmingham, or because Hall Pycroft the clerk is so colourless, the story is not highly regarded.

The Adventure of the 'Gloria Scott'. After ten brief paragraphs of introduction, this tale (first published in the *Strand* for April 1893 and *Harper's Weekly* for April 15, 1893) is told entirely in the voice of Holmes, reminiscing before the fire. It is as though the author, two years into his writings about Holmes, felt the need for some novelty. What he introduces is a flashback to the detective's youth, specifically to the incident that led him to make detective work his career. Like so many of the stories, the matter turns out to have its origin in distant regions and long-gone years — in a mutiny aboard a ship *en route* to Australia's penal colonies. The detection is of little interest, though there are some fine minor deductions about the person of old Trevor, and the most memorable aspect of the case in fact is the amusing if improbable cipher in which an important message is conveyed.

The Adventure of the Musgrave Ritual. A month after "The 'Gloria Scott'", in May 1893, the *Strand* presented a second story about Holmes's college years, one with many strong features. It also appeared in *Harper's Weekly* for May 13. This tale offers royalty, sexual intrigue, a first-rate antagonist for Holmes in the person of butler Brunton, and the "ritual" itself, a series of solemn questions and answers, so easily memorized, so hard to forget. Although the solution to the puzzle is somewhat artificial, involving trigonometry and arbitrary pacing of distances, the climactic scene in which a corpse is found under the flagstones of Hurlstone Manor is a fine one.

The Adventure of the Reigate Squires. This tale, set among the gentry of Surrey, appeared first in the *Strand* for June 1893, titled "The Adventure of the Reigate Squire", singular. *Harper's Weekly* published it June 17, 1893, as "The Reigate Puzzle", perhaps because Americans could not be expected to know exactly what a squire was (although there is some evidence that "Puzzle" was the author's intended title). In British book editions, the title became "The Reigate Squires", plural, but the "Puzzle" version has remained standard in the United States. By any title, the story is an undistinguished one, though it presents some memorable glimpses: of Holmes prostrate with depression even while Europe rang with his praises, of Holmes feigning illness to create a diversion, of Holmes knocking over a table and blaming Watson, of Holmes showing off his abilities at the analysis of handwriting. It takes no graphologist, however, to see that the fragments of a note that are reproduced with the tale, being the essential clue, are in the thinly disguised handwriting of Arthur Conan Doyle.

The Adventure of the Crooked Man. Published in the *Strand* for July 1893, and *Harper's Weekly* for July 8 of that year, this story returns to the Indian

Mutiny as background, and gives full scope for Doyle's fascination with physical distortion: the "crooked man" is an ex-soldier who is hideously crippled as the result of torture by the rebels outside Bhurtee. The tale is notable for the presence of Teddy the mongoose, for the Canon's only reference to regular church-going (in the Roman Catholic tradition, not that of the established church), and for the motive that lies behind the evil deeds it presents: a love triangle, the rivalry of two men for the love of the beautiful Nancy Devoy.

The Adventure of the Resident Patient. When this story first appeared in the *Strand* in August 1893, and *Harper's Weekly* for August 12, it began with a brief episode now unfamiliar to most Sherlockians. Holmes is at work on an "abstruse" chemical investigation, but "towards evening" he breaks a test tube, gives "an exclamation of impatience", and suggests to Watson that they go for "a ramble through London". In modern British editions of the story, that incident has disappeared, and the "ramble" is suggested in the same brief paragraph in which Watson speaks of "a close, rainy day in October". In American editions, it is also missing, but in favour of a three-page digression known as "the thought-reading episode", a passage that had previously been published in "The Cardboard Box". That episode was transplanted into "The Resident Patient", at the expense of the broken test-tube, when "The Cardboard Box" was suppressed, as it effectively was from 1894 to 1917. Such editions as the Doubleday *Complete Sherlock Holmes* continue to print it in full in both stories. In other respects "The Resident Patient" is less remarkable, though the opportunity it gave Doyle to use his knowledge of medical practice gives verisimilitude. The story deals with the mysterious behaviour of Dr. Trevelyan's resident patient, who proves to be in hiding from his former companions in crime; at last his sins find him out.

The Adventure of the Greek Interpreter. This tale dates from the *Strand* of September 1893, and *Harper's Weekly* for September 16. It is of interest chiefly because it introduces Mycroft Holmes, offering a long scene at the Diogenes Club in which he displays his eccentric brilliance. The case itself is set among foreigners rather than among Englishmen, and involves kidnapping and extortion of a most melodramatic kind. Little detection is involved, but there is a satisfactory rescue scene in which Watson has the opportunity to administer first aid in the form of brandy.

The Adventure of the Naval Treaty. So long is this story — some 12,700 words, compared with an average of 8,100 for the fifty-six short stories — that it was originally published in two instalments, in the *Strand* issues for October and November 1893. *Harper's Weekly* also published it in two instalments, October 14 and 21 of that year. (The first installment ended with Holmes's announcement that "We are now going to interview Lord Holdhurst, the Cabinet Minister and future Premier of England.") For the first time in the Canon, Holmes is involved with government secrets and affairs of state: a treaty has been stolen and war threatens if it is not recovered. The story has elements of the locked-room mystery, with a rather improbable floor plan of the Foreign Office, and of the purloined-letter tradition, as the treaty is found very close at hand. Its most memorable moment is, however, a digression, in which Holmes admires a moss rose and reflects that "Our highest assurance of the goodness of Providence seems to me to rest in the flowers."

The Adventure of the Final Problem. The title of this tale seems a redundancy — the more so as Holmes faces no "problem" in it, in the sense of a mystery to be solved. Rather, he has traced to his lair the mastermind of London criminality, Professor Moriarty, and must now conquer him or be conquered by him. To Watson's horror, detective and arch-criminal die together, falling over the falls of the Reichenbach, Switzerland, to which Moriarty has pursued the fleeing Holmes. Doyle wrote this story, and offered it for publication in the *Strand* (and also *McClure's*) for December 1893, simply as a way of killing off Holmes so that he might turn his authorial attention to other works. When it appeared, Doyle told audiences later, "if I had killed a real man I could not have received more vindictive letters than those which poured in upon me." It is said that young men about town wore black mourning-bands on their arms that winter. Their grief, real or assumed, is a tribute to the effect of the earlier Holmes stories and the pathos with which Doyle, in Watson's voice, writes a final tribute to "the best and wisest man whom I have ever known".

The Hound of the Baskervilles

Determined for some years to write nothing more of Sherlock Holmes, Doyle weakened in 1901 when he realized that Holmes was the perfect protagonist for a novel he wanted to write about a demon hound on Dartmoor. He did not, however, bring Holmes back to life, instead presenting his story as an adventure that had taken place some time before the encounter at the Reichenbach Falls.

It has become the most beloved and best-known of all the Sherlock Holmes tales, the name "Baskerville" being easily recognizable even to those who have never read a word of the story. It is also arguably the finest of the novels, perhaps of all the stories, in the eyes of those who know them well, for it displays a unity in time and texture, and a splendid series of perplexities and rising climaxes, unknown in any of the others. It has no long flashback (a device which disfigures all three other novels, as well as some of the short stories) but it does indulge in the luxury of varying points of view, several chapters being told as extracts from Watson's diaries or letters to Holmes, while others are his usual more leisured narrative.

The case takes Watson, and then also Holmes, to desolate Dartmoor, in the vicinity of the fearful prison at Princetown, to investigate the mysterious death of Sir Charles Baskerville, along with some peculiar collateral events. The plot is simple enough, although two sexual subplots complicate matters somewhat, but in this novel the atmosphere is immensely rich. There is the moor itself, with its relics of prehistoric man (emphasized by references throughout the story to anthropological studies and themes). There is the lurking presence of the prison, with Selden, the escaped murderer, a constant threat. There is the suffocating pettiness of village life; there is the gloom of Baskerville Hall, where the new squire, Sir Henry, announces at the end of the story that he is eager to install electric lights. A textual analysis of *The Hound* by Wendy Machen (in *Canadian Holmes*, 1989) finds that the dominant colours in this story are the black and white of night, the grey of uncertainty and the green of the moor's vegetation.

Doyle attributed the idea for *The Hound of the Baskervilles* to his friend Fletcher Robinson, declaring in a dedicatory epistle (of which three different versions appear) that Robinson had told him of "a west country legend". But scholarship has not turned up any Devonshire legend involving a dog, a wronged woman, and supernatural vengeance, though there are "black dog" legends aplenty. Tradition has pointed to a legend associated with the Cabell family of Buckfastleigh, Devon; but that legend cannot be traced before 1907 and may itself be based on the Baskerville story. The Baskerville and Vaughan families of Herefordshire apparently are associated with a longstanding Black Hound story, as Maurice Campbell argued in the *Sherlock Holmes Journal* in 1975. The safest conclusion is that *The Hound* has overlapping and multiple sources — as Janice McNabb argues in *The Curious Incident of the Hound on Dartmoor* (1984).

The story was first published as a serial in the *Strand*, between August 1901 and April 1902 (in the American edition, September through May). Chapters I-II appeared together; Chapters III-IV; Chapters V-VI; Chapters VII-VIII; Chapter IX alone; Chapters X-XI; Chapter XII alone; Chapter XIII and part of XIV; the remainder of XIV with XV. As soon as the final instalment had appeared, book editions were ready, from George Newnes, Ltd., in England and from McClure, Phillips & Co. in the United States. They were best-sellers, particularly after the American publisher obtained the manuscript, broke it into leaves, and distributed it to booksellers across the country as a publicity gesture. *The Hound* was also serialized in several American newspapers during the summer of 1902.

The Return of Sherlock Holmes

In 1903 Doyle was persuaded to bring Holmes back to life, or rather to invent a way in which his detective might have been alive all the time in spite of the report from Reichenbach. The persuasive influence was money, primarily from the American magazine *Collier's Weekly*, although the stories continued to appear in the British edition of the *Strand*. Doyle's own experience, and the emotional complexities he was undergoing during the first decade of the twentieth century, led him to write more realistic, more deeply coloured adventures for Holmes than anything the earlier two series had offered. *The Return of Sherlock Holmes* may be his finest work.

The thirteen stories in this sequence were collected in book form as soon as they had all appeared in magazines, and while they were still being republished in a group of American newspapers. The first edition appeared in the United States, from McClure, Phillips & Co., in February 1905; the rights were soon transferred to Doubleday, Page & Co. for subsequent editions. A British edition from George Newnes, Ltd., appeared in March, but the rights were soon taken over by Smith, Elder & Co. The American book edition was illustrated by Charles Raymond Macauley, and the British once again by Sidney Paget, whose drawings continued to appear in the *Strand* appearances. However, the illustrations most often associated with the stories in *The Return* are those of Frederic Dorr Steele, who drew dramatic covers for *Collier's* as well as black-and-white illustrations to accompany the stories inside that magazine.

The Adventure of the Empty House. This tale is rather a chapter of biography, or autobiography, than a mystery story in the accepted sense, for the mystery Holmes solves is incidental to other matters, and explained in only a few sentences. What matters is the return of Sherlock Holmes to London, and the unsuccessful attempt on his life by Colonel Sebastian Moran, right-hand villain to the late Professor Moriarty. The memorable scenes involve Watson's faint when he is confronted with his friend, whom he has presumed dead, and the vigil in the "empty house" across from 221B Baker Street while Moran tries to shoot the dummy which he supposes to be Holmes. The story first appeared in *Collier's* for September 26, 1903, and the *Strand* for October 1903.

The Adventure of the Norwood Builder. *Collier's* published this story October 31, 1903, and the *Strand* in November 1903. Its most memorable feature is the use of a thumbprint as a clue; the print never has to be matched with anything, for its very presence is sufficient to tell Holmes that something is wrong, but any reference to the uniqueness of fingerprints marks the story as modern (very modern, since fingerprinting, developed for police use in India, was introduced in England in a paper given to the British Association in 1899, and adopted by Scotland Yard in 1901). In other respects the story is of interest for its plot of sexual revenge, and for the device Holmes uses (an echo of what he tried in "A Scandal in Bohemia") of enticing a fugitive out of his hiding-place by raising an alarm of fire.

The Adventure of the Dancing Men. With this story Doyle returns to themes of adultery and love gone wrong, which evidently obsessed him during the early years of the century, while his own emotions were painfully divided. The "child's scrawl" that proves to be an underworld cipher, and the clue in a gory murder, makes this story one of the most memorable in the Canon, and one of the most frequently dramatized (although solving such a cipher is a far simpler matter than Holmes, or the author, makes out). Much attention has been given to Doyle's possible sources for the dancing men, and to the genuine existence of an ancient Cubitt family in Norfolk. For the first time since "The Five Orange Pips", Doyle uses an American background in this story, reasonably enough since he now had a major American audience. It appeared in *Collier's Weekly* for December 5, 1903, and in the *Strand* for December 1903.

The Adventure of the Solitary Cyclist. Violet Smith (who is not herself the solitary cyclist of Charlington; that was her pursuer) is the distressed damsel in this dramatic story, and the second of the four Canonical Violets. Like Violet Hunter in "The Copper Beeches", she is a career woman making her way in the world, and finding the atmosphere at a remote country house threatening. In short, the tale is as much a Gothic as it is a detective story. The dramatic wedding scene at the end is among the most exciting passages in the Canon. This story was first published in *Collier's* for December 26, 1903, and the *Strand* for January 1904.

The Adventure of the Priory School. A lonely little boy from a broken home runs away from school: the plot of this story must reflect Doyle's childhood fears. Its concluding scene, in which Holmes patronizes and swindles the rich and powerful Duke of Holdernesse, gives a convincing picture of the detective as iconoclast; the scene in which he arranges crumbs on the tablecloth to show Watson how the cow-tracks on the moor were arranged is a classic of detection, explication and dramatic sense. The story was first published in *Collier's* for January 30, 1904, and the *Strand* for February 1904.

The Adventure of Black Peter. Not, please, "the" Black Peter: the title indicates a person's name. The story appeared first in *Collier's* for February 27, 1904, and in the *Strand* for March 1904, and deals with a particularly violent murder — Holmes is first seen returning from an attempt to drive a spear through a pig's carcass, to estimate the force involved in the harpooning of Peter Carey. The whaling background doubtless owes something to Doyle's youthful experience in that industry.

The Adventure of Charles Augustus Milverton. Holmes has not much to detect in this case; he is employed instead as an agent to recover papers from Milverton the society blackmailer. To do so, he resorts to wooing Milverton's housemaid (a sordid episode which has led to much Sherlockian speculation and sniggering) and, in Watson's company, to burglary; in his presence, Milverton is shot dead by an unidentified woman who has been dubbed "Lady X". The case thus has much colour and action, as well as moral satisfaction, the noble Holmes vanquishing the snakelike Milverton. The tale was first published in *Collier's* for March 26, 1904, and the *Strand* for April 1904.

The Adventure of the Six Napoleons. The British fear of Napoleon, emperor of France, even eight decades after his death, figures large in this story, though ultimately only as a red herring: the gem might have been hidden in busts of anyone, but Napoleon is a plausible subject for monomania, on which everyone except Holmes blames the curious incidents of vandalism. The tale gives an opportunity for Holmes to display his clear reasoning and, in the scene at the end where he triumphantly produces the pearl, his flair for drama as well. "The Six Napoleons" was first published in *Collier's Weekly* for April 30, 1904, and the *Strand* for May 1904.

The Adventure of the Three Students. Improbable details abound in this story of a student who cheats on a university exam; the very procedure used to unmask the cheater, in which the don responsible calls in Holmes privately, is alien from the way a university would deal with such an incident. But as a logic puzzle the tale is splendid, giving Holmes the opportunity to choose from among three young men, the only possible suspects, and they confront the culprit, who confesses in a burst of emotion. The story first appeared in the *Strand* for June 1904 and *Collier's* for September 24, 1904.

The Adventure of the Golden Pince-Nez. Holmes is made to appear politically somewhat retrograde in this tale of Russian nihilists, exiled revolutionaries of the kind much feared in the England of that generation. The story is not of the first rank, despite Holmes's perception in understanding the dying words of the murdered secretary — "The professor, it was she" — and his ingenuity in scattering cigarette ashes so that the concealed murderess would leave footprints when she emerged. It was first published in the *Strand* for July 1904 and *Collier's Weekly* for October 29, 1904.

The Adventure of the Missing Three-Quarter. Doyle's beloved world of amateur sport (with which Holmes ostentatiously denies any familiarity) provides the background for this pathetic tale, in which mystery proves to be domestic tragedy. The comic portrait of the miser, Lord Mount-James, is hardly enough to make the tale a success. It appeared first in the *Strand* for August 1904 and *Collier's* for November 26, 1904.

The Adventure of the Abbey Grange. By 1904, Doyle had spent almost a decade tending a dying wife, while he was in love with another woman. Two years later he would become president of the Divorce Law Reform Union. Thoughts on such matters clearly lay behind the writing of this story, about a brave woman who helps her lover kill her aristocratic but drunken husband. The story is also notable for its picture of Holmes seeing more than the official police can see as he inspects the bloody room at the Abbey Grange, and for its juxtaposition of free-minded Australians with decadent English. "The Abbey Grange" was first published in the *Strand* for September 1904 and *Collier's* for December 31, 1904.

The Adventure of the Second Stain. The title of this story is as intriguing as the story itself; its resonance can be seen in its mention in "The Naval Treaty", along with the untold "Adventure of the Tired Captain". The second stain is a clue that helps Holmes solve his case, which involves not the usual murder but a matter of espionage and statecraft, again recalling "The Naval Treaty". By far the most interesting feature of the case is the beautiful Lady Hilda Trelawney Hope, who is faithful to her high-placed husband after her fashion. The story was first published in the *Strand* for December 1904 and *Collier's* for January 28, 1905.

The Valley of Fear

This novel may just be Doyle's masterpiece; it may even be two masterpieces, for it consists of two almost entirely separate mystery novels, and the second of them, "The Scowrers", is if anything more successful than the first, "The Tragedy of Birlstone", which involves Sherlock Holmes in a way the second does not. J. Bliss Austin, prominent collector and scholar in Pittsburgh, felt such an affinity for the second book that he managed to become owner of the entire manuscript of *The Valley of Fear* — but then he was a vice-president of United States Steel, a company whose shadow can easily be felt in "The Scowrers", a tale of the Pennsylvania coal and iron fields.

"The Scowrers" is set in the 1870's, in a time of technological and social change, and hence of conflict between the mostly Irish miners and labourers and their American-English bosses. One flower in the carbonized soil of the Shenandoah Valley (a metaphor repeatedly used in *The Valley of Fear*) was a fraternal and, eventually, terrorist group called the Mollie Maguires, largely a perversion of the otherwise legitimate Ancient Order of Hibernians. It has been the subject of several books, variously historical and fanciful, and of a 1969 film (*The Molly Maguires*, starring Sean Connery). The Mollies were eventually infiltrated by the new Pinkerton detective agency, in the person of agent James McParlan, and a number of them hanged for murder, including Jack Kehoe, the most prominent leader or "bodymaster". Doyle learned the story of the Mollies from a somewhat partial source, Allan Pinkerton's book *The Molly Maguires and the Detectives* (1877), and while *The Valley of Fear* is not precisely a *roman à clef*, it follows the Pinkerton version of the story closely. Sherlockians have enjoyed speculating about which of the coalfield towns — Tamaqua, Pottsville, Mauch Chunk (now Jim Thorpe) or Mahanoy City — is the original of "Vermissa". Bruce Kennedy and Robert Watson Douty explore such questions, and recreate the grim atmosphere of the Valley in those days, in their chapbook *In the Footsteps of Birdy Edwards* (1980).

But none of this background is apparent in the first half of *The Valley of Fear*, which begins as a country-house murder mystery with Professor Moriarty lurking in the background. The seven chapters of "The Tragedy of Birlstone" give some scope for a mystery and its solution to develop, and for personal touches of a kind impossible in a short story, such as the curious behaviour of the late John Douglas's devoted wife. The clue of the missing dumb-bell is one of the most amusing, and hence unforgettable, in the whole Canon. Eventually, after the seven "Scowrer" chapters, an "Epilogue" returns the scene to England, and Holmes is seen brooding when — astonishingly — Moriarty is victorious after all.

The Valley of Fear was serialized in the *Strand* magazine from September 1914 through May 1915, after most of the tales that would later appear in *His Last Bow*. In the United States it was not carried by *Collier's*, but instead appeared in the "Associated Sunday Magazines", a group of newspaper supplements, beginning on September 20, 1914, and concluding on November 22. In book form it appeared in February in the United States (from George H. Doran Co.), and in June in England (from Smith, Elder & Co.). As Gibson and Green note in their *Bibliography*, there are a number of deliberate textual variations, some caused by the war with Germany, in which Britain (but not America) was engaged beginning late in 1914, some "for greater accuracy" in the American details.

His Last Bow

This fourth collection of Canonical short stories is the smallest of all, containing but eight tales — and that figure includes "The Cardboard Box", originally published as one of *The Memoirs* but suppressed from 1894 until this volume appeared in 1917. The stories were somewhat rearranged from the order in which they had been originally published. The British edition was published by John Murray, apparently because Smith, Elder & Co. thought seven or eight stories too few to make a worthwhile book. The American edition appeared simultaneously, from George H. Doran Co. The subtitles of the two editions differ slightly: in Britain it was "Some Reminiscences of Sherlock Holmes", and in the United States "A Reminiscence of Sherlock Holmes". Many editions (but not, for example, the John Murray *Short Stories*) include a one-paragraph Preface signed by Watson: "The friends of Mr. Sherlock Holmes will be glad to learn that he is still alive and well. . . ."

Shortly after *His Last Bow* was published, Doyle wrote an article, "Some Personalia about Mr. Sherlock Holmes", which appeared in the *Strand* for December 1917. It was later revised as a chapter in his autobiography, *Memories and Adventures* (1924). Clearly intended as an epilogue to the entire Canon, the existence of this article makes it clear that *His Last Bow* was intended to be, indeed, Holmes's *last* bow. It leaves open, however, the question of which sort of "bow" the author had in mind: the kind an actor takes at a curtain-call, or the kind the dying Robin Hood drew to shoot an arrow to his final resting-place.

The Adventure of Wisteria Lodge. Like "The Naval Treaty", the only Canonical short story that is longer, this one was first published in the *Strand* in two parts: "The Singular Experience of Mr. John Scott Eccles", September 1908, and "The Tiger of San Pedro", October 1908. *Collier's Weekly* published the two parts August 15, 1908, under the title "The Singular Experience of Mr. John Scott Eccles". The two labels, for two halves of this story, survive in modern editions; the title "Wisteria Lodge" for the full story was first used when *His Last Bow* was published in book form. This tale was "a difficult story to write", Gibson and Green say *obiter* in their *Bibliography*, and it shows it, being long and confusing. The horrible face at the window and the shocking relics of voodoo that serve as clues along the way are hardly sufficient to redeem the story, nor is the sudden appearance of "Don Murillo", the deposed Latin American dictator.

The Adventure of the Red Circle. A background of Italian-American mafia activity makes this story a favourite with many readers, though its early pages, in which Holmes reassures a distressed landlady and puzzles over the identity of her mysterious lodger, is in fact more typical of the Canon. The "cipher" which proves to be Italian has excited much commentary; whichever way Holmes counted the letters, they don't seem to come out right. The story was first published in the *Strand* in two parts, in March and April 1911 (a month later in the American edition), and retains a division into parts I and II.

The Adventure of the Bruce-Partington Plans. Mycroft Holmes, last seen in "The Greek Interpreter", returns in this story, bringing his brother a case which, like two or three others, involves espionage and international intrigue rather than domestic crime. Apart from its supposed political importance, the case is of interest chiefly for the ingenious disposal of a body atop an Underground train — and of course for the presence of the dead man's fiancée, one of the four Canonical Violets. "The Bruce-Partington Plans" (the title referring to the blueprints for the Bruce-Partington submarine, a thoroughly up-to-date invention in 1908) appeared first in the *Strand* for December 1908 and *Collier's* for December 12 of the same year.

The Adventure of the Dying Detective. The title is sensational; the story is a splendid one, drawing on Doyle's medical background (and drawing in Watson's medical mediocrity) to present a Holmes who is feigning fatal illness to ensnare a clever adversary. Such detail is given about the ruse that there is hardly room for the mystery itself, and it is not even quite clear who Victor Savage was or why he was killed. "The Dying Detective" was first published in *Collier's* for November 22, 1913, and immediately offprinted as a Christmas greeting pamphlet from the advertising department of *Collier's*. It also appeared in the December 1913 issue of the *Strand*.

The Disappearance of Lady Frances Carfax. Comedy and Gothic melodrama figure more in this story than in most other Canonical tales — the comedy in Watson's clumsy attempts to play detective, acting on Holmes's behalf in Montpellier; the melodrama in Holmes's frantic prying-open of the coffin in which the missing lady is about to be buried alive. The story comes nearer than any other in the Canon to being about rape, rather than murder or theft. Its unusual title (without "The Adventure of") is no excuse for the *faux pas* that was made when it first appeared in the United States, in the *American Magazine* for December 1911; there it was headed "The Disappearance of Lady Carfax". Under its right name it appeared in the *Strand*, also for December 1911.

The Adventure of the Devil's Foot. As in "The Reigate Squires", Holmes in this case is taking a medically imposed vacation, this time in Cornwall, and conveniently finds himself in proximity to a mystery. Murder is not at first suspected in "the Cornish horror", a phenomenon that rather reminds one of a Spiritualist seance gone wildly wrong (but Doyle in 1910 was not yet active as a Spiritualist). The most memorable aspect of the story may be the hideously contorted faces of the victims of *radix pedis diaboli*, a root hitherto unknown to science, but its most important feature is the scene in which Holmes holds justice higher than law and lets the culprit go. "The Devil's Foot" was originally published in the *Strand* — in December 1910 in the British edition, in January and February 1911 in the American edition. (The first of those two episodes ended with "Hurry — hurry, before things get disarranged.")

His Last Bow. This story, which gives its title to the collection in which it later appeared, represents a departure from the style of all the previous Holmes tales. It is narrated in the third person, rather than by Watson; it introduces Holmes as a surprise, far into the narrative; it presents not the London-based consulting detective but a Holmes come out of retirement in Sussex; it is a story not of crime but of international espionage, with Holmes acting as a double agent on the eve of World War I. It takes place August 2, 1914, during the hours when the war was actually beginning, and it takes a jingoistic tone, having undeniably been written as war propaganda. One can hear Doyle's voice from the beginning ("the most terrible August in the history of the world") through the slurs on Germany, Irish separatists, and suffragist "Furies", to the peroration about a cleansing "east wind". Holmes as spy is little more convincing than Holmes as goateed American, under the pseudonym of Altamont, but readers in 1917 may have been grateful for whatever they might get. The tale was subtitled "The War Service of Sherlock Holmes" when it appeared in the *Strand* for September 1917 and *Collier's* for September 22, 1917, but became "An Epilogue of Sherlock Holmes" when *His Last Bow* appeared in book form. Doyle was indicating once again that he had had enough of him.

The Case-Book of Sherlock Holmes

The title is admirable, and two or three of the stories likewise, but in general this final collection is acknowledged to be weaker than the books that preceded it. Gibson and Green in their *Bibliography* say that Doyle was encouraged to write more about Holmes when he saw the early films that starred Eille Norwood as the detective, released beginning in 1921. "Norwood's disguises were remarkable," they say, "and his sphinx-like countenance suggested the idea for *The Crown Diamond*," which was first a play and then the first of this final dozen stories to see print.

The tales — written, or at least published, over a much briefer period than those in *The Return* and *His Last Bow* — were completely rearranged for book publication. They were introduced with a Preface, this time in Doyle's voice rather than Watson's, which first appeared in the *Strand* for March 1927, announcing a contest that invited readers to rank the stories and match Doyle's own assessment. It survives as the lovely brief essay that assigns Holmes to "some fantastic limbo for the children of imagination, some strange, impossible place" and yet fixes him firmly in history:

> He began his adventures in the very heart of the later Victorian Era, carried it through the all-too-short reign of Edward, and has managed to hold his own little niche even in these feverish days.

The first edition of *The Case-Book* was published in Britain by John Murray, and in America by George H. Doran Co., in the middle of 1927.

The Adventure of the Illustrious Client. Sex (indeed, probably, prostitution) is the atmosphere and motivation in this tale, which takes its name not from any element of the plot but from the (unidentified) noble party who asks Holmes to take the case. It is a matter outside his usual range, for there is no mystery to solve. Rather, Holmes is supposed to persuade a well-to-do young lady that Baron Gruner, with whom she is infatuated, is a cad and worse. She will have none of his reasoning (he carries it off with dignity, despite his inexperience in such affairs), but violence intervenes, in the nasty old-fashioned form of vitriol-throwing: Gruner is marked for life by the attack of the wild Kitty

Winter. This racy fare first appeared in *Collier's* for November 8, 1924, and the *Strand* for February and March 1925 (the first part ending with the dramatic words "Murderous Attack Upon Sherlock Holmes").

The Adventure of the Blanched Soldier. Current affairs find their way into the Canon more directly than usual in this tale; it deals with a consequence of the Boer War, specifically a medical matter, having its origin in a field hospital much like the one Doyle himself managed during that conflict twenty-five years earlier. Its strength is as a medical tale rather than an instance of detection, as there is little for Holmes to do save to discern the anti-climactic truth and arrange a happy ending for the family of the ex-soldier who believed him to have a dread disease. "The Blanched Soldier" first appeared in *Liberty*, a New York magazine, for October 16, 1926, and in the *Strand* for November 1926.

The Adventure of the Mazarin Stone. The first words of this story make it distinctive: it is written in the third person, not with Watson as narrator. It is in fact an adaptation of "The Crown Diamond", a play by Doyle about Sherlock Holmes that was first produced in May 1921. The story saw print in the *Strand* that October, and in *Hearst's International Magazine* in New York in November 1921. Not only because of its awkward style (rigidly observing the dramatic unities, it simply describes what might be seen on a stage set), but also for lack of originality in plot or circumstantial detail, it is widely recognized as probably the weakest of all the Holmes tales. Nevertheless, it deserves some acclaim as the first new tale to be published since "His Last Bow" four years previously.

The Adventure of the Three Gables. Unhealthy sexuality (a young man becomes fascinated by an older woman) and the misuse of wealth make the atmosphere of this story distasteful, and there is little detecting for Holmes to do. The issue in this affair, as in "A Scandal in Bohemia", is blackmail at the point where sex and money meet. The unusual character of Isadora Klein is probably the story's strongest feature, though there is also some interest in the way Holmes examines the attempt to buy Mrs. Maberley's house, contents and all, eventually realizing that a tell-tale manuscript is what the buyer was after. "The Three Gables" was first published in *Liberty*, New York, for September 18, 1926, and in the *Strand* for October 1926.

The Adventure of the Sussex Vampire. Written during Doyle's years as an advocate of Spiritualism, this tale nevertheless presents a firmly materialist Holmes: "No ghosts need apply." Among the *Case-Book* stories it is unusually strong and memorable, reminiscent of Holmes's early adventures, although the title is deliberately lurid, the story something of a trick, for Holmes finds that the woman who has been sucking blood from her stepson's neck is no sort of monster. "The Sussex Vampire" was first published in the January 1924 issues of both the *Strand* and (in New York) *Hearst's International Magazine*.

The Adventure of the Three Garridebs. The appeal of this story depends heavily on the novelty of the grotesque surname "Garrideb". Holmes is called in not to solve a crime but to render advice in the search for men of that name; when three of them stand in a row, a fortune is theirs to divide. Of course he finds the whole business to be a fraud, rather as was the League of the Red-Headed Men in a story written thirty years earlier, a story whose plot is largely borrowed for this one. The dramatic scene in which Watson is wounded is among the high emotional moments of the Canon. This tale was first published in *Collier's* for October 25, 1924, and in the *Strand* for January 1925.

The Problem of Thor Bridge. This story (which departs from the "Adventure of" style of title) presents a classic piece of deduction by Holmes, in which he works out from a chip on a stone bridge the true explanation for the death of Maria Gibson. It has to do with a gritty love triangle, a plot that seems unmistakably of the 1920's. The story also offers the Sherlockian one of the Canon's finest paragraphs about other cases which Holmes addressed, but for which the world is not yet prepared. "Thor Bridge" was first published in the *Strand* and in *Hearst's International Magazine*, both in the February and March issues of 1922; the first part ends with "We come at once upon a most fruitful line of inquiry."

The Adventure of the Creeping Man. Holmes makes his nearest approach to science fiction in this story, in which the unusual behaviour of a professor proves to be caused by a "serum" extracted from langur monkeys. Experiments with such injections of testicular extract began in the 1880's and attracted much attention in the 1920's, but they seem somehow too modern for Holmes's attention, in a case that requires little action from him but does lead him to some philosophizing, and a hint that he might soon retire. The story was first published in the *Strand* and in *Hearst's International Magazine*, both for March 1923.

The Adventure of the Lion's Mane. Sherlock Holmes himself is the narrator of this tale (his prose style is, however, revealingly similar to Watson's). Its events take place on the Sussex coastline, after Holmes's retirement to a "villa", and involve the strange death of Fitzroy McPherson, which proves to be the result of a natural phenomenon rather than of human violence. The story has novelty (not least, the absence of Watson) to recommend it, as well as the portrait of that "most complete and remarkable woman", Maud Bellamy. "The Lion's Mane" first appeared in *Liberty* for November 27, 1926, and in the *Strand* for December 1926.

The Adventure of the Veiled Lodger. Holmes waxes philosophical in this sad tale, as does Doyle, who wrote it near the end of his life (it was published in *Liberty* for January 22, 1927, and the *Strand* for February 1927). Readers might reasonably feel a little cheated, for Holmes is called on to do no detecting at all, only a little speculating and a good deal of listening as Eugenia Ronder tells the dramatic story of how her face was ruined, so that she now lives behind a veil.

The Adventure of Shoscombe Old Place. Original publication of the Canon came to an end with this story, appearing in *Liberty* for March 5, 1927, and the *Strand* for April 1927. It is a story of degeneration, death and old bones, with the suspected murder proving to be nothing more serious than a fraud born of desperation. Still, its final paragraph tries to offer hope, speaking of "a happier note than Sir Robert's actions deserved . . . an honoured old age". It harks back to

The Hound of the Baskervilles, with the association of mysterious dogs and spooky death, and its highlight is the brief exciting scene in which Holmes lets a spaniel loose to bark at the mysterious occupant of a carriage. (The story was originally announced as "The Adventure of the Black Spaniel", but never published under that title.) A return to the horse-racing milieu that gave "Silver Blaze" much of its novelty also adds interest to this story.

The Adventure of the Retired Colourman. Perhaps because of the word "retired" in the title, and because its theme is the hopelessness of old age, this story was put last in *The Case-Book*, although there were two tales still to come when it was first published in *Liberty* for December 18, 1926, and the *Strand* for January 1927. Doyle returns to his frequent theme of a love triangle, includes his only mention of chess ("one mark of a scheming mind"), makes Sherlock Holmes conduct one of his most clever, if inconsiderate, ruses, and offers perhaps the most chilling image in the entire Canon, the incomplete phrase scrawled on the wall of the death chamber by the two murder victims. The seven-word question with which Holmes nails the unsuspecting killer is a splendidly dramatic note for the story which a cover-to-cover reader of the Canon will encounter last.

Abbreviations for the Stories

The following abbreviations (given with the short title of the corresponding story) were devised by Jay Finley Christ and first published in connection with his *Irregular Guide to Sherlock Holmes*, 1947.

ABBE ♦ The Abbey Grange
BERY ♦ The Beryl Coronet
BLAC ♦ Black Peter
BLAN ♦ The Blanched Soldier
BLUE ♦ The Blue Carbuncle
BOSC ♦ The Boscombe Valley Mystery
BRUC ♦ The Bruce-Partington Plans
CARD ♦ The Cardboard Box
CHAS ♦ Charles Augustus Milverton
COPP ♦ The Copper Beeches
CREE ♦ The Creeping Man
CROO ♦ The Crooked Man
DANC ♦ The Dancing Men
DEVI ♦ The Devil's Foot
DYIN ♦ The Dying Detective
EMPT ♦ The Empty House
ENGR ♦ The Engineer's Thumb
FINA ♦ The Final Problem
FIVE ♦ The Five Orange Pips
GLOR ♦ The 'Gloria Scott'
GOLD ♦ The Golden Pince-Nez
GREE ♦ The Greek Interpreter
HOUN ♦ The Hound of the Baskervilles
IDEN ♦ A Case of Identity
ILLU ♦ The Illustrious Client
LADY ♦ Lady Frances Carfax
LAST ♦ His Last Bow
LION ♦ The Lion's Mane
MAZA ♦ The Mazarin Stone
MISS ♦ The Missing Three-Quarter

MUSG ♦ The Musgrave Ritual
NAVA ♦ The Naval Treaty
NOBL ♦ The Noble Bachelor
NORW ♦ The Norwood Builder
PRIO ♦ The Priory School
REDC ♦ The Red Circle
REDH ♦ The Red-Headed League
REIG ♦ The Reigate Puzzle
RESI ♦ The Resident Patient
RETI ♦ The Retired Colourman
SCAN ♦ A Scandal in Bohemia
SECO ♦ The Second Stain
SHOS ♦ Shoscombe Old Place
SIGN ♦ The Sign of the Four
SILV ♦ Silver Blaze
SIXN ♦ The Six Napoleons
SOLI ♦ The Solitary Cyclist
SPEC ♦ The Speckled Band
STOC ♦ The Stockbroker's Clerk
STUD ♦ A Study in Scarlet
SUSS ♦ The Sussex Vampire
THOR ♦ Thor Bridge
3GAB ♦ The Three Gables
3GAR ♦ The Three Garridebs
3STU ♦ The Three Students
TWIS ♦ The Man with the Twisted Lip
VALL ♦ The Valley of Fear
VEIL ♦ The Veiled Lodger
WIST ♦ Wisteria Lodge
YELL ♦ The Yellow Face

They are widely used in footnotes and sometimes even in text about the stories, either in this all-capital form or (less often) in the upper-and-lower format which Christ used: Abbe, Blac, Engr, RedC, 3Stu and so on.

Chapter II

Characters and Adventures

In writing the Sherlock Holmes tales, Arthur Conan Doyle invented the valuable literary genre of "linked" short stories: their plots are independent (so that they can be read in any order) but the central characters and settings continue. A detective is the perfect figure to appear in such a structure, for he remains unchanged while a succession of clients bring their various problems to him.

Because Holmes appears in all the stories, Watson in all but one, and several other characters repeatedly, it is easy for the reader to see them as fragments of biography. Enthusiasts have speculated and written endlessly about Holmes's accomplishments and character, and about the deeds he may have performed which Doyle (or Watson) unaccountably failed to record. In addition, it is easy to see themes and characteristics that appear in story after story, some with gradual changes over the decades from *A Study in Scarlet* to the final sad tales published in 1927.

Readers who see the Canon as a unit, rather than as unconnected stories, have felt the need for reference books that help them trace the developments and locate specific names or incidents. An early alphabetical guide of this kind was Jay Finley Christ's *An Irregular Guide to Sherlock Holmes of Baker Street* (1947). It was valuable, but idiosyncratic and, even with two Supplements, inadequate. A modern successor is *Good Old Index* (1987), by William D. Goodrich. Both are keyed to the Doubleday *Complete Sherlock Holmes*. Somewhat different is Jack Tracy's invaluable *Encyclopaedia Sherlockiana* (1977), which concentrates on proper names and some matters of Victorian daily life, defining them and indicating the story (but not the precise page) that gives each its interest to a reader of the Canon.

Sherlock Holmes

"What is it that we love in Sherlock Holmes?" asked Edgar W. Smith in his first essay as editor of the *Baker Street Journal* (1946). His answer began with discussion not so much of Holmes as of Holmes's time, but then it turned to the figure of the great detective himself:

> Not only there and then, but here and now, he stands before us as a symbol — a symbol, if you please, of all that we are not, but ever would be. His figure is sufficiently remote to make our secret aspirations for transference seem unshameful, yet close enough to give them plausibility. We see him as the fine expression of our urge to trample evil and to set aright the wrongs with which the world is plagued.

That is a lot to ask of a human being, or even of a literary approximation of a human being, and yet enthusiasts continue to ask it. Perhaps it would be better first to take the measure of Holmes as a man — "the best and wisest man whom

I have ever known", Watson is made to call him, borrowing a phrase first used by Plato about Socrates.

Holmes reports that his ancestors were "country squires" and that a grandmother was a sister of "Vernet, the French artist" (presumably Émile Jean Horace Vernet, 1789-1863). His older brother Mycroft appears in two of the stories. Otherwise, the reader knows nothing of Holmes's family or background beyond vague hints about his university education. The Canon provides an outline of his career, from his early cases as an amateur ("The 'Gloria Scott'" and "The Musgrave Ritual") through his establishment in London as a consulting detective; his meeting with Watson in (probably) January 1881; ten years of professional success; his encounter with Professor Moriarty at the Reichenbach in 1891; his return from supposed death three years later; a further nine years of professional work; his retirement to Sussex, from which he emerged for counter-espionage work ("His Last Bow") in 1912-14. During his active career he is said to have handled thousands of cases, only a handful of which are chronicled. The great stretches of time unaccounted for — if one accepts Holmes as a historical figure, and the tales as fragments of his biography — are an immense temptation to the tale-spinner and the scholar alike.

His limitations. Sherlock Holmes is first presented in *A Study in Scarlet* as a tall, thin, flamboyant, and eccentric student in the pathology laboratory of St. Bartholomew's Hospital, London, where he is developing a practical test for bloodstains. By Chapter II he is rooming with Watson at 221B Baker Street, and before long Watson, puzzled about his companion, tries to set out his "limits" in a famous chart:

    1. Knowledge of Literature. — Nil.
    2.   ”   ” Philosophy. — Nil.
    3.   ”   ” Astronomy. — Nil.

And so on. Eventually he discovers that Holmes is "a consulting detective", who believes in keeping in the "lumber-room" of his brain only such information as he is likely to need. As the acquaintance deepens, however, it becomes clear that Holmes is by no means so utilitarian in his thoughts, or so innocent of literature, philosophy, astronomy and the rest. Indeed, by the time of "The Lion's Mane" late in the Canon, the reader is not surprised to hear Holmes himself speaking of the vague and half-remembered information stored somewhere in the "box-room" that his mind has become.

Holmes's intellectual limits extend at least to these distances:

• A vast knowledge of (non-fictional) criminal literature and the history of crime and strange occurrences, which he was wont to cite for the bewilderment of professional detectives.

• Technical knowledge of tobacco ash, footprints, tattoos, ciphers, manuscript dating and other such subjects, on all of which he claimed to have written monographs — to say nothing of "the influence of a trade upon the form of the hand". At the end of his career he prepared *The Whole Art of Detection*.

• A detailed knowledge of London, including its geography and an extraordinary number of its people among all classes.

• An enjoyment of serious music and at least a superficial acquaintance with composers and performers, although it appears that he attended concerts as a means of relaxation rather than to be stimulated through close attention as a genuine musical aficionado might. He also showed the ability to play the violin passably, and the flexibility to extract noises from it while it was flung carelessly across his knee rather than held in the usual position.

• An acquaintance, perhaps broad rather than deep, with literature in a number of languages; he refers to Hafiz, Horace, Gustave Flaubert, George Sand, Goethe, and even the occasional English author, and claims at one point to be carrying "my pocket Petrarch".

• "A good practical knowledge of British law," as Watson puts it — the sort of familiarity that bred contempt, judging from a number of incidents in which Holmes lets malefactors go free, breaks into dwelling-houses in the night-time, extorts evidence in defiance of the Judges' Rules, and otherwise comports himself outside the law.

• Considerable knowledge of chemistry, to the point that he spent months (at least) conducting researches at Montpellier shortly before the affair of "The Empty House". He used chemistry in his professional work at times, probably chiefly to detect poisons, but also apparently did experiments to occupy his mind in the intervals between cases. He was frequently unable, however, to explain his work clearly to Watson, who describes him attempting to "dissolve" a hydrocarbon as though that were a difficult achievement.

• An unparalleled ability to observe trifles about a person, room or road and to apply logic and a knowledge of daily life in order to reconstruct the events of the past.

Holmes the man. But there is more to Sherlock Holmes than this intellectual catalogue; there remain the traits that caused Watson to label him "best and wisest". Such traits are not so easily listed, for they are conveyed to the reader — as they were to Watson — through long acquaintance and leisurely intercourse.

Christopher Morley, selecting episodes from the Canon and preparing a school edition of them in 1944, called his volume *Sherlock Holmes and Dr. Watson: A Textbook of Friendship.* The modern reader may snicker at the portrayal of a close, emotional friendship between two adult men, and certainly at such sentiments as Holmes and Watson express about one another in "The Three Garridebs" at the dreadful moment when Watson is wounded. Are they lovers? one may wish to ask. Of course they are not, although one or two pornographers have chosen to interpret them that way. They are simply close friends, demonstrating a kind of relationship that was common both in the literature and in the real life of the 1890's. It was an era when friendship between men and women on equal terms was virtually impossible, and when the bonds one might associate with soldiers under fire could also be formed between men in the world of London clubs and flats. The picture of it seen in Holmes and Watson appears wholesome indeed beside the male relationships in, say, George du Maurier's *Trilby* (1894).

Holmes evidently has some of the qualities one might want most in a friend, the right combination of loyalty (emphasized in "The Dying Detective" when Holmes is obliged to pretend betrayal) and independence. The mutual affection of Holmes and Watson is understated, both as a demonstration of the friendship's firmness and as a natural consequence of Victorian formality. "My dear Watson," and "My dear Doctor," Holmes still calls his colleague after twenty years of shared danger. He is obeying the conventions of his time and place, but no doubt the stress was all on the "dear".

How tolerable Holmes may have been as a companion is another question altogether. His "cat-like love of personal cleanliness" is balanced by a pack-rat love of clutter, an indifference to the proper places for household objects, a taste for strong tobacco to the point of filling his rooms with a thick blue haze of smoke. He is demanding, both of Watson and of strangers; he is secretive, preferring to spring surprises rather than take a companion into his confidence. He is also a captive of many Victorian prejudices, seen in their ugliest form in his baiting of a black man in "The Three Gables" and one or two remarks that may be anti-Semitic. At times he fawns on the rich and aristocratic, although he can be contemptuous of those, such as the King of Bohemia, who do not live up to *noblesse oblige*, and he can occasionally be very gentle with the lowly.

Most notably, Holmes is moody, alternating periods of energy, enthusiasm and prodigious work with periods of languor, inactivity and apparent depression. Alan Bradley and William Sarjeant in *Ms. Holmes of Baker Street* (1989), affecting to believe that the detective was secretly a woman, attribute this alternation of moods to the influence of a strong menstrual cycle. Most other commentators have unhesitatingly seen it as a manic-depressive personality at work. Holmes could be arrogant (though rarely as disagreeable to Watson as Basil Rathbone makes him in his films of the 1940's) and nervous (though not nearly so full of tics, shrill cries and mindless movement as Jeremy Brett makes him in the television series of the 1980's).

In the early stories, most explicitly *The Sign of the Four*, Holmes is seen as a user of drugs, "a seven-per-cent solution" of cocaine, which is a stimulant and anti-depressant. Watson scolds him for this abuse of his body, but seems resigned to it. Use of such drugs was legal in the England of the 1890's, and is used to emphasize Holmes's mercurial personality and his pose of sophisticated eccentricity. Many details are elucidated by Jack Tracy and Jim Berkey in *Subcutaneously, My Dear Watson* (1978):

> Holmes's cocaine habit was in no way unlawful. . . . Not until 1916 was the sale of cocaine restricted to a doctor's prescription. . . . If Holmes made use of a 10- to 20-mg. dose in each of his three-times-daily injections, then his habit was costing him between 2¢ and 4¢ a day. . . . 10% became the official strength of solution in the *British Pharmacopœia* in 1898. . . . One grain, or 65 mg. — legally purchased from the neighbourhood chemist — would then provide three ample doses, one

day's supply, and a grain a day was often mentioned in the literature of the time as a recommended dosage for the treatment of melancholia.

The horrified reaction of modern readers, aware of contemporary drug abuse, is a misunderstanding of the character as Doyle was drawing him and his habits.

Holmes and women. "Women have seldom been an attraction to me," Holmes says in "The Lion's Mane", "for my brain has always governed my heart." But the converse is far from true; something in Holmes's character has attracted the opposite sex since the days when the first stories were being published, and Doyle received proposals of marriage on his character's behalf. One contemporary woman has observed that "I feel sorry for men Sherlockians, because they don't have Sherlock Holmes to fall in love with." Even within the Canon, such women as Violet Hunter ("The Copper Beeches") and Mary Morstan (who eventually marries Watson) show some attraction to Holmes. He does not reciprocate, making a number of derogatory remarks about women, although he does demonstrate an expert knowledge of perfumes and millinery when they are relevant to his investigation. The apparent exception, on which many Sherlockians have written at length, is Irene Adler of "A Scandal in Bohemia", significantly a story written before Holmes's character was fully formed and demonstrated. He calls Irene Adler "*the* woman", giving a lasting impression of infatuation even though Watson assures the reader that there was nothing emotional in Holmes's admiration of her. She is an extraordinary woman compared to the damsels in distress who populate many of the other tales, and those who insist that Holmes should have a mate could do worse than settle for her.

"May I marry Holmes?" William Gillette is said to have telegraphed to Doyle when he was writing his play *Sherlock Holmes* at the turn of the century, meaning that he felt the need to introduce a love interest. Doyle's response: "You may marry him or murder him or do what you like with him." Gillette did, and numerous dramatizers and authors have followed suit, including Jerome Coopersmith, who explained what he had done in the musical *Baker Street* (1965): "I gave Sherlock Holmes a girl friend, and that is as it should be." But in the Canon itself, the fair sex is, as Holmes says, Watson's department. (Holmes's love life, and related issues, are treated at length in Christopher Redmond's *In Bed with Sherlock Holmes*, 1984.)

The great hiatus. No aspect of Holmes's life is odder than the three years that are said to have elapsed between May 1891 and April 1894, that is, between the events of "The Final Problem" and those of "The Empty House". The latter story offers Holmes's brief narrative: after escaping Professor Moriarty at the Falls of the Reichenbach, he travelled to Tibet, conducted explorations under the name of Sigerson, visited such exotic sites as Mecca (where non-Muslims are not welcome) and Khartoum (capital of the Sudan, during an interlude between bitter wars against Britain), and spent time at Montpellier doing laboratory research into "the coal-tar derivatives".

The reader who sees the stories as biography demands a better truth, an explanation that adds something to the understanding of Holmes's personality.

The fascination with the Great Hiatus (a term for this three-year interlude apparently coined by Edgar W. Smith in a 1946 article in the *Baker Street Journal*) may also proceed from a wish to know exactly why and how Holmes changed — why, as folklore insists that a contemporary reader told Doyle, "Sherlock Holmes may not have died when he fell down that waterfall, but he was never the same man afterwards." Jack Tracy, in his *Encyclopaedia Sherlockiana* (1977), says quite truthfully: "In the absence of supporting evidence, an enormous number of alternate theories have been formed to account for Holmes's activities during this period, each more outrageous than the others." For example, the story of his involvement in the August 4, 1892, murders at Fall River, Massachusetts, in which Lizzie Borden was acquitted, has yet to be told. The events of "Wisteria Lodge" are alleged to have taken place in 1892, clearly an impossibility.

A figure of real life. William S. Baring-Gould's *Sherlock Holmes of Baker Street* (1962) is a full-length "biography", with this significant auctorial note: "No characters in this book are fictional, although the author should very much like to meet any who claim to be." He thus takes to its extreme the Sherlockian game of treating Holmes as a historical figure, skillfully blending inferences from the Canon with information from more conventional historical sources. He begins with Holmes's birth, continues with his hypothetical education and his known early cases, and goes through the dramatic points of his career as narrated in most of the sixty stories. Final chapters deal with his retirement and with his imagined death on January 6, 1957, on a clifftop in Sussex.

Along the way, Baring-Gould introduces a number of ideas that are sometimes accepted by Sherlockians as authentic parts of Holmes's life, although they are best classified as folklore:

• That Professor Moriarty was his mathematics tutor in his youth.

• That Holmes had a second brother, Sherrinford (a name taken from Doyle's earliest notes for *A Study in Scarlet*, which used the name "Sherrinford Holmes" for the detective himself, and "Ormond Sacker" for Watson).

• That Holmes toured America as a young actor in 1879-81.

• That he assisted in the solution of the Jack the Ripper murders in 1888.

• That he enjoyed a dalliance with Irene Adler in Montenegro shortly after his supposed death at the Reichenbach Falls.

At the same time he gives the status of history to speculations that have been vaguely accepted by Sherlockians, such as a birthdate for Holmes of January 6, 1854. The year seems plausible from several Canonical references. The month and date are attributed to Christopher Morley, who apparently chose them to match those of his brother Frank, and to refer to *Twelfth Night*, a play which Holmes twice quotes. A later scholar has seen significance in Holmes's behaviour on a January 7 in *The Valley of Fear*: he shows signs of suffering from a hangover.

Doyle might well have been astonished by such detailed imagining about his creation, although he saw something of Holmes's power in the indignant letters he received after "The Final Problem" killed off the detective, as well as the proposals of marriage that arrived for Holmes at other times in his career. Letters in fact still arrive for Holmes at his address of 221B Baker Street (London NW1 6XL); a selection of them was published as *Letters to Sherlock Holmes* (1985). They are a tribute to the plausibility of the figure Doyle originally created, although the image of Holmes that now lives in the public mind is much less subtle and complex than the one that lives in the pages of the Canon.

John H. Watson

The Canon, save for three short stories and a few other passages, is presented as memoirs by John H. Watson, a former army doctor who was the companion of Sherlock Holmes for most of his working life. Indeed, the first half of *A Study in Scarlet* is subtitled as "a reprint from the reminiscences" of the good doctor, leading playful bibliographers to speculate about the very limited press run those *Reminiscences* must have had. Watson thus must be considered first as an "author" (in which case Arthur Conan Doyle is relegated to the status of Literary Agent, a title some Sherlockians have been happy to give him) and then as a character.

As author — biographer, one might say — Watson is a trifle self-conscious; several Canonical stories mention exchanges between him and Holmes about the narratives he has published, which Holmes says are full of "romanticism" and empty of detective logic. "I could not tamper with the facts," Watson indignantly replies in *The Sign of the Four*. But there is much evidence that he does tamper with them, both deliberately and accidentally. "The Second Stain", for example, acknowledges the need to be "vague in certain details", to avoid betraying state secrets, and the frequent references to towns and streets that do not exist, politicians who did not hold office, and weather that does not match the records in *The Times*, all suggest similar concealment. Other inconsistencies, such as the jump from June to September within a few hours in *The Sign of the Four*, can be attributed to carelessness. Sherlockians have taken joy for several decades in identifying and explaining such little errors, often blaming them on a medical man's dreadful penmanship. Late in the Canon, Watson is very bold about addressing his audience directly, as when he uses the introductory paragraph of "The Veiled Lodger" to announce that a certain story will be made public if illicit attempts to get at his papers are not abandoned. By that time, the relationship between Holmes and Watson is one of equals, the author having an established position just as the detective has. Holmes himself observes that "I am lost without my Boswell," alluding to the companion and biographer of Dr. Samuel Johnson. Certainly Holmes without Watson is far different, far less comprehensible, the forlorn eccentric of "The Lion's Mane" with no one to narrate the tales — and, more important, no one to serve as reliable setting for his sparkling gem.

Watson has been called "boobus Britannicus", a phrase originated by Edmund Pearson (in *The Bookman*, 1932), who blamed illustrator Arthur Keller for making Watson look truly stupid. That was before Nigel Bruce's bumbling portrayal in the 1940's films where he is made a constant fool, the better to set off Basil Rathbone's Holmes. But the original Watson is no boob. Holmes is perhaps generous in telling Watson that "though you are not yourself luminous, you are a conductor of light," but beyond doubt Watson is a man of common sense — as a physician, and certainly an army doctor, must be — and of other good qualities which Holmes often recognizes. He may patronize Watson for lacking intellect to match his own, sometimes descending to cruelty, but it seems clear in most of the stories that he also respects Watson's judgement. A passage in *The Valley of Fear* is particularly telling. Holmes has spun an elaborate web of speculation about the case, and Watson is doubtful:

> "We have only their word for that."
> Holmes looked thoughtful. "I see, Watson. You are sketching out a theory by which everything they say from the beginning is false. . . . Well, that is a good sweeping generalization. Let us see what that brings us to. . . ."

Watson proves to be wrong and Holmes right, of course, but the mutual respect remains. Holmes also finds his companion valuable as a reliable ally in time of emergency, the man who carries the gun in several crises and who will keep his wits about him. Indeed, there is more. At the end of "The Abbey Grange" he addresses his friend: "Watson, you are a British jury, and I never met a man who was more eminently fitted to represent one." Readers of the stories have generally agreed, as did Edgar W. Smith in one of his eloquent editorials in the *Baker Street Journal* (1955), observing that it is the admirable Watson, rather than the unpredictable Holmes, who would make the more welcome friend. He may be ancestor of a hundred foolish companions to brilliant detectives (a cliché which also owes something to early Westerns), but he is himself an admirable fellow.

Biographical details about Watson are few. Of his family, the reader hears only about the "unhappy brother" whose alcoholism and death are chronicled in the early pages of *The Sign of the Four*. Watson took his medical degree in 1878 from the University of London (which validated credentials earned through hospital study, rather than providing medical instruction of its own), entered the army, and served with it during the Second Afghan War. British troops were in Afghanistan for the defence and consolidation of the Empire, and in particular to deter Russia from menacing India through the mountains. A treaty signed in 1879 with local puppet rulers got little respect from the heavily-armed populace, and a powerful force massed in the spring of 1880. As Watson reports in *A Study in Scarlet*, he was wounded at the Battle of Maiwand, which took place July 27, 1880, and was an utter rout from the British point of view; he was unusually lucky to survive in the slaughter and terrible heat, and to be carried to safety at Kandahar and eventually returned to England. Although Watson claims that the Jezail bullet which hit him struck his shoulder and grazed the subclavian artery, there are references in later Canonical tales to a wound in his leg, or in one instance to an injured Achilles tendon. A number of Sherlockians have tried to reconcile all those references, suggesting two wounds, a faulty memory, malingering, or a bullet with an ingeniously complicated trajectory.

Repatriated to England, Watson soon met Holmes (on January 1, 1881, according to at least some scholars) and took up residence with him at 221B Baker Street. He remained there, apparently, for about seven years, until his marriage to Mary Morstan, at the end of *The Sign of the Four*. Thereafter, in several cases that are part of *The Adventures*, Watson is clearly living with a longsuffering wife, presumably Mary, and has entered private medical practice. Repeatedly he leaves Mary (and turns over the practice to an accommodating colleague, Jackson or Anstruther) briefly to accompany Holmes on some adventure. But by the time of "The Empty House", which takes place in 1894, Watson has suffered a bereavement, and is free to move into the old rooms again, abandoning medicine for biography, when Holmes returns to London after a three-year absence. Still later, in "The Blanched Soldier", Holmes speaks of Watson having "deserted me for a wife", and one infers a second marriage. Sherlockians enjoy drinking a toast to "Dr. Watson's second wife", and a number of them have tried to identify her. The chronology is impossibly complicated, with inconsistencies that can be attributed to Watson's muddled thinking or, more realistically, to Doyle's complete indifference to such details. Of course it is more fun for Sherlockians to speculate that, as one of them has put it, "Watson had as many wives as Henry VIII."

The fair sex is his department, as Holmes says; but he is chivalrous about it, and decent in every way. (Rex Stout's article "Watson Was a Woman", in the *Baker Street Journal* in 1946, was only a joke.) He seems to be the ideal Britisher, whom the author holds up to the reader as the measure of the less conventional Holmes. Indeed, one might say, he seems to be the author's representative. Says Peter Costello in *The Real World of Sherlock Holmes* (1991): "Dr. Watson, whatever other models he may have had in real life, such as Conan Doyle's own secretary Major Wood, is largely drawn from Doyle himself. For a start both are medical men of much the same age with sporting interests. Both have a bluff, hearty appearance. Both seem conventional, Imperialist in politics, non-intellectual men of action. Dr. Watson even shares Conan Doyle's love for Southsea, and his literary tastes." If Holmes is Arthur Conan Doyle's mentor, Joseph Bell, surely Watson is Doyle himself.

The Supporting Actors

Professor James Moriarty. For all the reputation he has developed as Holmes's arch-enemy, Professor James (if that was in fact his given name) Moriarty figures in only two stories — three if one counts "The Empty House", in which the truth of his death, occurring in "The Final Problem", is told. Countless cartoonists and parodists have drawn Moriarty into their creations; such respectable Holmesians as the producers of the Granada television series of the 1980s have succumbed to the temptation, making Moriarty the genius behind the events of "The Red-Headed League", an idea for which there is no justification in the original story.

Moriarty is presented, in "The Final Problem" and the second chapter of *The Valley of Fear*, as the master-criminal behind "half that is evil and . . . nearly all that is undetected" in London:

> He sits motionless, like a spider in the centre of its web, but that web has a thousand radiations, and he knows well every quiver of each of them. He does little himself. He only plans. But his agents are numerous and splendidly organized. Is there a crime to be done, a paper to be abstracted, we will say, a house to be rifled, a man to be removed — the word is passed to the professor, the matter is organized and carried out.

In short, Moriarty is the modern Jonathan Wild, a successor to the criminal leader who operated in London at the beginning of the eighteenth century (he was hanged in 1725) and is known chiefly from Henry Fielding's 1743 satire *The Life and Death of Jonathan Wild the Great*. Alec MacDonald, the Scotland Yard inspector in *The Valley of Fear*, vaguely dismisses Wild as "someone in a novel". Holmes, of course, noting that Wild was real, adds that "The old wheel turns, and the same spoke comes up." In "The Final Problem" he calls Moriarty "the Napoleon of crime".

He is presented as a professor of mathematics, formerly of "one of our smaller universities", dismissed as the result of "hereditary tendencies" which led him into unspecified wickedness. "At the age of twenty-one he wrote a treatise upon the binomial theorem which has had a European vogue," Holmes says, referring to one of the basic principles of algebra. More ominously, he elsewhere refers to Moriarty's work on *The Dynamics of an Asteroid*, which has been interpreted as having to do with space travel or even atomic energy (and may in fact be a study of the notoriously complicated three-body problem of gravitational attraction). Of his personal life the only other information provided in the Canon is that one brother was "a station master in the west of England" and another, also named James, a colonel. The professor's physique was remarkable, as Holmes describes it in "The Final Problem", as he was "extremely tall and thin", with a great domed forehead, rounded shoulders, and a habit of oscillating his face "from side to side in a curiously reptilian fashion".

Some close readers of the text have suggested that Moriarty never existed — that he was a fantasy of a drug-addicted Holmes, or at least that he was an innocent man, all his crimes imagined by Holmes in some paranoid delusion. Nicholas Meyer used that idea to good advantage in his highly successful novel *The Seven-Per-Cent Solution* (1974), and Jeremy Brett's play *The Secret of Sherlock Holmes* (1989) offers a variation on it. That extreme is no more reasonable than the popular Sherlockian belief that everything evil has Moriarty behind it, and the vague impression among the public that the Holmes stories are about one struggle after another between the detective and the professor, rather as Denis Nayland Smith endlessly battles Fu Manchu in the writings of Sax Rohmer.

Irene Adler. "She is the daintiest thing under a bonnet on this planet," Holmes reports in "A Scandal in Bohemia", before setting eyes on Irene Adler. No matter: the description has been generally accepted, as has Watson's report that Holmes characterized her as "*the* woman". She is mentioned in one or two other stories, but only in reference to the adventure of which she is the central figure, "A Scandal in Bohemia".

Early in that story, Holmes looks her up in a reference book and reports that she is an operatic contralto, born in New Jersey and now retired from the international stage. He patronizingly calls her a "young person"; the King of Bohemia, who feels the threat of blackmail from her, calls her a "well-known adventuress". Holmes is engaged to recover the compromising papers from her clutches, and quite fails to do so. By the end of the tale, having seen the lady in person, he is so impressed — perhaps with her courage and intelligence, perhaps with her beauty — that he asks for her photograph as a souvenir, and allows Watson to record that he had been "beaten by a woman's wit".

Irene Adler lives in St. John's Wood, the fashionable London neighbourhood in which wealthy men did typically install their mistresses. She is presumably modelled on the women known as adventuresses, *grandes horizontales*, or "pretty horsebreakers" — courtesans more realistically associated with the 1860's, such as Laura Bell, Cora Pearl, Catherine Walters and Caroline Otero. *Fanfare of Strumpets* (1971), a non-Sherlockian book by that venerable Sherlockian Michael Harrison, is full of anecdotes about them. In Irene Adler there may also be a whiff of the scandalous Sarah Bernhardt (1844-1923) and of Lillie Langtry (1852-1929), "the Jersey Lily" who became a mistress of Edward, Prince of Wales. Yet another original is clearly Lola Montez (1818-1861), whose intrigues with Louis of Bavaria had been notorious five decades earlier. At a less exalted level, Sherlockians associate Irene Adler with "Aunt Clara", the spoilt heroine of a 1940's comic song, the full story of which is told in *We Always Mention Aunt Clara* (1990) by W. T. Rabe.

There is little in the text of the story to justify attaching to Irene Adler either the social standing or the morals of such women. A feminist interpretation of her life (as put forward, not surprisingly, by some of the Adventuresses of Sherlock Holmes) makes her an early career woman, misused and cast aside by a snob of a Bohemian prince. Carole Nelson Douglas interprets her in that way with particular sensitivity and conviction in the novel *Good Night, Mr. Holmes* (1990) and two sequels. But most readers, it seems, have preferred to see her as the woman Sherlock Holmes loved and lost (or, in a minority view, loved and later won). Belden Wigglesworth celebrated her in a poem in the *Baker Street Journal* in 1946, one of many such apostrophes:

> I wonder what your thoughts have been,
>   Your inmost thoughts of him, Irene,
>   Across the years? . . .
>   Did you forget?
>   Did Baker Street *quite* lack a Queen?
>   I wonder.

These and other imaginings are discussed at length, as are all aspects of Irene Adler, in chapters of *In Bed with Sherlock Holmes* (1984) by Christopher Redmond. There is much to say about her, and much that has already been said, but the Canon provides little basis for either sentimental or prurient speculation about a Holmes-Adler connection.

Mycroft Holmes. The brother of Sherlock Holmes, older than he by seven years, figures in two cases, both of which he brings to the detective's attention. One is "The Greek Interpreter", in which the client, Mr. Melas, happens to lodge in the same building as Mycroft. The other is "The Bruce-Partington Plans", a government affair in which Mycroft, on behalf of the highest authorities, demands his brother's assistance — for Mycroft, who "audits the books in some of the government departments" in the first case, turns out in this later one to have a much more crucial position. "Occasionally he *is* the British government," Holmes tells an astonished Watson:

> We will suppose that a minister needs information as to a point which involves the Navy, India, Canada and the bimetallic question; he could get his separate advices from various departments upon each, but only Mycroft can focus them all, and say offhand how each factor would affect the other. . . . Again and again his word has decided the national policy.

Such a description foreshadows the computerized "expert systems" of modern times, and indeed Robert A. Heinlein (in *The Moon Is a Harsh Mistress*, 1966) found it appropriate to name an omniscient computer Mycroft.

Watson describes Mycroft's body as "gross", his fat hand "like the flipper of a seal". His habits are unvarying and unathletic — "Jupiter is descending," says Holmes when his brother condescends to call. Otherwise, "Mycroft has his rails and he runs on them. His Pall Mall lodgings, the Diogenes Club, Whitehall — that is his cycle." (The Diogenes Club, described in "The Greek Interpreter", is a club — which Sherlock Holmes finds "soothing" at times — for unclubbable men, forbidden by by-law to take any notice of one another, or to talk, save in the Strangers' Room.) But his detective powers are immense. "It was Adams, of course," he says to his more active brother about a case the latter has been working to solve. Action, of course, is "not my *métier*", but theorizing and thought from an armchair — in that, Mycroft Holmes excels. The passage from "The Greek Interpreter" in which the brothers compete in deductions about a stranger on the street is a classic, so much so that Doyle used it as one of his "readings" when he lectured in North America in 1894:

> "An old soldier, I perceive," said Sherlock.
> "And very recently discharged," remarked the brother.
> "Served in India, I see."
> "And a non-commissioned officer."

And so on. Not for nothing has it been suggested that Nero Wolfe, the corpulent, chair-bound detective created by Rex Stout in the 1930's, is a relative of Mycroft Holmes.

Mrs. Hudson. The best appreciation of Holmes's landlady, Mrs. Hudson, is an article by Vincent Starrett that appeared in the 1944 anthology *Profile by*

Gaslight. He writes of her possible background, her management of the house at 221B Baker Street, her staff, and her loyalty to Holmes, shown particularly in her patience with his foibles. Other writings about her have interpreted her relationship with the detective in various ways, some suggesting that it was peculiarly personal. Certainly the kind of devotion seen in "The Empty House", in which she repeatedly crawls to Holmes's wax bust "on my knees" and in danger of her life to adjust its position, suggests something more than the usual relationship between tenant and landlady.

But "landlady" may be slightly misleading. In story after story, Mrs. Hudson is presented as the "housekeeper", and it seems possible that rather than owning the house outright, she had it on a long-term lease and proceeded to rent rooms to gentlemen. Watson does speak, in "The Dying Detective", of Holmes's "princely" rental payments to her. On the other hand he frequently treats her as an employee, demanding refreshment and ignoring scheduled mealtimes, and abuses the fabric of the building when it suits him. The most famous instance is his indoor target practice, in which he shoots the initials V.R. (for Victoria Regina) into the wall — an activity which must at least have filled the house with plaster-dust.

There may well have been a housemaid at 221B, although she is never mentioned, and certainly there was Billy the pageboy, at least during some periods. Other staff are uncertain; Holmes in "Thor Bridge" speaks of a "new cook", which may imply that there had been a former cook, or may mean that Mrs. Hudson had finally delegated the kitchen duties to an employee. The incident (in "The Three Students") when Mrs. Hudson promises "green peas at seven-thirty" gives no indication that they were to be prepared by anyone other than herself. Breakfast may have been her forte; it is mentioned in story after story, and in "The Naval Treaty" Holmes offers the high praise that Mrs. Hudson has "as good an idea of breakfast as a Scotchwoman", a comment that has led to the general impression that she was in fact Scots. Then there is the famous reference in "A Scandal in Bohemia" to "Mrs. Turner", one of those cruxes that Sherlockians love; it has been variously interpreted as meaning a cook, a temporary replacement while Mrs. Hudson was holidaying or unwell, or simply absent-mindedness on someone's part.

Of the woman herself we know little, not even her first name, although on no evidence she has been identified with the "Martha" who is the housekeeper in "His Last Bow". Holmes once speaks of cronies, but their identity is as unknown as Mrs. Hudson's taste in amusement, food, or furnishings. Even her physique can only be inferred from a reference to her "stately tread". What matters to the reader of the Sherlock Holmes tales is her reliable maintenance of the house in Baker Street, and her presence (in only fourteen of the sixty stories) as the motherly figure without whom the sometimes childlike Holmes would be lost in London. For that role, readers remember and honour her. Vincent Starrett again: "It is proverbial that landladies never die."

Billy. The pageboy of 221B Baker Street appears in ten of the stories, only three times by name. The "Billy" who ushers in visitors in *The Valley of Fear*, circa 1889, can hardly be the same boy who is there for "Thor Bridge" and "The Mazarin Stone" more than twenty years later. A succession of boys is the obvious explanation, and it may be as few as two of them, since the appearances are clustered, most in stories that take place in the 1880's, two in the early 1900's. Among the latter is the passage in "The Mazarin Stone" that has made Billy the object of great affection among readers:

> It was pleasant to Dr. Watson to find himself once more in the untidy room of the first floor in Baker Street. . . . Finally, his eyes came round to the fresh and smiling face of Billy, the young but very wise and tactful page, who had helped a little to fill up the gap of loneliness and isolation which surrounded the saturnine figure of the great detective.
> "It all seems very unchanged, Billy. You don't change, either. . . ."

A mythical character can remain unchanged for a quarter of a century; perhaps Billy now deserves that title.

The Baker Street Irregulars. The youngsters who helped Holmes in a few cases would be of the smallest importance to modern readers, had not the American Sherlockians of the 1930's chosen the name "Baker Street Irregulars" for their organization. They might almost have been the same people, for the children of (say) 1890 were middle-aged folks in 1934, when the American BSI had its beginning.

But the original Irregulars were Londoners (one presumes Cockney accents), urchins or "street arabs" in the contemporary phrase. They are seen in *A Study in Scarlet* and *The Sign of the Four*, where their wages are fixed at one shilling a day; after these two early cases they return only in "The Crooked Man". Their leader in the first two stories is Wiggins; in "The Crooked Man" he is Simpson, the earlier generation of boys having presumably grown past the age when they could be of use to Holmes as unobtrusive spies. In one other case, *The Hound of the Baskervilles*, Holmes uses a boy (Cartwright), but as a lone agent on Dartmoor rather than as the leader of a London gang.

"Irregulars" are combatants not from the regular army (George Washington used the word about his own ragged troops). Applying it to the boys of Baker Street (and there may have been girls too; the text is indefinite), Holmes means investigators who are independent of the police. He uses the same word in "Lady Frances Carfax" to mean himself and Watson.

The Unpublished Cases

Throughout the tales, Watson is made to drop hints about other cases in which Sherlock Holmes was engaged. Usually he makes mention of the other business that was under way at the time, but sometimes he compares the current case to some other, and on several occasions Holmes does the same thing, drawing both on his direct experience and on his reading.

Such allusions range from the generic ("a very commonplace little murder", Holmes calls his current business in "The Naval Treaty") to the memorable:

> As I turn over the pages, I see my notes upon the repulsive story of the red leech and the terrible death of Crosby, the banker. Here also I find an account of the Addleton tragedy, and the singular contents of the ancient British barrow. The famous Smith-Mortimer succession case comes also within this period, and so does the tracking and arrest of Huret, the Boulevard assassin — an exploit which won for Holmes an autograph letter of thanks from the French President and the Order of the Legion of Honour. ["The Golden Pince-Nez"]

Listing the unpublished cases in *The Tin Dispatch-Box* (1965), Christopher Redmond defined them as "any criminal investigation or professional business in which Holmes was involved or took a particular contemporary interest. Using this definition, there are altogether 111 cases." (The listing which led to that total has a few omissions.) Such cases are of interest to the would-be biographer as clues to filling in the great stretches of Holmes's career not covered in the published stories, and as instances in which he made use of his powers to solve mysteries about which the reader would love to hear.

The unpublished cases have provided motifs for a number of "pastiches", or imitations of the original tales, including several of the *Exploits of Sherlock Holmes* (1952-53) by Adrian Conan Doyle and John Dickson Carr. They were also the basis of many scripts by Edith Meiser (1932-43) and her successors for a long-running series of American radio dramatizations. For such purposes the unpublished cases are ideal, since generally there is merely a thought-provoking phrase, rather than a plot to which the writer must stick.

A surprising amount can, however, sometimes be deduced about an unpublished case. Edward F. Clark, Jr., in the *Baker Street Journal* in 1963 offered a careful exegesis of a few words in "The Final Problem": "I knew in the papers that [Holmes] had been engaged by the French republic upon a matter of supreme importance." A number of scholars have toyed with "the papers of ex-President Murillo", mentioned in "The Norwood Builder", identifying that gentleman with various former South American leaders. Exploration of what Watson meant to say begins to overlap with investigation of Doyle's sources, as when "the peculiar persecution of John Vincent Harden" is said to have been suggested to the author's mind by his reading about Texas bandit John Wesley Hardin. Some of the unpublished cases refer to historical people, including the Pope (presumably Leo XIII) and Vanderbilt (one of the New York railroad clan). Others contain intriguing but inexplicable names, personal or geographical, including "Isadora Persano" and "the island of Uffa". In a class by itself is "the giant rat of Sumatra", a phrase that has intrigued not only pasticheurs and scholars but also the designers of new hazards in the popular game "Dungeons and Dragons".

The Rooms at 221B Baker Street

The arrangement of Holmes's (and, in some of the stories but not all, Watson's) rooms is unclear, and in any case may have changed over the years. "The Mazarin Stone", a story that is a one-act play lightly rewritten, contains what amount to stage directions, calling for exits and entrances hardly compatible with a conventional suite in Baker Street. It is better to build up the lodgings — and particularly the sitting-room, where most of the action takes place — in the mind's eye. Still, a creditable job has been done by the proprietors of several restorations, particularly the one at the "Sherlock Holmes" public-house in Northumberland Street, London, and the one improbably located at a Holiday Inn in San Francisco. Illustrators, stage designers and television producers have faced the same challenge, generally emphasizing whichever features of the room, authentic or otherwise, are needed for their immediate purposes.

A monstrous amount of furniture must be fitted into that room if every sentence in the Canon is to be taken as true. The chairs on either side of the fire, in which one imagines Holmes and Watson sitting to chat, are a bare beginning: Don MacLachlan, writing in *Canadian Holmes* in 1989, includes in the inventory "12 chairs, two stools, one sofa, and something sittable-on by the window. Enough seating for at least 17 people." But there are many other objects in the room as well, from the dining-table to the workbench with Holmes's chemicals, not to mention a bearskin rug, a safe, a sideboard, and the coal-scuttle in which Holmes kept his cigars. A plausible floor plan was drawn by Julian Wolff to accompany his analysis of the rooms in the *Baker Street Journal* in 1946. He includes a bathroom adjacent to the sitting-room — a facility that may have amounted to a luxury in 1895. He also puts Holmes's bedroom (which figures in "The Dying Detective" in particular) adjacent to the sitting-room, relegating Watson to an upper storey (British "second", American "third", floor).

The dominant feature of the suite at 221B must have been clutter. Holmes had "a horror of destroying documents", Watson reports, and attached his unanswered letters to the mantelpiece with his jack-knife. Chemical experiments were often in progress, discarded newspapers and telegrams littered the floor, and relics of cases were, Watson says, wont to turn up in the butter-dish. There may have been a little space left for Watson's cherished portrait of General "Chinese" Gordon, but the conventional decorations of a Victorian sitting-room, the antimacassars and ostrich eggs, must have been almost entirely absent. For it is probably a mistake to imagine a spacious room; the chamber of a pair of bachelors was surely rather cosy than elegant.

Holmes's Methods

"You know my methods," Holmes repeatedly told his companion. If the reader does not know them — as sometimes, it seems, Watson did not — they are evident in passages throughout the Canon, or systematically set out in Brad Keefauver's book *The Elementary Methods of Sherlock Holmes* (1987). Keefauver considers Holmes's immense general knowledge, his reference library, his readiness to compare the present case to precedents in criminal activity, his use of disguise, and other stratagems and resources. But the essence of Holmes's detective ability lay in the data he was able to collect and the reasoning in which he engaged.

Chiefly, Holmes worked from facts. "I cannot make bricks without clay," he said once; and over and over again, "It is a capital mistake to theorize in advance of the facts." And for him facts were usually tiny things — a burnt match in the mud, the torn and ink-stained finger of a glove:

> I can never bring you to realize the importance of sleeves, the suggestiveness of thumb-nails, or the great issues that may hang from a bootlace. . . . Never trust to general impressions, my boy, but concentrate yourself upon details. My first glance is always at a woman's sleeve. In a man it is perhaps better first to take the knee of the trouser. ["A Case of Identity"]

In using such a procedure to size up a client or a suspicious character, Holmes is following the example of Doyle's medical mentor, Joseph Bell. It is a technique exactly suited to the Victorian age, a period of many specialized trades, and to the British multiplicity of social classes and local customs. In a modern, homogenized North America, where all classes dress alike and only a few people work in trades that leave such marks as the weaver's tooth or the compositor's left thumb, a Sherlock Holmes might have a much more difficult task.

The observation of trifles is not limited to assessing profession and character. Holmes uses it particularly in examining the scene of a crime, engaging in the famous "floor-walk" with his "powerful convex lens" in search of tiny objects: a pill in *A Study in Scarlet*, "what seemed to me to be dust" (but was tobacco ash) in "The Boscombe Valley Mystery". Footprints and other traces are a specialty. The ability to see details, rather than "general impressions", makes it possible for Holmes to understand the significance of a chip on a railing in "Thor Bridge", and of beeswing in a wine-glass in "The Abbey Grange".

Finally, of course, Holmes has the knowledge of previous cases, and his general knowledge of society, to help him focus his attention:

> "How did you see that?"
> "Because I looked for it." ["The Dancing Men"]

What he does not have is the improbable, detailed knowledge of every science, craft and art seen in such later detectives as R. Austin Freeman's Dr. Thorndyke. Holmes is widely read and experienced, but chiefly in the areas that he knows will come in handy. His methods strongly resemble those of the physician, writes Kathryn Montgomery Hunter in *Doctors' Stories* (1991) — he compares the symptoms of his current case to those of many previous cases, his own and those of other investigators, before making a diagnosis and prescribing treatment.

The form of reasoning Holmes used, which he variously calls "deduction", "logical synthesis", and "inference", is certainly not the same as the traditional formal logic, which is a form of mathematics developed in the middle ages, concerned not with truth but with consistency. The simplest example of a "syllogism", the form into which logic casts its ideas, is this:

> All dogs are mortal.
> The Hound of the Baskervilles is a dog.
> Therefore the Hound of the Baskervilles is mortal.

The first two statements, or "premises", lead to the conclusion; thus the syllogism is logically sound. A second syllogism,

> Scotland Yard inspectors are detectives.
> Sherlock Holmes is a detective.
> Therefore Sherlock Holmes is a Scotland Yard inspector.

is unsound because of what logic calls "the fallacy of the undistributed middle". The premises may or may not be true, but either way they do not prove the conclusion. On the other hand, a logically sound syllogism can have wildly untrue premises, and thus demonstrate nothing about the truth of the conclusion.

Holmes rarely works in this way, although he speaks of it: "From a drop of water, a logician could infer the possibility of an Atlantic or a Niagara." If traditional logic is "deduction", a moving from the general to the specific, from cause to effect, then Holmes's method is really "induction", moving from the specific to the general, from effect to cause. "The grand thing is to be able to reason backwards," he says in *A Study in Scarlet*. Such a process is prone to error, as an effect can have many causes. As Keefauver demonstrates, Holmes frequently worked through "deduction" in a different sense: imagining as many explanations for the facts as possible, then deducting (eliminating) the less promising. In his most famous dictum ("The Beryl Coronet") he alludes to this process: "When you have excluded the impossible, whatever remains, however improbable, must be the truth." The danger of course is deeming something "impossible" when it is not. Holmes often does that, but such is the art of the detective story that he never goes wrong in his leaps.

Overtones in the Stories

The myth and the hero. To call Sherlock Holmes the "hero" of the Canonical stories is more than simply to observe that he is the central figure. A hero is someone who acts in a cause, such as freedom or justice, and according to certain conventions. One classic statement of the hero "pattern" is that of Lord Raglan (in *The Hero*, 1936), who finds twenty-two common features in the stories of figures from Oedipus to King Arthur. Holmes can be seen to have about thirteen of those features, a higher score than Siegfried's, and equal to that of Robin Hood. He "prescribes laws", for example (*The Whole Art of Detection*), nothing is known of his childhood, nothing is known of his death.

Many of Raglan's "heroes" are supposed gods. Holmes is not presented as a god (although G. K. Chesterton wrote about his apotheosis in "Sherlock Holmes the God" as early as 1935), or even as a king, but merely as "the head of his profession". However, it is hard to deny that some of his appeal derives from his conformity to the classic pattern. Most important is his "death" at the Reichenbach and his "resurrection" three years later. (A fall from grace and a mysterious death at the top of a hill are involved in several of Raglan's points.) The spring dates of Holmes's death and resurrection, and the name of the adversary whom he conquers (Moriarty, suggesting *moriar*, "I shall die"), remind the attentive reader of Easter, and the Christian story of the death and resurrection of Jesus (who incidentally scores at least sixteen points on Raglan's scale). Springtime resurrection is of course not unique to Christianity, for most religions include some hint of it, based on the natural cycle of vegetation.

Holmes's heroic qualities are such that enthusiasts have tried to associate him with practically every known hero and other prominent figure, pretending that he is the descendant of Shakespeare, the colleague of Marconi, the lover of Sarah Bernhardt, the antagonist of Hitler, the father of Nero Wolfe and the near relative of Mr. Spock of "Star Trek". All such speculations are feeble attempts at describing the emotional, even spiritual, significance of a figure like Sherlock Holmes, who bestrides his world, and the world of the imagination, like a colossus. There are various short catalogues of the figures who, though fictional, have become universally known; they may perhaps include Robinson Crusoe, Romeo, and Ronald McDonald, but there is no doubt whatever that they include Holmes. It is also said that only two characters from literature regularly receive mail. One is Juliet, whose correspondents are lovelorn teenage girls, and the other is Sherlock Holmes.

Sexual implications. Although one might expect a "detective story" to be concerned only with crime and adventure, in fact the Sherlock Holmes tales are rich in love and sexual elements as well. They can be seen from the earliest tales to the latest: *A Study in Scarlet* is about a murder prompted by sexual jealousy, as is "The Retired Colourman", last story in *The Case-Book*.

Holmes's own love life receives much attention, chiefly through attempts to read more into his relationship with Irene Adler than the text warrants; many Sherlockians have also attempted to link him with Violet Hunter of "The Copper Beeches", largely through such paragraphs as this one, identified by David Hammer in *Baker Street Miscellanea* (1991):

> I remember nothing until I found myself lying on my bed trembling all over. Then I thought of you, Mr. Holmes.

Taking sentences out of context can, of course, be a delight — John Bennett Shaw, the master of that craft, collected many examples in a paper he titled "To Shelve or to Censor" (1971). A classic is Holmes's remark in "The Speckled Band" that "Mrs. Hudson has been knocked up," an idiom with quite different meanings in America and England.

Legitimate romance plays an important part in *The Sign of the Four*, in which Watson's love affair with Mary Morstan alternates with Holmes's detective work as the plot develops, and in such short stories as "The Noble Bachelor". Less proper relationships drive the plots of "A Case of Identity", "The Crooked Man" and "The Cardboard Box". In *The Hound of the Baskervilles*, much of the dramatic complexity comes from the relations between the sexes: the apparently wholesome attraction between Sir Henry Baskerville and Beryl Stapleton, the sadomasochistic relationship between Beryl and Jack Stapleton, the sad if not scarlet past of Laura Lyons. Then there are any number of stories in which romance provides a subplot, a "love interest" to vary the pace, from Arthur Cadogan West's desertion of his fiancée in "The Bruce-Partington Plans" to Violet Smith's engagement in "The Solitary Cyclist" (a matter which leads Holmes to make a remark that makes the lady blush coyly).

Not surprisingly, traces of the author's own life and relationships can be seen in all these features. Mary Morstan in *The Sign of the Four* is in many respects a portrait of his first wife, Louise; the solid bonds of love between John and Ivy Douglas in *The Valley of Fear* strongly suggest those between Doyle and his second wife, Jean, to whom he had been married seven years when the book was published. Most important in reflecting the author's experience and feelings, however, are a cluster of stories published in the first decade of the twentieth century, during and just after a difficult period in his life, while he was married to the dying Louise but already in love with Jean. In these tales — "The Norwood Builder", "The Solitary Cyclist", "The Devil's Foot" and others — sex is a source of trouble, and repeatedly there are men obliged to choose between two women, or women obliged to choose between two men. In the most dramatic example, "The Abbey Grange" (published in 1904, two years before Louise's death), Doyle puts in the mouths of his characters eloquent arguments for divorce-law reform. Such motifs appear in his stories as late as 1922, when he published "Thor Bridge" and pictured the illicit lady-love of Holmes's client, Neil Gibson, as a woman much like Jean, and every bit as acceptable for him as his true wife.

Sexual motifs have been examined by a number of Sherlockian writers, but chiefly for prurient effect, or as a way of demonstrating that Victorian life was by no means sexless. The latter point has been made in such non-Sherlockian volumes as *The Worm in the Bud* (1969) by Ronald Pearsall and *The Other Victorians* (1974) by Stephen Marcus. It was an era of fashionable mistresses and *grandes horizontales*, pervasive street prostitution and some white slavery, and lavish pornography. That sexual enthusiasm prevailed, but public discussion of sexual matters was impossible, goes far to explain the origins of the kinds of crime Holmes is seen investigating. Sex in the Sherlockian Canon is discussed at full length in *In Bed with Sherlock Holmes* (1984) by Christopher Redmond.

Chapter III

Sherlock Holmes in Print

The publishing of Sherlock Holmes has been a substantial industry for a hundred years. Each of the sixty stories, though it may appear fixed and inevitable on the printed page, finds its present form — its content, its text, its typography, its illustration — as the result of choices and chances not only on the part of Doyle but on the part of publishers, editors, typographers and readers over the decades.

An understanding of the stories' origins, the circumstances of their writing, and the details of their transmission from the author's pen to the modern printed page, is valuable in understanding their intentions and their ingenuity. The reader must sometimes be a bibliographer, sometimes a critic, and sometimes a connoisseur of language and of art.

There is no single bibliographical listing of editions of the Canon, and one would be immensely difficult to compile. Some editions, especially early ones, appear in Green and Gibson's *Bibliography of A. Conan Doyle* (1983) and other works on Doyle. Ronald B. DeWaal's *World Bibliography of Sherlock Holmes* (1974) and *International Sherlock Holmes* (1980) include the stories separately and in collections, but the descriptions provided are sparse and unhelpful. Before DeWaal's work, the leading Sherlockian bibliography was *Baker Street Inventory*, edited by Edgar W. Smith (1945, with regular supplements appearing in the *Baker Street Journal*, which also published valuable bibliographical notes from time to time in its early years). There are also the two editions (1973 and 1977) of *A Checklist of the Arthur Conan Doyle Collection* at the Metropolitan Toronto Library, compiled by Donald Redmond.

Sources

A direct source for *The Hound of the Baskervilles* is generally believed to exist, in a "west country legend" told to Doyle (for so he himself says) by a friend, Fletcher Robinson. At best, however, he worked from a complex of "black-dog" legends associated with unpopulated parts of England, including Dartmoor. Janice McNabb explores those sources in *The Curious Incident of the Hound on Dartmoor* (1984). In *A Study in Surmise* (1984), Michael Harrison sets out in detail what he previously argued elsewhere: that *A Study in Scarlet* is extensively based — indeed, that the existence of Sherlock Holmes is based — on "the vanishing, from his shop in the St. Luke's district of London, of a German baker, Urban Napoleon Stanger. This was in 1881." *The Valley of Fear* is largely based on the doings of the "Mollie Maguires" in the coal country of Pennsylvania in the 1870's. A few other direct sources for large portions of Doyle's plots can be identified.

It has become clear that Doyle not only read voraciously but stored what he read, at least half-consciously, to reuse and recombine names and details years

later. Donald Redmond has written extensively on specific sources as they can
be unearthed:

> Holmes "spoke [in *The Sign of the Four*] on a quick succession of subjects"
> including the Buddhism of Ceylon and miracle plays. In fact, it seems that he was
> only relating what he had read in the papers. For *The Times* (London) had on 15
> June 1888 reported upon the Congress of Protestant Foreign Missions, then in ses-
> sion, with a long account: "Wednesday afternoon's conference . . . subject was
> 'Buddhism and other kindred heathen systems: their character and influence com-
> pared with those of Christianity' . . . Sir Monier Monier-Williams [the president of
> the conference] at once proceeded to place in contrast the Bible of Christianity and
> the Bible of the Buddhists." Among other matters in the account, evident anti-
> Catholic accounts would have attracted Conan Doyle's attention. As to miracle
> plays, Geoffrey S. Stavert, in his recent *A Study in Southsea*, points out that the
> Rev. H. Shaen Solly of Southampton spoke to the Portsmouth Literary and Scien-
> tific Society (in which Conan Doyle was very active) on this exact subject. . . .
>
> After Mary Morstan had left their sitting-room, Sherlock Holmes was probably
> striving for effect when he "smiled gently" at Watson's shocked reaction to
> Holmes's languid put-down, and cried, "I assure you that the most winning woman
> I ever knew was hanged for poisoning three little children for their insurance-
> money. . . ." In the *Sherlock Holmes Journal* (vol. 11, Summer 1973, pp. 58-63) I
> looked at this remark, with instances.

Many such connections are of course conjectural. In the absence of a full reading of everything Doyle can have read over a period of several decades — or,
still better, the unveiling of his notebooks — much will emerge only by chance.
And it is often unclear whether a correspondence between something in the
news, or in an earlier author, and something in Doyle is deliberate allusion,
unconscious repetition, or pure coincidence. The researcher can easily be
tempted to substitute wishful thinking for evidence. Patterns do, however,
emerge. Donald Redmond reports in *Sherlock Holmes: A Study in Sources*
(1982) that at least eight of the Scowrers, and some twenty-three other characters in *The Valley of Fear*, appear to be named after medical acquaintances of
Doyle. Many characters in *A Study in Scarlet* share surnames with neighbours of
Doyle in Southsea and Portsmouth, where he lived when he wrote that book.
Often, it appears, a character is named for more than one original, or takes a
name from one and an attribute ("club foot" or "tiger hunter") from another.

Sherlock Holmes's own name has been the subject of much interest, especially in the light of his first incarnation as "Sherrinford Holmes" in a page of
Doyle's handwritten notes. The author claims that he took the "Sherlock" from a
bowler of the Marylebone Cricket Club against whom he once had a run of luck
— although the eighteenth-century theologian Thomas Sherlock lurks in the
background, and James McCord revealed in the *Baker Street Journal* in 1992
that Jane Sherlock Ball was the mother of one of Doyle's aunts. "Holmes",
meanwhile, is popularly assumed to come from Oliver Wendell Holmes the
elder, the American doctor and author, whom Doyle much admired. Another
possibility is a physician friend and neighbour of Doyle's. Dr. John H. Watson
probably takes his name from Dr. James Watson, a medical colleague of Doyle's

in Southsea; the first Moriarty ever encountered by Doyle was a master at his school, Stonyhurst College.

Joseph Bell. Doyle always maintained that Sherlock Holmes was modelled on Dr. Joseph Bell (born 1837, died October 4, 1911), professor of surgery in Edinburgh, and the teacher who impressed the young Doyle most. He wrote in his autobiography, *Memories and Adventures*, that when he came to create Holmes, "I thought of my old teacher Joe Bell, of his eagle face, of his curious ways, of his eerie trick of spotting details." Elsewhere in the same book he tells an anecdote or two about Bell the master of diagnosis, including the famous exchange, quoted in many writings about Doyle, in which Bell begins by greeting a patient: "Well, my man, you've served in the army.... Not long discharged?... A Highland regiment?" And so on.

Ely M. Liebow accepts that attribution in his biography *Dr. Joe Bell: Model for Sherlock Holmes* (1982), although he acknowledges that Holmes had other origins as well. Bell was editor of the *Edinburgh Medical Journal* from 1873, and a teacher from 1878, as well as an expert consulted by the police in forensic matters, but it was as a practising surgeon that he was best known. Says Liebow:

> Joe Bell was an operator, a great one. He was in all probability better than Syme, better than Lister or Annandale, or any other contemporary, with the exception of the great-but-silent Patrick Heron Watson. While he was in the post-Listerian age, and the post-Simpson age, he would be operating many times in his life without anesthesia and when septicemia still plagued the hospitals. "Rapidity," writes a colleague, "was his keynote, swiftness in operating."

Doyle, as a medical student, was chosen to be clerk for Bell's clinics at the Royal Infirmary, and heard the great man assess patients with rapid perceptions that he would later put into Holmes's mouth: "This man's limp is not from his hip but from his foot. Were you to observe closely, you would see there are slits, cut by a knife, in those parts of the shoe where the pressure of the shoe is greatest against the foot. The man is a sufferer from corns, gentlemen." Such flashes of insight made an impression, and when Doyle created about Holmes he wrote to Bell, "I do not think that his analytical work is in the least an exaggeration of some effects which I have seen you produce in the out-patient ward." Bell's compassion, and his thirst for justice, may also be reflected in Sherlock Holmes.

Manuscripts

Doyle wrote his stories in longhand, in a firm, squat, generally legible script but with apparent disdain for the rules of punctuation and capitalization. There is evidence in the known manuscripts that his first draft was also generally his last; on occasion he left a space in which he would later fill in a name or phrase.

The manuscripts have been thoroughly dispersed by the publishers or by the author's heirs, and the whereabouts of some is unknown. A number, including *The Sign of the Four* and *The Valley of Fear*, are in private hands. Others are in public collections — "The Red Circle" at Indiana University, "The Solitary Cyclist" at Cornell University, three short stories and a chapter of *The Hound of the*

Baskervilles at the New York Public Library. The British Museum (now the British Library) had none until a consortium of American Sherlockians bought "The Missing Three-Quarter" and made a gift of it in 1959. In 1990, "The Dying Detective" and a portion of "The Crooked Man" were placed on permanent loan with the Sherlock Holmes Collection at the Marylebone Library, London. A census of the manuscripts by Peter E. Blau appeared in *Baker Street Miscellanea* in 1978.

Portions of many manuscripts have been reproduced in facsimile in Sherlockian journals, and two complete manuscripts have been published in book form: *The Adventure of the Priory School: . . . A Facsimile of the Original Manuscript in the Marvin P. Epstein Sherlock Holmes Collection* (1985) and a facsimile of "The Dying Detective" published by the City of Westminster and the Arthur Conan Doyle Society (1991).

Publishing and Textual Transmission

A publisher is someone, an individual or more commonly a firm, who takes the responsibility for having an author's book printed and distributed. The usual arrangement is that the author receives "royalties", a percentage of the sale price of the book, often with a minimum payment represented by an "advance" or cash payment when the manuscript is submitted. A 10 per cent royalty is a rule of thumb, but the figure can vary: in 1902 Doyle was receiving 25 per cent of the sale price on copies of his best-selling *The Hound of the Baskervilles* in Canada. In some cases — rarely today, but more commonly in the nineteenth century — the publisher buys the book outright. The publishers of *Beeton's Christmas Annual* paid Doyle £25 (a not ungenerous $2,000 in today's currency) for the ownership of *A Study in Scarlet*. The author may choose to sell only certain "rights" to a publisher, restricted by geography ("North American rights") or limited to a period of time. Whatever the exact terms of the contract, it becomes the publisher's obligation to pay for the printing of the book, which may be done in his own plant or elsewhere, and the publisher makes a profit or takes a loss depending on how well the book sells. A publisher employs editors who do their best to improve the text of the book before it is printed, and staff whose job is to send copies to reviewers, encourage booksellers to stock the book, and so on.

Doyle dealt with several publishers in the course of his career, some briefly and others over long periods. Among the latter were George Newnes, whose interests included book publishing as well as the *Strand*, and the great family firm of Lippincott in Philadelphia, who also published both books and magazines. Much information about the publishing and distribution of Doyle's works is found in the fine print of Green and Gibson's *Bibliography of A. Conan Doyle* (1983). Astonishingly much, however, is not known, for publishers do not necessarily keep the records of their former projects. By the early 1890's, Doyle was conducting financial negotiations with his publishers through the intermediary of A. P. Watt, a professional literary agent, and it was to Watt that (for example) the Toronto publisher George N. Morang & Co. sent substantial sums as royalties. (Records of those are in the Berg Collection of the New York Public Library.)

Most of the Sherlock Holmes stories were published first in magazines; the author would have sold "serial rights", for magazine publication, before the "book rights". The manuscripts went first to an editor, such as Greenhough Smith of the *Strand*, and from the editor to a typesetter, whose mercy and competence largely determine the text known to succeeding generations. There is evidence, as from the manuscript of "The Three Students" (now at Harvard University), that the typesetter was given much latitude for making sense out of Doyle's erratic punctuation and capitalization. Negative evidence, such as the survival of many inconsistencies in the stories, as well as the lack of markings on them, suggests that an editor's hand touched the manuscripts little or not at all.

The mechanics of printing were little different in the 1890's from what they had been in Shakespeare's day. Machinery was now powered by steam rather than by muscle, but type was for the most part still set by hand, letter by letter, allowing full scope for typographical errors of a kind now extinct, such as "wrong font" and inverted characters. The detailed study of these mechanics, as described in the definitive *An Introduction to Bibliography for Literary Students* by Ronald B. McKerrow (1962), is applied to portions of the Sherlockian Canon by Donald Redmond in *Sherlock Holmes Among the Pirates* (1990). A typographical error, unless very obvious, could easily be perpetuated in subsequent editions of the same text, as the new typesetter might well work from a previous printed page rather than from a reliable manuscript. The consequence is that mistakes and variations throughout the Canon survive to bedevil researchers; and a new generation of such errors has been created when the text is "scanned" into computer memory, with technology that is still somewhat fallible.

The Strand Magazine. All the Sherlock Holmes stories except the first two novels had their first British publication in the *Strand*, a monthly magazine founded at the beginning of 1891 by George Newnes (1851-1910). Newnes, originally a Manchester merchant, had become a publisher in 1881 with the creation of *Tit-Bits*, a weekly paper of entertainment and miscellaneous information for the lower middle class, which was becoming steadily more literate after the reforms of the 1870 Education Act. He introduced the *Strand* as a more respectable product, with a title taken from a fashionable west-end street just around the corner from the magazine's offices. It boasted modern-looking typography and (a policy from the beginning) an illustration on every double page, and it quickly became enormously successful, reaching a circulation of half a million. In its heyday, it sold a hundred pages of advertising every month. George Newnes Ltd. went on to publish dozens of other periodicals, and briefly an American edition of the *Strand*. The British magazine survived until 1951, when it became a victim of financial losses and a change in public reading habits.

Although Newnes (later Sir George for his contributions to journalism) was nominally editor of the *Strand*, its day-to-day manager was H. Greenhough

Smith (1855-1935), the "literary editor" from the magazine's beginnings, who continued at its helm until 1930. Reginald Pound in *Mirror of the Century: The Strand Magazine 1891-1950* (1966) describes him:

> Tall, lean, sandy-moustached, with freckles to match on a pallid expressionless face, he surveyed the world with kindly scrutineering eyes through rimless *pince-nez*. His distrust of emotion gave an impression of a temperament that did not fully warrant the nickname by which he was known to his fellow clubmen, "Calamity" Smith. . . . Wary of originality, he was prepared to encourage it but not at the expense of readability or of the reputation of the magazine.

He encouraged H. G. Wells, Grant Allen, E. Nesbit, Rudyard Kipling, E. W. Hornung, W. Somerset Maugham, and countless other important figures of Victorian writing; the *Strand* was noted for good story-telling rather than for ground-breaking literature. It carried articles about travel, science, the aristocracy, and public affairs as well, and deferential interviews with prominent persons, all in a generally complacent tone but without entirely concealing the problems of British society. Newnes, always insisting that he represented "the common man" but resplendent in the snug waistcoat of the successful businessman, cultivated — and received — the approval of prominent figures, including Queen Victoria, who more than once gave the magazine access to the royal apartments and scrapbooks.

A story by Arthur Conan Doyle, "The Voice of Science", appeared in the first volume of the *Strand*, but his importance to the magazine — and its to him — began in Volume 2 no. 1, July 1891, when Smith received the first episodes of what became *The Adventures of Sherlock Holmes* and labelled them "a gift from Heaven". At first Doyle was paid £5 per thousand words for the stories of Sherlock Holmes; by the end, nearly forty years later, he received £648 14s just for "Shoscombe Old Place". Doyle also wrote dozens of non-Sherlockian tales for the *Strand*, and his credibility with the magazine was such that when he appeared in 1921 with an article maintaining that two little girls' photographs of fairies in their garden were authentic, Smith swallowed hard and published it. A collection of letters from Doyle to Smith, now at the Metropolitan Toronto Reference Library, was discussed by Cameron Hollyer in *Baker Street Miscellanea* in 1985.

The *Strand* is of more than bibliographical interest for students of Sherlock Holmes, for it perfectly reflects his Victorian and Edwardian times, in its fiction, its articles and even its advertisements. It seems likely that Doyle read it closely, and even alluded to it, as when Watson in "The Five Orange Pips" speaks of "Clark Russell's fine sea stories"; he may have been thinking of "Captain Jones of the 'Rose'", which the *Strand* published in May 1891. *An Index to the Strand Magazine, 1891-1950*, compiled by Geraldine Beare, was published in 1982.

The American magazines. The stories of *The Adventures* and *The Memoirs*, and *The Hound of the Baskervilles*, were first published in the American edition of the *Strand* magazine, which was begun along with the British *Strand* in 1891 and was discontinued in 1916. When "The Empty House" appeared in 1903, however, and was followed by the other stories that would soon make up *The Return*, they appeared not in the *Strand* but in *Collier's Weekly*, which was one of the two leading magazines in the United States (the other, about equally popular, being the *Saturday Evening Post*).

It had been founded in 1888 by Peter Fenelon Collier, as a weekly in the nineteenth-century tradition of *Frank Leslie's*, and from 1898 was managed by his son, Robert J. Collier, fresh from Harvard College and keen to give American journalism "a little true literary flavor". He commissioned stories by Henry James but also by Rudyard Kipling and Hall Caine as well as Doyle, and he paid Charles Dana Gibson $1,000 apiece for a hundred of his double-page "Gibson girl" drawings. He also, in 1902, hired Norman Hapgood to be the editor, chiefly to take charge of the editorial page and to direct the magazine's muck-raking coverage of public affairs. Its war coverage, its articles on labour problems, and its exposés of patent medicines gave *Collier's* much of its popularity. In 1904 it changed its title from *Collier's Weekly, An Illustrated Journal* to *Collier's, The National Weekly*.

When the stories of *His Last Bow* began to appear in 1908, *Collier's* published the first two ("Wisteria Lodge" and "The Bruce-Partington Plans"). But the magazine's interest in fiction was fading, as were its fortunes in general after the death of Peter Collier in 1909, and for the next couple of stories Doyle's agent returned to the American edition of the *Strand*: ("The Devil's Foot" and "The Red Circle" in 1911). Later that year one story, "Lady Frances Carfax", appeared in the *American Magazine*. Holmes returned to *Collier's* for "The Dying Detective" in 1913, "His Last Bow" in 1917, and "The Three Garridebs" and "The Illustrious Client" in 1924. They would be the last of Holmes's adventures to appear there. The magazine was sold in 1919, suffered financial and production difficulties, but recovered in the 1920's to have reasonable influence in public affairs and reasonable success in publishing such stories as Sax Rohmer's adventures of Fu Manchu. In 1952-53 it would publish the stories by Adrian Conan Doyle and John Dickson Carr that became the *Exploits of Sherlock Holmes*. *Collier's* ceased publication in 1957.

The stories of *The Case-Book*, apart from those two in 1924 that were claimed by *Collier's*, appeared in two American magazines: four in *Hearst's International* from 1921 through 1924, and six in *Liberty* in 1926 and 1927. *Hearst's International* was originally an educational journal (*Current Encyclopedia*, founded in 1901), and in 1911 was taken over by William Randolph Hearst, who turned it into a public-affairs monthly. Before long it became clear that there was more money in fiction, and the magazine published prominent authors both American and European. At first it was *Hearst's Magazine*, then simply *Hearst's*, and from 1921 *Hearst's International*. In 1925 it was merged into *Cosmopolitan*, another title in the Hearst publishing empire (and ancestor of the racy modern magazine for single women).

Liberty, having begun publication in May 1924, was only two years old when it began carrying Canonical stories. Already it was among the three leading weeklies in the United States, having joined *Collier's* and the *Saturday Evening Post* in selling more than a million copies of each issue. What it did not do was make money for its proprietors, Robert McCormick of the Chicago *Tribune* and Joseph Patterson of the New York Daily News. They sold it in 1931; successors kept trying to make it pay, but gave up and closed the magazine in 1951.

Copyright

Copyright is literally the right (owned by an author unless it is specifically assigned or sold to someone else) to copy — that is, to publish — an author's written words. The law of copyright is byzantine and, to most lay people, dull, but even an amateur can learn not to violate copyrights simply by not copying and distributing the works of another. The chief exception to copyright protection is popularly known as "fair dealing", and includes making a single copy (such as a photocopy) for private use, or quoting a reasonable passage (300 words is often cited) in an article or subsequent book.

In Britain and Canada, copyright generally expires fifty years after the author's death; Doyle's stories thus were free of copyright in 1980. In the United States, however, the standard term of copyright is seventy-five years from a work's first publication, a rule that since 1891 has applied to the works of foreigners as well as those of Americans. Accordingly, as of 1993 all the stories originally published after 1918 were protected by copyright. That includes only the stories in *The Case Book*. The result, however, has been a Doubleday monopoly on publication of the complete stories, although *The Adventures*, *The Hound of the Baskervilles* and other earlier works are available in dozens of editions — anyone can legally publish them.

The American copyrights which remain are owned by Dame Jean Conan Doyle, only surviving child of the author. "The Estate of Sir Arthur Conan Doyle", an entity tangled in litigation, owns some manuscripts and other properties, but no copyrights, at least in works that have been published. Dame Jean has also attempted to assert a common-law property right (not a copyright) in the characters and names of Sherlock Holmes and Dr. Watson; the extent to which such a right is enforceable, allowing her to prevent the writing of new tales using the characters, is legally unclear, but at present American publishers are complying with Dame Jean's wishes, to be on the safe side.

Editions of the Stories

The original magazine publication, and the newspaper syndication that followed in most cases, did not exhaust publishers' interest in the Canonical stories, as they were republished in American and British newspapers from the early 1890's through the early years of the twentieth century. The *New York World* Sunday magazine rediscovered the *Adventures of Sherlock Holmes* in 1905, for example; the *Boston Sunday Post* published the stories of *The Return* as "Masterpieces of Sherlock Holmes" in 1911. A few stories were published yet again in periodical format, the oddest examples being an excerpt from *The Sign of the*

Four and the full texts of "A Scandal in Bohemia" and "The Copper Beeches", which graced the first three issues of *Playboy* magazine (1954). Many of the stories have been used in anthologies, from "The Dancing Men" in *Famous Stories of Code and Cipher* (1947) and "A Scandal in Bohemia" in *With All My Love: An Anthology* (1945) to "The Five Orange Pips" in *Masterpieces of Mystery & Detection* (1965). Unusual publications also include *The Blue Carbuncle* (1948), a collector's item published by the Baker Street Irregulars.

Partial collections of Canonical stories have appeared over the decades with such titles as *Conan Doyle's Stories for Boys* (1938), *Famous Tales of Sherlock Holmes* (1958), and *Sherlock Holmes' Greatest Cases* (1966). In the early years some such collections were piracies; with the expiry of American copyrights, that word no longer applies, but often the collections are as cheap in every way as were the piracies of the 1890's. In that period, *The Sign of the Four* (in more than 200 unauthorized editions) and *A Study in Scarlet* were extensively pirated by American publishers operating in a free-for-all atmosphere. The later books of the Canon were not extensively pirated, so that the multiple editions of *The Adventures*, *The Hound of the Baskervilles* and the rest come from a limited number of authorized publishers. Still, a full bibliographical listing of them will be immensely difficult to compile.

Some of the Sherlock Holmes tales appear in the authorized "Author's Edition" of Doyle's works (1903). All are among the twenty-four volumes of the "Crowborough Edition", begun before Doyle's death in 1930 and published posthumously in a limited edition of 760 sets; many copies include signatures which the author affixed to pre-publication sheets. Also approved was *Sherlock Holmes and Dr. Watson: A Textbook of Friendship* (1944), edited by Christopher Morley and including two novels (one abridged), five short stories and extensive notes. Supposedly definitive editions, under the editorship of Edgar W. Smith, were published by The Limited Editions Club (1950-52, eight volumes) and The Heritage Press (1952-57, three volumes). In 1928, when the Canon was first complete, *The Complete Sherlock Holmes* was published in eight volumes by P. F. Collier & Son in the United States. A six-volume edition followed in 1936.

In Britain, a two-volume set appeared from the old publishing firm of John Murray. It remains the standard British edition of the stories, as *The Complete Sherlock Holmes: Long Stories* and *Short Stories*, cited as "S" and "L" with a page-number in some British writings. An eight-volume edition has been published jointly (1974) by John Murray and Jonathan Cape. A multi-volume edition of the Canon, with annotations by British scholars, is expected in 1993 or 1994 from Oxford University Press.

In North America the title *The Complete Sherlock Holmes* has been applied to a series of editions from Doubleday (also variously known as Doubleday Doran and Garden City Publishing). The first was the "Memorial Edition", shortly after Doyle's death in 1930, which had erratic and repetitive pagination because it was printed from the plates previously used for separate volumes of the various tales. It also presented "In Memoriam Sherlock Holmes", an eloquent if maudlin Introduction by Christopher Morley, which has been a fixture ever since. A one-volume edition of *The Complete* followed in 1936. Early Sherlockian writings frequently refer to its 1,323-page layout, also published as "the Literary Guild Edition" and "the De Luxe Edition" in two-volume and one-volume formats. One-volume and two-volume editions in a new format of 1,122 pages were introduced in 1960 and remain standard. The Book-of-the-Month Club continues to distribute many thousands of the most recent impression. The one-volume edition has also appeared as a paperback, under the Penguin imprint. These editions have been, for their times, the North American standard, to which reference works have generally been keyed. Doubleday was also responsible for the ten-volume "Literary Guild" edition in 1933, of which reprinting has frequently been suggested.

Latterly, the Sherlockian fancy has been for facsimile editions in which the original *Strand* appearance of the stories, including Sidney Paget illustrations, is reproduced. The best-accepted of these is a heavy volume of 1,126 pages, *The Original Illustrated 'Strand' Sherlock Holmes*, with the *Strand* pages enlarged from their original size (and *A Study in Scarlet* and *The Sign of the Four*, which never appeared in the *Strand*, set in a similar typeface and format). Unlike some earlier facsimiles, this one manages clear and bright reproduction of the drawings by Paget and his successors. The British edition appeared from Wordsworth in 1989, the American from Mallard Press in 1990.

The Annotated Sherlock Holmes. The complete Canon was published with a vast apparatus of notes under the title *The Annotated Sherlock Holmes* (Clarkson N. Potter, 1967; a British edition followed in 1968 from John Murray, and there is also a one-volume reprint). Its editor was William S. Baring-Gould, whose death while the book was still in proof prevented the correction of some errors and imperfections. Even so, the *Annotated* has been indispensable for a generation of Sherlockian scholars, and a new edition is greatly to be wished. Enthusiasts headed by Jack Tracy of Gaslight Publications, Bloomington, Indiana, have expressed the hope of preparing an update in computer-disk format.

Its two volumes (688 pages in the first, 824 pages in the second) provide hundreds of illustrations — often murkily reproduced — and marginal notes explaining Victorian terms, pointing the reader to related passages in other stories, and providing a wealth of background and enrichment. In addition, there are nineteen chapters on general subjects, all Baring-Gould's work: on Sherlockian parodies, on films, on Watson, on the snake in "The Speckled Band", on Watson's wounds, on Watson's marriages, on the Great Hiatus, and so on. These chapters are interspersed with the stories, in facsimile from the John Murray collected edition, arranged in the order in which Baring-Gould deemed them to have taken place. Thus "The 'Gloria Scott'" comes first and "His Last Bow" last; the first volume goes as far as *The Sign of the Four*. Constant recourse to the table of contents is unavoidable. The *Annotated* holds unswervingly to the pretence that Sherlockian imagination is historical scholarship, thus slighting Doyle and limiting its use for some kinds of study.

Illustration

It is difficult to think of Sherlock Holmes without his deerstalker hat, which is never mentioned in the Canon, but was the inspiration of an early illustrator, Sidney Paget. That lasting gift from artist to character is one example of how important illustration has been in establishing the myth of Sherlock Holmes, and in making the stories successful and memorable. No wonder, then, that Walter Klinefelter found it easy to devote a full volume to Sherlockian illustration: *Sherlock Holmes in Portrait and Profile* (1963). Admirable so far as he goes, he only scratches the surface, for there have been dozens of illustrators whom he has no room to mention.

There is more to illustrating Holmes than the presence of the deerstalker hat and its usual companions the magnifying glass, the curved pipe, and the Inverness cape, unless one is merely a cartoonist. Still, some modern illustrators (even those who appear to have the basic qualifications such as the ability to draw human figures in the right proportions) do no more than that when they try to interpret Holmes visually. One expects from an illustrator the discernment of an artist, revealed in features, expressions and gestures that match the Holmes described in the text. It is for achieving those expressions and gestures, in particular, that two early artists — Paget and Steele — are acknowledged to be great interpreters of Holmes, while others are nearly forgotten. In addition, the reader deserves authenticity in Victorian clothing and furnishings; the scenes illustrated should be ones that are not merely exciting and action-filled but significant to the progress of the story; the illustrations should be placed on the page or in the volume in such a way that the story is not spoiled for the first-time reader; and their reproduction should be clean and clear.

The first person to draw Sherlock Holmes for print was D. H. Friston, whose illustrations for *A Study in Scarlet* appeared in *Beeton's Christmas Annual* for 1887. (It is not clear that the often-reproduced cover of *Beeton's* is intended to represent Holmes or have anything to do with *A Study in Scarlet*.) Klinefelter is critical of Friston's Holmes, calling it "a travesty", not so much in physiognomy as in clothing and headgear. Those illustrations were abandoned when *A Study in Scarlet* was republished, and in Friston's place stood the author's father, Charles Doyle, by 1888 confined to a mental institution and exercising his talent rather for therapy than professionally. Gibson and Green, in their *Bibliography of A. Conan Doyle*, observe that "The six frail drawings bear no relation to later conceptions of the subject but are of interest none the less." Later illustrators for the same novel included George Hutchinson.

Sidney Paget. Always admired, the drawings of Sidney Paget for the original publication of about half the Canon have been more widely known since facsimile editions became available. One or two of them, such as a drawing for "Silver Blaze" of Holmes and Watson together in a railway carriage, and one for "The Naval Treaty" of Holmes sniffing a rose in a moment of ecstasy, have become virtual icons. Others, less often reproduced, still capture moments of characteristic action, or aspects of Holmes's milieu, as no other illustrations have been able to do. It can be seen as a tribute to Paget's mastery of his medium, and of his Victorian subject as well, that selected illustrations have twice been reproduced by the spicy British magazine *Mayfair* with off-colour captions replacing the original Canonical ones.

Gibson and Green in their *Bibliography* explain the conjunction of Paget and the Canon thus: "George Newnes wanted the [*Strand*] magazine to have a picture at every opening, and to achieve this appointed W. H. Boot as the art editor. He in turn chose one of the Paget brothers for this series, intending it to be Walter Paget, though in fact the offer went to Sidney Paget. The choice was a good one and met with the author's approval, though he had envisaged a 'more beaky nosed, hawk-faced man'." Tradition says that Walter Paget became, rather than the artist, the model for Holmes.

It was Paget who introduced the deerstalker hat to Sherlock Holmes, identifying the detective's "travelling cap" as the headgear he himself favoured: a cloth cap in plain or (often) houndstooth fabric, with fore-and-aft peaks and with earflaps that could be tied up or down. He drew it only five times, but that was enough, especially as one of the five deerstalkers is seen falling from Holmes's head into the gorge of the Reichenbach in an illustration for "The Final Problem". Other artifacts of the Paget household can also be identified in some of the illustrations.

Sidney Paget did a total of 356 illustrations for the Canon, to accompany the magazine publication of *The Adventures*, *The Memoirs*, *The Hound of the Baskervilles*, and *The Return*. (Many of them were carried along when those texts were published in book form.) Ann Byerly, writing in *Baker Street Miscellanea* in 1983, described his technique:

> Employing the black-and-white watercolor technique, he worked [the illustrations] up on a kind of cardboard about 6″ X 8″ in size, first pencilling in his composition, next filling in the background with a light wash, then applying black watercolor paint to dark areas in the picture, and finally, filling in the details with black and white after that had dried. . . . Much more of his draftsmanship is evident when an original is tilted to the light to catch the glint of the pencilling than is apparent in the reproductions.

(Still less, of course, can be seen in most modern facsimiles.) Some of the drawings were reproduced from engravings, others from (cruder) woodcuts. Warren Scheideman, writing in the same issue of *BSM*, notes that some of Paget's genius resides in the "creative rather than formal" shape of his drawings, which lack hard edges: "The lines drift into the text, sometimes like smoke, clouds, dreams, or thoughts, often in physical conjunction with the words they illustrate."

Sidney Paget was born October 4, 1860, and was a young painter and newspaper artist when he was accidentally chosen to illustrate "A Scandal in Bohemia" and the stories that followed it. He went on to produce drawings for many other stories by Doyle, and for other authors' works in the *Strand* and elsewhere. In October 1897, it is reported, he painted Doyle's portrait. He suffered from a "chest complaint" in the early years of the twentieth century, gradually doing less and less work, and died January 28, 1908. He and his wife, Edith Hounsfield, whose wedding-present from Doyle was a silver cigarette-case inscribed "From Sherlock Holmes", had six children; one of them, Winifred, has written about her father and was a member of the Sherlock Holmes Society of London from its founding until her death in 1978. "Only a handful" of his original drawings are known to exist, Ann Byerly reported in 1983.

Frederic Dorr Steele. The leading American illustrator of the Canon was in fact its illustrator only for the final three volumes of short stories. Walter Klinefelter, in *Sherlock Holmes in Portrait and Profile* (1963), introduces the contributions of Frederic Dorr Steele thus:

> For the text of the stories of *The Return*, which made its first American appearances in various numbers of *Collier's Weekly* from September 26, 1903, to January 28, 1905, Steele drew forty-six illustrations. The master detective's visage appears in twenty-six of them. For each story Steele also provided individual headpieces and decorative initials. But at the most these drawings, though of very special merit, comprise the lesser part of this artist's contribution to the embellishment of *The Return*. The choicest of his drawings for this section of the canon consist of the ten gorgeous portraits which he executed in color for the front covers of a like number of the issues of *Collier's* in which Watson's stories appeared. These portraits were the finest of Holmes done up to that time, perhaps the finest that ever were or ever will be done of him.

Steele went on to do similar work for most of the stories that would make up *His Last Bow*, and for two of the *Case-Book* stories. He later illustrated one story (with cover) for the *American Magazine*, four (without covers) for *Hearst's International*, and six (again without covers) for *Liberty*. A number of newspaper illustrations were also his work.

The cover illustrations are, indeed, Steele's most important Sherlockian work, from the deerstalkered figure at the Reichenbach for "The Empty House" to his gaunt, bedridden Holmes for "The Dying Detective" and the aging figure of Holmes in retirement for "His Last Bow". For "The Norwood Builder", Steele drew Holmes looking not at a thumb-print but at an entire bloody handprint on the wall, perhaps his only concession to melodrama; for a pamphlet edition of "The Dying Detective" some years later, the same drawing was used, with a sketched portrait of Doyle replacing the handprint on the wall under Holmes's piercing scrutiny. It seems clear that the model Steele used for Holmes was William Gillette, who toured America through the early decades of the century presenting the great detective on stage. Walter Klinefelter identifies the *Collier's* cover for "The Priory School" as being the most like Gillette; indeed, that picture of Holmes staring away across the moor does bear a striking resemblance to pictures of Gillette that appeared on publicity material for his play and also as a frontispiece in some contemporary editions of the Canon.

Frederic Dorr Steele, born August 6, 1873, was primarily a book illustrator, having worked with texts by such authors as Richard Harding Davis, Mark Twain, Rudyard Kipling and O. Henry. He was winner of the bronze medal at

Sherlock Holmes as seen by two great portraitists. Left: by Sidney Paget, for "The Man with the Twisted Lip", 1891. Right: by Frederic Dorr Steele, for "The Norwood Builder", 1903 — said to be the first time he drew Holmes from a photograph of actor William Gillette. Neither artist gives Holmes the curved pipe that later became associated with him.

the St. Louis Exposition of 1904, and spent his working life in New York, where he was a member of the elite Players Club; his obituary in *The New York Times* said he was also a member of the Baker Street Irregulars, but that does not seem to have been the case, although he certainly was a friend of such early Sherlockians as Vincent Starrett and Gray Chandler Briggs. The *Times* also reported that shortly before his death (July 5, 1944) he had been working on illustrations for the projected Limited Editions Club version of the Canon, which was to appear beginning six years later. He was survived by his wife, Mary. A collection of anecdotes about Steele and appreciations of him and his work appeared in a 1991 issue of *Baker Street Miscellanea.*

Later illustrators. American magazines which published the stories in the early years of the century, but did not accompany them with Steele's drawings, used such other illustrators as Arthur I. Keller, G. Patrick Nelson, W. T. Benda and John Richard Flanagan. The American book edition of *The Return* was illustrated not by Steele but by Charles Raymond Macauley. As for British editions after Paget, the editors of the *Strand* had similarly played the field, entrusting the illustration to Arthur Twidle, Gilbert Holiday, Joseph Simpson, H. M. Brock, Frank Wiles, Howard Elcock, Alec Ball, A. Gilbert, and even Paget's brother Walter, who had been intended as the original illustrator two decades earlier.

By the twentieth century it was no longer fashionable for books to contain illustrations. *The Valley of Fear* had only a frontispiece (by Wiles) in England, although the American edition had a few Keller drawings scattered through the text. *His Last Bow* and *The Case-Book* had no illustrations at all in either American or British editions. The collected editions of the Canon, the Doubleday *Complete Sherlock Holmes* and the *Long Stories* and *Short Stories* published by John Murray, do not have illustrations, nor do most of the paperback volumes available.

There has been no well-known illustrator of the Canon since Paget and Steele; images of the detective since the 1920's have been based on the faces and postures of actors, primarily (at least in North America) Basil Rathbone. The Paget illustrations, little-known in the United States until the appearance of *The Annotated Sherlock Holmes* with its many reproductions, are now often seen. A number of undistinguished illustrators have made attempts at Holmes for various post-copyright editions of the stories, often not rising above the deerstalker-and-calabash level of caricature also seen in countless cartoons and advertisements. Perhaps the most successful Sherlockian artist in recent decades has been Dan Day, whose work in the 1980's was not for book illustration but for comics.

Translations
The stories of Sherlock Holmes have appeared in languages from French and German to Sinhalese and Urdu, despite the vast difficulties in conveying the nuances of British life and the subtleties of Holmes's work to readers in far dif-

ferent cultures. It is said — although such statements are difficult to verify — that portions of the Canon have been put into more tongues than any other work save the Bible. There is a persistent story that in some language, in some country (Egypt?), the Canon has been used as a textbook for detectives, but the facts have never been demonstrated. Certainly the Canon has often been a textbook for the learning of English; student editions with notes and apparatus in French, Russian, Swedish, and other languages are known.

Translation into French began before the turn of the century, with *The Sign of the Four* appearing from Hachette in 1896 as *La Marque des Quatre: Roman Anglais* (1896). The bibliographical record is nearly as confused as its English-language counterpart, with partial, probably unauthorized translations appearing frequently. There is the further complication of variant titles: *A Study in Scarlet* is found both as *Une Etude en Rouge* and as *Les Débuts de Sherlock Holmes*. The full Canon appears along with other works of Doyle in his *Oeuvres Complètes* from Robert Laffont (1956-58) and subsequent collected editions.

German translations may have appeared in North America before they were seen in Germany itself: *A Study in Scarlet* and *The Sign of the Four* are known from Milwaukee newspaper serializations in 1903, under the titles *Späte Rache* ("Belated Revenge") and *Das Zeichen der Vier*. Milwaukee and Pittsburgh also saw early publications of *Der Hund von Baskerville*. Publishers in Germany, particularly Robert Lutz of Stuttgart, were bringing out portions of the Canon between 1906 and 1910, and many editions followed, leading to the *Sämtliche Romane* and *Sämtliche Stories* in the 1960's.

The earliest Japanese translations date from the 1890's; more appeared in the 1920's (*Shinku No Isshi* is a 1923 version of *A Study in Scarlet*), and they became numerous after World War II. A complete Canon in thirteen volumes, *Sherlock Holmes Zenshû*, appeared in 1951-52 from Getsuyô-shobô in Tokyo.

Russian is a special case. The first translations came early, about 1903, as Anatole Chujoy recalled in the *Baker Street Journal* in 1953. But they were less than perfect:

> In *A Study in Scarlet*, for instance, Dr. Watson's jezail bullet became a piece of shrapnel, and the valiant Murray's name is changed to Miurrai. The providential meeting between Watson and young Stamford takes place not at the Criterion Bar, as we have always believed, but in the street. The reason for this is perhaps that the institution we know under the appellation "bar" was foreign to Russians, and the paraphrast probably could not find a suitable definition for "bar" in the dictionary.

Multiple editions in Russian appeared in later decades, including an eight-volume edition in 1966 (Ogonyok Library) and a 1945 edition of "The Man With the Twisted Lip" as part of The Little Library of the Journal of the Red Army Soldier. It was said that 11 million volumes of the Canon had been sold in the two years before a 1959 lawsuit in which Doyle's estate asked a Soviet court to award it royalties on those books. The suit was unsuccessful because the Soviet Union, unlike most other countries, was not then party to any of the international copyright conventions.

Most European languages had accepted Holmes early: *Le Avventure di Sherlock Holmes* (Milan) dates from 1895, *De Fires Tegn* (Christiania, i.e. Oslo) from 1891. The full history of translation remains to be unearthed, as many items are doubtless unknown to bibliographers, and many items that have been listed are undated or only vaguely described. Translation remains an area where collectors can specialize, explore, and point to novelties — a Ukrainian edition of *A Study in Scarlet* published not in Ukraine but in Edmonton, Alberta; Hebrew editions of the Canon (mostly published in Tel Aviv in the 1950's) in which, for lack of the initial letter H, the great detective is named Golmes.

Other formats. Apart from conventional print, portions of the Canon have been commercially published in Braille (*The Adventures* in Britain in 1920, selected *Cases of Sherlock Holmes* in the United States in 1965). A more common novelty on collectors' shelves is an edition in shorthand, either Gregg or Pitman. Several have been produced for practice by novice stenographers; the earliest Pitman version, of *The Sign of the Four*, appeared in England shortly after the original book's first edition.

Audio-tapes of the stories may be of benefit to blind readers, but in recent years their chief consumers, apart from passionate collectors, are commuters who listen to tapes in their cars. Some tapes may be copies of material originally intended for radio broadcast; others were made with direct sale in mind. Among the classic recordings, available through various distributors, are those by Basil Rathbone of "The Speckled Band", "The Final Problem", "The Red-Headed League", "A Scandal in Bohemia", and "Silver Blaze"; those by John Brewster of "A Scandal in Bohemia", "The Red-Headed League", "The Speckled Band" and "The Final Problem"; a large number by Robert Hardy; and those by Patrick Horgan of *A Study in Scarlet* and *The Hound of the Baskervilles* (both abridged). Tapes of this kind should not be confused with tapes of dramatizations, chiefly from radio broadcasts, which are also widely available.

Machine-readable text. The text of the Canon has doubtless existed in computer-readable form, in some publisher's typesetting machinery, for years, but enthusiasts who wanted to perform computer analysis on the Canon, search for lost phrases, or even compile a concordance were faced with the prospect of typing its more than four million characters themselves. In 1987, however, Psy-Logic Systems (PO Box 315, Tolland, Connecticut 06084) began to distribute *An Electronic Holmes Companion*, a Canonical text on diskettes suitable for use in a PC-compatible or Macintosh computer, along with documentation and a number of programs for text analysis. The text was created by optical character scanning, a process with a notoriously high error rate, and despite proofreading may still contain some anomalies. More recently a CD-ROM (compact disk) of the entire Canon has been offered by at least two entrepreneurs. A group of enthusiasts headed by George Vanderburgh (PO Box 204, Shelburne, Ontario L0N 1S0) has announced preparation of an electronic version of all Arthur Conan Doyle's published works, including the Canon, with text, commentary and many illustrations, for use in a PC-compatible computer.

Arthur Conan Doyle in early middle age — reproduced from an engraving in a 1900 edition of *The Refugees*. According to his daughter, Doyle stood six feet, one and a half inches tall. A recording betrays more than a hint of a Scots burr in his speaking voice even in later life.

Chapter IV

Arthur Conan Doyle

For fifty years Sherlockians have dismissed Arthur Conan Doyle half-seriously as "the Literary Agent", but acknowledging his authorship, and the life behind it, does give the stories of the Canon an additional richness. Even outside Sherlockian circles, he is chiefly known only for Sherlock Holmes, to the point that the detective's name almost invariably appears in the titles of books about Doyle. But there is more to him than his nine volumes of Holmes — more even than all his literary writings, models though they are of English prose. Doyle is of importance as a social reformer, a religious leader, and a public figure generally. An increasing number of articles in Sherlockian journals (especially *Baker Street Miscellanea*) give Doyle his due. In 1989 an Arthur Conan Doyle Society was founded, chiefly in England though with many members elsewhere. (Its president is Christopher Roden, Ashcroft, 2 Abbottsford Drive, Penyffordd, Chester CH4 0JG, England.) It publishes a twice-yearly *Journal* and a newsletter, *The Parish Magazine*, both dedicated to scholarship about Doyle and news about activities in his memory. Some of the material takes a slightly desperate tone, faced as Doyleans are with the necessity of rescuing the author from the shadow of his creation.

There is an irreconcilable difference of opinion about the preferable form of the great man's name. He always signed himself "A. Conan Doyle", which leaves doubt whether he considered "Conan" a given name or the first part of a compound surname. His father was simply "Doyle", but his children have been determinedly "Conan Doyle". Cataloguers for the Library of Congress and the British Library have chosen "Doyle" to stand alone as the surname.

Life and Medical Career

Arthur Conan Doyle was born May 22, 1859, at 11 Picardy Place, Edinburgh, a lower-middle-class row house in the capital city of Scotland. The family were Roman Catholics, members of a not insignificant minority in Presbyterian Scotland. Doyle's father was an Englishman: Charles Doyle, youngest son of the prominent cartoonist John Doyle — an artist himself, but unsuccessful, whose work was as a draftsman in the Scottish Office of Works. His mother was Mary, née Foley, a strong-minded Irishwoman with a strong, even imaginative, sense of family tradition. They had ten children:

- Annette, born 1856, who became a governess (in Portugal for one period) and probably gave Doyle the sympathetic interest in governesses reflected in "The Copper Beeches". She died, unmarried, in 1889.
- Catherine, born 1858, died in infancy.
- Arthur, born 1859.
- Mary, born 1861, died in childhood.
- Caroline, born circa 1866, died in childhood.

● Constance, born circa 1867, also worked as a governess for a time. In 1893 she married Ernest William Hornung, who went on to create A. J. Raffles, the celebrated gentleman-burglar, in *The Amateur Cracksman* (1899) and to elaborate him in *The Black Mask* (1901), *A Thief in the Night* (1905), and *Mr. Justice Raffles* (1909). She died in 1924.

● Lottie (Caroline), born 1869, again a governess at one period. She married Leslie Oldham, a military man who became a major in the Royal Engineers and was killed in World War I.

● Innes Hay, born March 31, 1873, who lived with Doyle when he was a young doctor in Southsea. Innes entered the army and rose during World War I to be a brigadier-general; he died in February 1919. His son, John Doyle, also became a brigadier-general, and a keeper of Doyle memorabilia; he died in 1990.

● Ida, born 1875. Later Mrs. Foley, she died in 1937.

● Bryan Mary ("Dodo"), born 1877. In 1899 she married the Rev. Cyril Angell, who officiated at Doyle's second wedding. She died in 1944.

The Doyles' genteel poverty became something worse as Charles Doyle became unable to work. He was both epileptic (a condition poorly understood in the middle of the nineteenth century) and, from some point during Arthur's childhood, alcoholic. Although there are no first-hand descriptions of life in the Doyle home in the 1870's, one may see reflections of it in some of the tales in which Doyle, as an adult, wrote with horror about the effects of drink (including "The Abbey Grange"). Charles Doyle was finally institutionalized in 1883; the story of his descent was revealed by Michael Baker in the Introduction to *The Doyle Diary* (1978), a facsimile of a sketchbook dating from Charles Doyle's years of confinement. He died October 10, 1893.

It was Arthur's mother, Mary (Foley) Doyle, who held the family together and who became, by general consent, the dominant figure in his life, even if John Dickson Carr (in *The Life of Sir Arthur Conan Doyle*, 1947) exaggerates the relationship and invents out of whole cloth the title "the Ma'am" for her. Irish by extraction, she was rigid in moral and social standards, and mindful of a proud ancestry which most researchers now think she largely imagined. It appears that Doyle wrote to her constantly ("Dearest Mam", the letters began) until her death December 30, 1920, only ten years before his own death; most of those letters are believed to survive among the Doyle papers which are currently sequestered as the subject of litigation. Doyle's mother was unquestionably the chief source of his life-long interest in history, as well as of his character and chivalric standards. Bryan Charles Waller (1853-1932), a family friend who was a few years ahead of Doyle at medical school, influenced him both towards medicine and towards literature, and apparently contributed to supporting the family after Charles Doyle was incapacitated; Mary Doyle spent her later years living on Waller's estate at Masongill, Yorkshire.

After early schooling in Edinburgh, Doyle was sent to prominent Roman Catholic "public" (boarding) schools in Lancashire: to Hodder School in 1868, to nearby Stonyhurst College in 1870. There he survived physical abuse, played sports with determination, read adventure stories voraciously, and perhaps learned a little of what the Jesuit masters sought to teach him — enough, anyway, that they sent him to their school at Feldkirch, Austria, for a year (1875-76). He returned to Edinburgh to begin medical studies at the age of seventeen, at what was probably the leading medical school in Europe. Ely M. Liebow, in *Dr. Joe Bell: Model for Sherlock Holmes* (1982), gives a picture of life at the University of Edinburgh:

> One had to learn much self-discipline, Doyle noted, for once the timid young freshman turned over his £1 note to the bursar he was practically on his own. While there certainly was a number of required courses in the arts as well as in medical school, the students were free to attend what lectures they pleased (text books, especially in the medical school, were practically non-existent until the 1880s). . . . Doyle, who was trying to compress five years' study into four to save money, admits quite readily that he was "always one of the ruck, neither lingering nor gaining — a 60 per cent man at examinations." . . . Doyle, like many a student in the 1870s, not only took courses from University professors, but often took classes on the same subject from an extra-curricular lecturer.

The most famous "extra-curricular lecturer" to instruct Doyle was Dr. Joseph Bell, to whom (Liebow reports) Doyle paid £4.4s for surgical teaching at Edinburgh's new Infirmary, where Bell became senior surgeon in 1878. Other professors, at the university or the surrounding hospitals, who made an impression on Doyle included Dr. Patrick Heron Watson, Bell's senior and a brilliant surgeon, and Dr. William Rutherford, whose voice and physique provided the model for Professor Challenger in stories Doyle would write decades later.

Graduating with a Bachelor of Medicine (M.B.) degree in 1881, Doyle — who had already, between terms as a student, served as "surgeon" on an Arctic whaling vessel — took a similar post on a ship voyaging to west Africa. Then he served briefly in Birmingham under an established doctor for whom he had also worked as a student. And then, early in 1882, he went into partnership in Plymouth, in southwestern England, with Dr. George Turnavine Budd, a former fellow-student whose medical acumen was tinged with charlatanism. Doyle made something out of the unsuccessful partnership later, thinly disguising the persons and circumstances in his novel *The Stark Munro Letters* (1895), but professionally it did little for him. He moved to Southsea, a resort town on the south coast of England, and went into medical practice alone. But patients were few and money scarce. The idle hours in his surgery gave him time to prepare a thesis for the degree of Doctor of Medicine ("An Essay upon the Vasomotor Changes in Tabes Dorsalis", i.e. aspects of syphilis) from Edinburgh in 1885. He also found time to begin writing fiction.

He was married August 6, 1885, to Louise Hawkins, sister of a patient (who died while under Doyle's care). Their courtship and marriage are the basis for another of his early novels, *A Duet with an Occasional Chorus* (1899). For the next few years he continued in medical practice at 1 Bush Villas, Elm Grove, Southsea, while also developing a literary reputation. In 1890-91 he went to Vienna for advanced study in ophthalmology, and with Louise and their daughter, Mary, he moved to London, taking lodgings at 23 Montague Place and professional quarters in Devonshire Place. "Not one single patient" ever appeared, he later wrote. Within weeks he had decided to give up medicine for literature; the family took a house at 12 Tennison Road, in the distant suburb of South Norwood, south of London, and Doyle settled down to be a writer.

A son, Kingsley, was born November 15, 1892. Less than a year later, Louise was diagnosed with tuberculosis, and the family went to Davos, Switzerland, for 1893-94 in the hope that the cool dry climate would do her good. While there, he introduced the incredulous Swiss to skiing, a form of recreation and transportation he had picked up on a visit to Norway. For a period in 1895-96 they toured Egypt, for its healthful dryness and also for adventure, and in October 1897 the family moved into a large house built to their specifications at Hindhead, Surrey, which they called "Undershaw".

On March 15, 1897, Doyle met a young woman who lived in London: Jean Leckie, intelligent, musical, beautiful, fourteen years younger than he. They fell in love instantly, and began to spend time together, with the approval of Doyle's mother and of the lady's parents. All biographers are agreed that nothing sexual passed between them, however, because Doyle's code required complete fidelity to his invalid wife, Louise. She died July 4, 1906, at Undershaw. Doyle and Jean Leckie were married September 18, 1907, at St. Margaret's Church, Westminster. Doyle had been knighted (made "Sir Arthur") in 1902; the marriage gave Jean the title "Lady Doyle".

They made a home near Crowborough in eastern Sussex, near the New Forest, buying and enlarging a house called "Windlesham". Three children were born there: Denis (March 17, 1909), Adrian (November 19, 1910), and Lena Jean (December 21, 1912). It remained Doyle's headquarters for the rest of his life; he wrote there, conducted his correspondence (with the help of a secretary, Major Alfred Wood), entertained, returned after the exertions of travel. He maintained a flat in Buckingham Palace Mansions, Victoria Street, for convenience when he was in London, and from 1925 the family had a summer home at Bignell Wood in the New Forest. Doyle died at Windlesham at breakfast-time on July 7, 1930.

Through a long career in literature and public affairs, Doyle came to know hundreds of prominent people, and they to know him, as did ordinary people worldwide. He was described, late in his life, as "the most prominent living Englishman". His correspondence, accumulated in files that are now part of the Estate's sealed papers, included letters from Edward VII, Cardinal Newman, George Bernard Shaw, Theodore Roosevelt, H. Rider Haggard, Noel Coward and Ramsay MacDonald. He took tea with George Meredith, he collaborated on a play with Sir James Barrie, he worked on Spiritualist matters with Sir Oliver Lodge. On an 1894 tour of America (discussed in detail in *Welcome to America, Mr. Sherlock Holmes* [1987] by Christopher Redmond), he played golf with Rudyard Kipling and drank with James Whitcomb Riley. About such a man, it is difficult to say which acquaintances were true friends. At Doyle's second wedding in 1907, Barrie was present, as was Bram Stoker, Sir Henry Irving's former secretary and the author of *Dracula* (1897). So too were two important figures from Doyle's literary youth, the 1892 founders of *The Idler* — Robert Barr, Canadian expatriate, and Jerome K. Jerome, author of *Three Men in a Boat* (1889), who had unsuccessfully courted Doyle's sister Connie.

Literary Work

Sherlockians affect to say that the tales of Sherlock Holmes are history, not fiction. Even if one accepts that postulate, it is still reasonable to describe Doyle as a prominent author of fiction, for the sake of his many other writings. Apart from the Canon, only *The White Company* and (intermittently) the stories of Brigadier Gerard are generally in print, but when antiquarian editions can be found, nearly all his books are worth the reading. Not only are they of interest for plot and character; Doyle's prose is clear and workmanlike, its effects coming from the marshalling of ordinary, mostly short, concrete words. Occasional descriptive passages provide relief from the brisk progress of a tale through dialogue, and the names of people and streets, specific numbers and dates, keep the narratives anchored in everyday reality.

Following is a list of Doyle's fiction, plays, and poetry with the heading numbers assigned by Green and Gibson in their *Bibliography*:

A1. *A Study in Scarlet*. 1887.
A2. *The Mystery of Cloomber*. 1888.
A3. *Micah Clarke*. 1889.
A4. *Mysteries and Adventures*. (Also published as *My Friend the Murderer and Other Stories, The Gully of Bluemansdyke and Other Stories*.) 1889.
A5. *The Captain of the Polestar and Other Tales*. 1890.
A6. *The Firm of Girdlestone*. 1890.
A7. *The Sign of Four*. 1890.
A8. *The White Company*. 1891
A9. *The Doings of Raffles Haw*. 1892.
A10. *The Adventures of Sherlock Holmes*. 1892.
A11. *The Great Shadow*. 1892.
A12. *The Refugees*. 1893.
A13. *The Great Shadow and Beyond the City*. 1893.
A14. *The Memoirs of Sherlock Holmes*. 1893.
A15. *An Actor's Duel and The Winning Shot*. 1894.
A16. *Round the Red Lamp*. 1894.
A17. *The Parasite*. 1894.
A18. *The Stark Munro Letters*. 1895.
A19. *The Exploits of Brigadier Gerard*. 1896.
A20. *Rodney Stone*. 1896.
A21. *Uncle Bernac*. 1897.
A22. *The Tragedy of the Korosko*. (Also published as *A Desert Drama*.) 1898.
A23. *Songs of Action*. 1898. (Poetry.)
A24. *A Duet with an Occasional Chorus*. 1899.
A25. *The Green Flag and Other Stories of War and Sport*. 1900.
A26. *The Hound of the Baskervilles*. 1902.
A27. *Adventures of Gerard*. 1903.
A28. *A Duet*. 1903. (Drama.)
A29. *The Return of Sherlock Holmes*. 1905.

A30. *Sir Nigel.* 1906.
A31. *The Croxley Master.* 1907.
A32. *Waterloo.* 1907. (Drama.)
A33. *Round the Fire Stories.* 1908.
A34. *Songs of the Road.* 1911. (Poetry.)
A35. *The Last Galley.* 1911.
A36. *The Speckled Band.* 1912. (Drama.)
A37. *The Lost World.* 1912.
A38. *The Poison Belt.* 1913.
A39. *The Valley of Fear.* 1915.
A40. *His Last Bow.* 1917.
A41. *Danger! and Other Stories.* 1918.
A42. *The Guards Came Through and Other Poems.* 1919. (Poetry.)
A43. *The Poems of Arthur Conan Doyle — Collected Edition.* 1922. (Poetry.)
A44. *Three of Them.* 1923.
A45. *The Land of Mist.* 1926.
A46. *The Case-Book of Sherlock Holmes.* 1927.
A47. *The Maracot Deep and Other Stories.* 1929.

(Gibson and Green continue the listing with posthumously published books and re-collected stories.) These titles include the nine volumes of Sherlock Holmes, four books of poetry, and three plays, one of them the 1912 *Speckled Band.* Those aside, there are thirty-one books of fiction, chiefly novels.

General fiction. Doyle's first published novel was *A Study in Scarlet* (1887), but it was not the first written. Of his surviving work, the earliest is *The Firm of Girdlestone*, written in 1884-85 but published only in 1890. Like most writings by young novelists, it is somewhat autobiographical, drawing on Doyle's Edinburgh background. The same might be said for some of his later, more substantial novels: *The Stark Munro Letters* draws on his experiences as a young doctor, *A Duet with an Occasional Chorus* on his courtship of his first wife. Both combine corroborative detail — pictures, presumably accurate, of middle-class life in the 1890's — with frequent flashes of humour. In the same category is the much later *Three of Them*, a barely fictionalized description of the childhood of Denis, Adrian, and Lena Jean.

Middle-class life is also portrayed in *Beyond the City*, which is of special interest for its early picture of an unconventional, self-supporting professional woman. Doyle, though never a sympathizer with feminists (he opposed extension of the vote to women), had a life-long admiration for strong women, presumably because of his mother's influence. (Biographer Owen Dudley Edwards deals with this point in "The Hero as Woman", second chapter of *The Quest for Sherlock Holmes* [1983].) He makes an admiring point about women in his own profession, medicine, in "The Doctors of Hoyland", an 1894 short story.

In a class by itself is the collection of short stories in which "The Doctors of Hoyland" appears, *Round the Red Lamp*. These are medical tales, revealing so much about Doyle — and about the medicine of the later Victorian era — that they are to receive elaborate attention in an annotated version now being prepared by Alvin E. Rodin and Jack D. Key, who have already collaborated on other analyses of Doyle and medicine. Their volume *Medical Casebook of Doc-*

tor Arthur Conan Doyle (1984) includes a detailed discussion of these stories, which range from the gentle to the chilling. Doyle's medical background is evident in many of his other writings as well, including several of the Holmes tales ("The Resident Patient" most obviously). One can also see, in all his fiction, a preoccupation — verging on the morbid — with injured or amputated legs and with scarred or mutilated faces; surely his tolerance for descriptions that distress some squeamish readers was a result of his experiences in medical school and professional practice.

Not all Doyle's early writings were about the experiences of people like himself, however. There is a strong element of sensation, seen also in the early Holmes tales. *The Mystery of Cloomber*, probably written early although not published until 1888, reflects the author's interest in blood revenge, mysticism and exotic India. "It was not among the author's favourite works," Green and Gibson note in their *Bibliography*, "as he considered it very immature." Most commentators have concurred. *The Parasite* is also sensational, although scientific hypnotism takes the place of eastern religion, and is one of the most overtly sexual of Doyle's writings, though they do return again and again to themes of obsession and jealousy, as they also do to motifs of the supernatural, eerie and inexplicable, with a strong presence of evil. More wholesomely, *Rodney Stone*, perhaps unjustly neglected, is a tale of boxing in the Regency era — a period Doyle clearly enjoyed — as is *The Croxley Master*.

Dozens of Doyle's short stories, many of them collected in such books as *The Captain of the Polestar*, *The Green Flag*, and *The Last Galley*, are about swashbuckling adventure. He did well to have many of them reissued late in his life (1922) as *Tales of Pirates and Blue Water*, *Tales of Terror and Mystery*, *Tales of Twilight and the Unseen*, *Tales of Adventure and Medical Life*, *Tales of Long Ago*. These tales include such classics as "A Straggler of '15", about a survivor of the Battle of Waterloo; "J. Habakuk Jephson's Statement", about a ship which is found abandoned, a tale that was widely taken as non-fiction when it first appeared in 1884; and "The Man from Archangel", a reflection of his youthful experiences in Arctic waters. Stories that did not appear in collected form have been searched out by Doyle's admirers in recent years, and many are now available for the first time in a century, in the pages of *Uncollected Stories* (1982), edited by Gibson and Green as a byproduct of their *Bibliography*. Adventure at novel length is found in such books as *The Tragedy of the Korosko*, about a party of English men and women in dire straits in the Egyptian desert; strikingly, the one character who emerges well from the ordeal does so by drawing on a Roman Catholic faith, the religion in which Doyle was raised but which he abandoned.

Napoleonic works. Repeatedly Doyle wrote about the era of Napoléon Bonaparte (1769-1821), Emperor of France. Napoléon conquered most of Europe between 1800 and 1814, was defeated in that year and forced to abdicate, but returned from his exile on Elba to rally his army; he was finally defeated at Waterloo June 18, 1815. The fifteen years of the Napoleonic wars against

France were stressful and memorable for England, and the figure of Napoléon — "Boney" — was still a bogeyman eighty years later. It is thus no surprise that Doyle made those wars the subject of several pieces of writing. He was, however, sufficiently sympathetic to France, if not to Napoléon, that he treats the wars as much from the French point of view as from the English, and that his central Napoleonic figure, Brigadier Etienne Gerard, attracts the reader's admiration and affection.

Doyle's first Napoleonic work was a short story, "A Straggler of '15", about the aftermath of the Battle of Waterloo. Published in 1891, that tale led to the one-act play *Waterloo*, which opened September 21, 1894, with Henry (later Sir Henry) Irving in the principal role. Then came *The Great Shadow*, set chiefly in Scotland but with its climax on the battlefield of Waterloo. Yet another novel with a Napoleonic background was *Uncle Bernac*, this one interpreting the emperor and his era in a comic tone.

But by far the most important of Doyle's Napoleonic work are his stories of Brigadier Gerard — seventeen short stories altogether, eight that were quickly collected in *The Exploits of Brigadier Gerard*, eight more in *Adventures of Gerard*, and a seventeenth, "The Marriage of the Brigadier", eventually appearing in *The Last Galley*. The tales are based more or less on the memoirs of Jean Baptiste de Marbot (1782-1854), a genuine Napoleonic general and baron. (Gerard never achieves either rank, although the emperor does decorate him for valour, if not for brains.) Marbot's memoirs were published in French in 1891 and in English the following year, and signalled an avalanche of military reminiscences and history, as well as such Napoleonic fiction as Doyle's. Gerard is given more bluster and more heroism than the blustering, heroic Marbot, whose experiences the tales follow with a wry fidelity that makes them read better in fiction than they do in sober history. Many readers think the stories of Gerard are, in fact, Doyle's finest work, their strength being in the use of irony (shading into comedy), the depiction of a larger-than-life personality, the choice of the perfect detail to illuminate a man, an event and an age.

Historical novels. Doyle believed that his reputation would rest on his four major historical novels, above all on *The White Company*, which is rich in historical detail about English and French life of the fourteenth century. He read exhaustively, exhaustingly, to collect the material for it, drawing also on the stories of chivalry his mother had told him in childhood:

> I had recourse to the study of 115 books before I could put a pen to paper. It was very much as Charles Reade had said of *The Cloister and the Hearth*: "I milked three hundred cows into my pail, but the butter was my own for all that."

Doyle is supposed to have added that when he wrote the book's final words he cried "That's done it!" and flung his pen across the room, staining the blue wallpaper of his study. The final words are a hymn of praise to England, in which the author escapes from narrative to say (rather self-consciously, the modern reader may think) what noble meanings he attaches to English virtue:

The sky may darken, and the clouds may gather, and again the day may come when Britain may have sore need of her children, on whatever shore of the sea they be found. Shall they not muster at her call?

Writing in 1948, Doyle's biographer, John Dickson Carr, was thrilled by *The White Company*, and saw it above all as honest: "What his characters would have done, *he* would have done. And did do, until the end of his life."

But the book has weaknesses, so that it has largely fallen out of favour. Its plot is weak; it follows young Alleyne Edricson from the abbey of Beaulieu (in the New Forest, where all his life Doyle longed to live) into worldly life, to the wars in France under the banner of Sir Nigel Loring, and home again to success in love. The climax is a minor battle in Spain, in which the "white company" of archers in which Alleyne has enlisted is gloriously annihilated. Most of the characters are cartoons, and the language is cloying, with voices crying "Nay!" and "By the rood!" However, the author displays an intimate, or at least convincing, knowledge of mediaeval archery, heraldry, underclothing, horsemanship, politics, stained glass, social hierarchy, medicine, and bad language, and misses no opportunity to demonstrate his versatility with them all. The most interesting figure in *The White Company* is Sir Nigel Loring, who became the central figure in another novel in which Doyle tried to repeat his success. *Sir Nigel*, published fifteen years later, shows Nigel Loring as a younger man, not yet with the bald head he boasts in *The White Company*. A second well-drawn figure joins him in this book — his grandmother, Dame Ermyntrude, generally considered to be a portrait of the author's mother, Mary Foley Doyle.

Doyle's earliest historical novel was given a pseudo-antique title which at least indicates its subject well:

> *Micah Clarke His Statement as Made to His Three Grand-Children Joseph, Gervas & Reuben During the Hard Winter of 1734 Wherein is Contained a Full Report of Certain Passages in His Early Life Together with Some Account of His Journey from Havant to Taunton with Decimus Saxon in the Summer of 1685. Also of the Adventures that Befell Them During the Western Rebellion, & of their Intercourse with James Duke of Monmouth, Lord Grey, & Other Persons of Quality Compiled Day by Day, from His Own Narration, by Joseph Clarke, & Never Previously Set Forth in Print. Now for the First Time Collected, Corrected, & Re-Arranged from the Original Manuscripts by A. Conan Doyle.*

The book is, of course, entirely fiction, set in the tumultuous period (much less well known than the English Civil War forty years earlier) of Monmouth's rebellion, crushed by James II, who thus managed to reign four more years before the "Glorious Revolution" saw him deposed. Monmouth and his followers were Puritans, close kin to the Presbyterians of the Scotland in which Doyle grew up; James and his followers were Roman Catholics, competing with the Puritans for control of the Church of England. So it is fitting that the most dramatic battle in *Micah Clarke* — next to the disastrous one at Sedgemoor (in which Monmouth was captured, July 6, to be executed nine days later) — takes place inside the thirteenth-century cathedral at Wells. *Micah Clarke* contains the same balance of character, compulsive historical detail, and episodic adventure as Doyle's later historical novels, and is as rarely read today.

The fourth of those major historical books is *The Refugees*, set at exactly the same date as *Micah Clarke*, but this time in France (chiefly at the court of Louis XIV) and in America, both in Québec and in the forests of what is now northern New York. The plot, more suited to a serial, with repeated cliff-hangers, than to a novel, deals with Huguenot (Protestant) lovers escaping from Roman Catholic oppression. Doyle gives himself the opportunity to describe every class of society, as well as the excitement of ocean travel, the baseness and nobility of various parts of the church, love and lust, and the drama of the frontier. His Iroquois are bloodthirsty torturers (the book includes mutilation scenes of a kind that were always dear to Doyle) and his whole picture of America is drawn, none too reliably, from the early historian Francis Parkman, whose books were among his youthful enthusiasms.

Science fiction. Educated to be a doctor, Doyle had something of the scientific temperament as well as some scientific knowledge. Medicine figures in many of his stories, but so do other sciences and technologies, particularly electricity, with which he seems to have been fascinated. As early as 1891 he wrote the short story "The Voice of Science", about the gramophone, invented just a decade before. "The Japanned Box" (1899) returns to the subject of sound recording, which was still new enough to amuse readers of Sherlock Holmes in "The Mazarin Stone" in 1921. The titles of other short stories indicate the range of the sciences on which they touch: "An Exciting Christmas Eve, or, My Lecture on Dynamite"; "The Great Keinplatz Experiment" (hypnotism); "The Beetle-Hunter"; "The Great Brown-Pericord Motor". Of special interest is "The Horror of the Heights" (1913), a story about aircraft pilots who find more at high altitudes than they had bargained for. Doyle had his one and only experience of airplane flight in 1911, at Hendon, and was exhilarated but terrified; he also had some experiences of ballooning.

The Best Science Fiction of Arthur Conan Doyle (1981), edited by Charles G. Waugh and Martin H. Greenberg, reprints some of these stories as well as others, including two from the Sherlock Holmes Canon: "The Devil's Foot" and "The Creeping Man". Both are about the effects of chemicals on human behaviour. The editors might have included "The Lion's Mane" as well, and there is a modern flavour to "The Bruce-Partington Plans", with its talk of double valves with automatic self-adjusting slots.

Much the most important of Doyle's science fiction, however, is the little body of material — three novels and two short stories — about Professor George Edward Challenger. The greatest of these is *The Lost World*, the story of an expedition to South America, where dinosaurs prove to have survived into modern times on an isolated plateau. Two young and practical men (Edward Malone, the newspaperman narrator, and adventurer Lord John Roxton) are juxtaposed with two elderly scientists — Professor Summerlee and the incomparable Challenger. The name of the latter is presumably taken from HMS *Chal-*

lenger, the ship that had spent 1872-76 circumnavigating the world and collecting data about the ocean bed and its inhabitants. The physique (short, broad, with "the face and beard of an Assyrian bull") and to some extent the personality are taken from William Rutherford, one of Doyle's professors at Edinburgh. But no medical professor abused his wife, bit his housekeeper, broke a newspaperman's skull, interrupted public meetings, boasted, bellowed, dared and discovered as Challenger does. He is, if not the most realistic character in Doyle's writings, the most memorable after Sherlock Holmes himself.

The Lost World, says Charles Higham in his biography of Doyle, "is a masterpiece of imaginative fiction, reminiscent of Jules Verne but not suffering from the comparison". (Verne [1828-1905] was the author of, among other works, *Twenty Thousand Leagues Under the Sea* [1869].) Doyle based it on anthropological and travel writings of the time — South American exploration was fashionable — and his own keen interest in evolution. That interest has led to accusations that he was the originator of the Piltdown Man hoax, fabricator of the skull and jaw bones discovered near Doyle's Sussex home in the same year in which *The Lost World* was published. Although the Piltdown hoaxer has never been identified, Doyle is convincingly acquitted in *The Curious Incident of the Missing Link* (1988) by Douglas Elliott. Whether the science in *The Lost World* is any more authentic than that of Piltdown, or that in Verne, is questionable, but the adventure story is first-rate (the love story rather less so), and the book was a success. It was filmed in 1925, with Wallace Beery as Challenger, and with creaky animated dinosaurs by the technician who later created King Kong. (A 1960 remake starred, rather oddly, Claude Rains.) A verse by Doyle that is sometimes quoted as if it were about Holmes was in fact the epigraph for *The Lost World*:

> I have wrought my simple plan
> If I give one hour of joy
> To the boy who's half a man,
> Or the man who's half a boy.

To add to the fun, Doyle costumed himself as Challenger to pose for a photograph that appeared as frontispiece to the book's *Strand Magazine* serialization (April-November 1912) and first British edition.

A year after *The Lost World*, Doyle brought Challenger back in *The Poison Belt*, this time proclaiming an unpopular but correct theory in astronomy rather than in palaeontology. The world is about to pass through a belt of poison in the "ether", with disastrous consequences expressed in rather the same tones as modern warnings about the ozone layer and global warming. Challenger and a few friends seal themselves in a cozy room (the story may owe a little to Poe's "The Masque of the Red Death") in order to survive.

The professor is the central character of a third novel, *The Land of Mist*, which, though it may be classed as science fiction, is really an apologia for the beliefs of Spiritualism, to which Doyle adhered in the 1920's. In that 1926 book, the iconoclastic and ultra-rational Challenger is converted to Spiritualism — a conversion which, strikingly, Doyle never attempted to force on Sherlock Holmes. Finally, "When the World Screamed" (1928) and "The Disintegration Machine" (1929) are short stories also involving Challenger.

Novel-length science-fiction works by Doyle which do not use the Professor as their protagonist include *The Doings of Raffles Haw*, a slight story of chemistry and social-climbing; *The Parasite*, an early and rather creepy novel about hypnotism and sexual obsession; and his last published work of fiction, *The Maracot Deep*, a rather feeble adventure in which a party of explorers finds the advanced civilization of Atlantis. The idea is by no means original, and the purpose of the book seems to be to preach Spiritualism (a belief whose truth the Atlanteans are able to demonstrate) rather than to entertain.

Doyle's science fiction is discussed in detail in *Lost Worlds in Time, Space and Medicine* (1988) by Alvin E. Rodin and Jack D. Key. They divide his stories in this genre according to the sort of science involved: Electrical Energy, Alien Creatures, Geographic, and of course Medical. They also suggest that science fiction is a reasonable product for an author who also excelled in mystery writing: "Both genres have in common the elements of adventure, danger, suspense, heroes and villains." It could also be said that a great deal of Doyle's writing is, if marginal as science fiction, unquestionably about the occult, for ghosts, mummies, uncanny influences and other such phenomena abound.

Drama and poetry. Doyle's three published plays are all reworkings of his fiction — *A Duet*, "A Straggler of '15" (a major success in 1894-95 and several subsequent productions, starring Henry Irving), and "The Speckled Band". He was also author of several unpublished plays of the same kind, including "Brigadier Gerard", performed in London in the spring and summer of 1906, with a brief run in New York that autumn. The Green and Gibson *Bibliography* mentions a dozen plays that were performed in Doyle's lifetime, and another half-dozen that were unfinished or never produced. One play of some importance is "Jane Annie, or, The Good Conduct Prize", a comic opera jointly by Doyle and J. M. (later Sir James) Barrie, produced in London and Newcastle in 1893 (text published the same year).

Doyle's four volumes of poetry — three significant collections and a "collected edition" with a little new material — are among his least-known work, and rightly so. Says biographer and critic Pierre Nordon in *Conan Doyle* (1966): "Anecdotes, ballads, odes, comic verse or doggerel, their unpretentiousness charmingly excuses their insignificance. But if they mark the lowest level of Conan Doyle's inspiration, they also stress the diversity of his ambitions and literary activities." The poems include "The Song of the Bow" (originally from *The White Company*), "The Storming Party", "A Ballad of the Ranks", "The Guns in Sussex" (reflecting the martial mood of 1917), "The Wreck on Loch McGarry", and other such topics, as well as a few more philosophic verses. Only one poem is quoted with any frequency, and that is "The Inner Room", dating at least from 1898, when it first appeared in *Songs of Action*. Its significance for understanding Doyle, or understanding Doyle's image of himself, is greater than its poetic virtues:

> It is mine — the little chamber,
>   Mine alone.
> I had it from my forbears
>   Years agone.
> Yet within its walls I see
> A most motley company,
> And they one and all claim me
>   As their own.
>
> There's one who is a soldier
>   Bluff and keen;
> Single-minded, heavy-fisted,
>   Rude of mien.
> He would gain a purse or stake it,
> He would win a heart or break it,
> He would give a life or take it,
>   Conscience-clean.
>
> And near him is a priest
>   Still schism-whole;
> He loves the censer-reek
>   And organ roll. . . .
>
> If the stark-faced fellow win,
>   All is o'er!
> If the priest should gain his will,
>   I doubt no more!
> But if each shall have his day,
> I shall swing and I shall sway
> In the same old weary way
>   As before.

Peripheral works about Holmes. The Sherlockian Canon of novels and short stories might seem complete and self-contained, but other fragments about Sherlock Holmes also came from Doyle's pen. They appear, with slightly different inventories, in three modern collections: *Sherlock Holmes: The Published Apocrypha* (1980), edited by Jack Tracy; *The Final Adventures of Sherlock Holmes* (1981), edited by Peter Haining; and *The Uncollected Sherlock Holmes* (1983), edited by Richard Lancelyn Green, whose well-informed 140-page Introduction to the volume is a sympathetic and valuable biographical study of Doyle. These are the most important "apocrypha" from Doyle's pen:

- "The Field Bazaar", a parody of a Baker Street breakfast scene, written in 1896 to help raise funds for a sports field at his old university. It was published in a special issue of the *Student* magazine.
- "How Watson Learned the Trick", another breakfast parody, written for a dollhouse created for Queen Mary in the 1920's, and published in 1924 in *The Book of the Queen's Dolls' House Library*.

• *The Speckled Band*, a play first produced at London's Adelphi Theatre on June 4, 1910, based on the short story of some eighteen years earlier. The best-known difference between story and play is in the proper names: Dr. Roylott becomes Rylott, and Helen Stoner becomes Enid Stonor; her deceased sister, Julia, now bears that favourite Doylean name Violet. The play was originally to be titled "The Stonor Case", research has revealed. Holmes, appropriately, has the curtain line at the end of the second act:

> Watson *(looking at snake):* The brute is dead.
> Holmes *(looking at Dr. Rylott):* So is the other. *(They both run to support the fainting lady.)* Miss Stonor, there is no more danger for you under this roof.
> *Curtain.*

• *The Crown Diamond*, a one-act play first produced in the spring of 1921. Its plot is that of the short story "The Mazarin Stone", published later in that year, and the stagelike quality of the story strongly suggests that it was adapted from the script rather than the other way around. The most striking difference is that the villain is not Count Negretto Sylvius, as in print, but Colonel Sebastian Moran, already familiar from "The Empty House", which shares an essential plot feature — the wax bust — with "The Mazarin Stone".

• "The Man with the Watches" and "The Lost Special", a pair of short stories first published in the *Strand Magazine* for July and August 1898, respectively, and later included in *Round the Fire Stories*. Both are mysteries that baffle the authorities but are solved, in letters to the newspapers, by an "amateur reasoner of some celebrity" whose style makes clear that he must be Sherlock Holmes. Writes Jack Tracy, introducing the stories in his anthology: "Nearly five years after . . . the supposed death of his detective creation, Conan Doyle could still neither forget Sherlock Holmes nor even resist the urge to write about him."

• "Angels of Darkness", a play based on the second part of *A Study in Scarlet*. It was never produced and has not been published, but the manuscript is at the Metropolitan Toronto Reference Library, and scholars have had a look and dropped hints: it seems that in this variant on Canonical history, Holmes is not involved in the case, but Watson is, and has a serious romantic interlude in America.

In addition to such apocrypha, Doyle wrote about Holmes a number of times in his own person. The most important such piece is "Some Personalia about Mr. Sherlock Holmes", published in the *Strand Magazine* in December 1917. There is also a plot for a Holmes story Doyle never wrote, involving a man who proves to have committed his crime with the help of stilts. Finally, there is a verse, "To an Undiscerning Critic", first published in the magazine *London Opinion* for December 28, 1912:

> Have you not learned, my esteemed commentator,
> That the created is not the creator? . . .
>
> He, the created, the puppet of fiction,
> Would not brook rivals nor stand contradiction.

He, the created, would scoff and would sneer,
Where I, the Creator, would bow and revere.

General Interests

To describe Doyle as an author is to neglect his many other activities and contributions to the public good — although, to be sure, he carried on many of them through the written word, not only in books but in pamphlets, letters to the newspapers, and a heavy private correspondence. *Letters to the Press* (1986), edited by John Michael Gibson and Richard Lancelyn Green, gives glimpses of a Doyle who was as interested in rifle shooting, retail closing hours, photography, inoculation, divorce law, cricket, income tax, war, motor-cars, prostitution, and the Olympic Games as he was in conventional literary work.

His interest in literary topics led him to take a prominent part in the Society of Authors and to appear on public occasions of a literary kind. He spoke on "the literature of the Scottish border" at a banquet of the London Scottish Border Counties Association in 1904, and took the chair at a dinner honouring the 1909 centenary of Edgar Allan Poe. In 1899 he was in print in the *Daily Chronicle* on "The Ethics of Criticism", and in 1911 in the *Bookman* about bogus literary agents. And repeatedly he wrote about other authors and their works, both his contemporaries and those who had influenced him in his early years. *Through the Magic Door* (1907), based on a series of 1894 magazine articles that had been titled "Before My Bookcase", is an appreciation of such writers as Scott, Carlyle, Macaulay, Parkman, and Poe — his childhood favourites.

Late in his life he wrote not only an autobiography (*Memories and Adventures* [1924, revised edition 1930]) but several books of travel and commentary: *Our American Adventure* (1923), *Our Second American Adventure* (1924), *Our African Winter* (1929). The latter books also include long defences of Spiritualism, to which he had by that time been converted. The autobiography includes many of Doyle's opinions and experiences, but is markedly lacking in personal insight and in reference to his emotional or private life. It shows him as clearly a public man — a role he played for some forty years.

Sports. Every form of sport was of interest to Doyle, and often as a participant, though he also became known as that vaguely defined thing, "a sportsman". At the 1908 Olympic Games, held in London, he was on hand to report for the *Daily Mail* at the finish line of the marathon race (the first race to use the now standard marathon distance of 26 miles 385 yards). When the Italian competitor, Dorando Pietri, who had led most of the way, collapsed just short of the finish line, was helped up by officials and was dragged across the line, but disqualified after a protest, Doyle immediately led a movement to present him with a cash purse (which reached £308) to honour his courage. A few years later he was in the newspapers repeatedly as Britain debated the merits of participation in the projected 1916 Olympics and the best way of organizing a team. A chapter entitled "Some Recollections of Sport" in Doyle's 1924 autobiography *Memories and Adventures* ranges from fishing to billiards, to say nothing of the Prince Henry International Road Competition in 1911, in which Doyle was one of nearly 100 drivers who spent three weeks touring Germany, Scotland and England.

The major sports in England were and are cricket, a bat-and-ball game, and football, of the kinds known in North America as rugby and soccer. Doyle played all three. Cricket, he wrote in the autobiography,

> has on the whole given me more pleasure during my life than any other branch of sport. I have ended by being its victim, for a fast bowler some years ago happened to hit me twice in the same place under my left knee, which has left a permanent weakness. ... I fulfilled a secret ambition by getting into the fringe of first-class cricket, though rather, perhaps, through the good nature of others than my own merits. However, I can truly say that in the last season when I played some first-class cricket, including matches against Kent, Derbyshire, and the London County, I had an average of thirty-two for those games. ... I was more useful, however, in an amateur team, for I was a fairly steady and reliable bowler.

He once performed a hat-trick, that is, bowled three "clean" wickets in a row; he once bowled the great W. G. Grace, equivalent to striking out Ted Williams in baseball; he once hit a century (100 runs) at Lord's, the shrine of cricket-grounds. As an amateur he was a member of a team of literary and artistic men organized by J. M. Barrie: the Allahakbarries, or Gawd-help-us-es, whose style on the playing field seems to have reflected their name.

Oddly, there is nothing of cricket in the Sherlockian Canon, save a mention that young Gilchrist of "The Three Students" played the game. That is hardly surprising, for he was an all-round athlete, whose visits to the clay-bottomed jumping pit helped lead to his undoing. Football, on the other hand, figures importantly in one story, "The Missing Three-Quarter"; its plot has to do with the disappearance of a star player on the Cambridge University team just before a big game.

> My ramifications stretch out into many sections of society [says Holmes], but never, I am happy to say, into amateur sport, which is the best and soundest thing in England. However, your unexpected visit this morning shows me that even in that world of fresh air and fair play, there may be work for me to do.

That is Doyle speaking, about the game he played as a young man at Edinburgh, his position being forward. This football is rugby, the collegiate game of the time and still frequently played by amateurs in England, though there is also a professional league. The major form of professional football is "association", or soccer, so called for the governing body established for it as a new sport in 1863. In Portsmouth, Doyle helped organize a new club for association football, and played for several seasons as a fullback and occasionally goalkeeper (usually under the discreet nom-de-plume of Smith). His autobiography deals with football in complimentary terms:

> If boxing is the finest single man sport, I think that Rugby football is the best collective one. Strength, courage, speed and resource are great qualities to include in a single game. I have always wished that it had come more my way in life. ...

I took to Association, and played first goal and then back for Portsmouth, when that famous club was an amateur organization. Even then, we could put a very fair team in the field, and were runners-up for the County Cup the last season that I played. In the same season I was invited to play for the county. I was always too slow, however, to be a really good back, though I was a long and safe kick. After a long hiatus I took up football again in South Africa and organized a series of inter-hospital matches in Bloemfontein.

Many other sports are reflected in the Canon, with only eleven of the sixty stories lacking some reference to a sport or athletic activity, according to Mark Alberstat in an unpublished study of *Sherlock Holmes, the Canon and Sports*. Most dramatically there is racing in "Silver Blaze", a sport of which Doyle confessed that he knew little (an ignorance confirmed by the story's many solecisms). "I never could look upon flat-racing as a true sport," he wrote in *Memories and Adventures*. "Sport is what a man does, not what a horse does."

He is equally critical of hunting ("I cannot persuade myself that we are justified in taking life as a pleasure"), and there is little of hunting in the Canon. Fishing does figure here and there, to the point that Donald G. Jewell was able to find material for a monograph about it: *A Trout in the Milk: A Monograph on Fish and Fishing in the Time of Sherlock Holmes* (1991), and Doyle did occasionally indulge in that form of killing. He also voyaged to the Arctic on a whaling ship in his youth.

The greatest sport, in his estimation, was boxing, which had been reorganized by the introduction of the Marquess of Queensberry rules (1867) and the foundation of the Amateur Boxing Association (1884). With these innovations boxing became less deadly than it had been, not only because of a spirit of fair play but because padded gloves were now required. Doyle boxed himself (as a "fair average amateur", he wrote) and loved to watch boxing; in 1909 an American promoter invited him to referee a heavyweight championship bout between Jack Johnson and James J. Jeffries, but he had to decline. (Johnson knocked out Jeffries in fifteen rounds July 4, 1910.) Doyle wrote about boxing in his novel *Rodney Stone*, set in the bare-knuckle days of the late eighteenth century, and in the novelette *The Croxley Master*, with a contemporary setting (the Queensberry Rules are mentioned). There is also a play, "The House of Temperley", performed in 1910 but never fully published; it is vaguely based on *Rodney Stone*. Boxing plays no large role in the Sherlockian Canon, but Holmes is described by Watson as an "expert" boxer, and on a few occasions he has to apply his pugilistic skill in situations much removed from sport.

Among Doyle's many other sporting interests was rifle-shooting. The Conan Doyle Cup is an event held annually as part of the National Rifle Association's meeting; a friend of Doyle's donated the prize in 1906. He was also associated with skiing:

I can claim to have been the first to introduce skis into the Grisons division of Switzerland, or at least to demonstrate their practical utility as a means of getting across in winter from one valley to another. It was in 1894 that I read Nansen's account of his crossing of Greenland, and thus became interested in the subject of ski-ing. It chanced that I was compelled to spend that winter in the Davos valley, and I spoke about the matter to Tobias Branger, a sporting tradesman in the village, who in turn interested his father. We sent for skis from Norway, and for some weeks afforded innocent amusement to a large number of people who watched our awkward movements and complex tumbles.

That experience may have prepared him for the hilarity with which the folk of Brattleboro, Vermont, received him and Rudyard Kipling when they tried golfing near Kipling's home there in November 1894. The two of them took eighty-four strokes over nine holes, and Doyle recorded later that he had never become much of a golfer.

The pursuit of justice. Biographers have been fond of describing Doyle's intervention in two prominent criminal cases, those against George Edalji and Oscar Slater. But a remarkable book by Peter Costello, *The Real World of Sherlock Holmes* (1991), reports dozens of crimes in which Doyle took an interest, and sometimes an active role. Costello manages to include the affair of Jack the Ripper in this category, on the strength of an investigation carried out in 1905 — seventeen years after the murders took place — by the Crimes Club, a private group of connoisseurs of which Doyle was a member. Beyond doubt, Doyle was interested in crime, and occasionally intervened casually in a case, as in an 1896 letter to *The Times*:

> Apart from the evidence of medical experts, it is inconceivable that any woman in her position in her sane senses would steal duplicates and triplicates — four toast-racks, if I remember right. Small articles of silver, with the hotel mark upon them, so that they could neither be sold nor used, were among the objects which she had packed away in her trunk. It can surely not be denied that there is at least a doubt as to her moral responsibility.

As Doyle became famous for creating a detective, he was in demand for such opinions; Costello discusses the Frank Westwood murder in Toronto in 1894, noting that Doyle gave it passing attention because he was badgered into doing so by reporters while he was visiting Toronto that year.

Although he deprecated his own detective skills, he could demonstrate vigorous common sense in attacking the salient points of a problem. More important, he was tireless, and applied his energy fearlessly to what he thought was right. In the Edalji and Slater cases, he was the chief advocate of men wrongly accused, and in each case he managed to earn something like justice for them after long periods of effort.

• George Edalji was a young solicitor in Birmingham who had served part of a seven-year prison sentence after being convicted in a series of knife attacks on farm animals near his home village of Great Wyrley, Staffordshire, in 1903. He maintained his innocence, and Doyle realized as soon as he met Edalji that the young man, being nearly blind, could not have committed the outrages under cover of rural darkness. Doyle easily uncovered an ugly tale of anonymous letters and decades-long harassment: Edalji's father, the vicar of the little community, was a Parsee, so that race prejudice lay at the root of the affair. After investigating, he wrote a pair of articles which appeared in *The Daily Telegraph* January 11 and 12, 1907 (and in *The New York Times* February 2 and 3); they were quickly republished in pamphlet form as *The Story of Mr. George Edalji*. He reported that the police and Home Office had been unsympathetic to requests that the case be reopened, and declared that he was now taking it to "a tribunal that never errs", namely public opinion. Immense excitement and controversy followed, and a government investigation led to a pardon for Edalji in May 1907. But Doyle was not satisfied — the real mutilator, and author of the nasty letters, remained to be found. Later that year he submitted a detailed accusation of the man he believed guilty; it was never acted upon.

• Oscar Slater had served more than three years of a life sentence for murder when his case came to Doyle's attention in 1912. The victim was Marion Gilchrist, an elderly woman in Glasgow, who was beaten to death in her flat December 21, 1908; a diamond brooch was apparently stolen, but other valuable jewellery left behind. Slater, a shady gem dealer, was arrested in New York. The case against him was built on a diamond brooch he had pawned in Glasgow (which was eventually proven not to have been the missing item), on identifications by unreliable witnesses, and on his general shady reputation as a crook and pimp (as well as on his German-Jewish origins). After the conviction there was an outcry, leading to the publication of a book by William Roughead, *The Trial of Oscar Slater*. Doyle's interest was attracted, and he contributed a pamphlet, *The Case of Oscar Slater* (1912). Two years later new information surfaced, with a hint that Marion Gilchrist's downstairs neighbour had suppressed the identity of a man who had been seen in the hallway just after the murder. Doyle and others pressed for official action, but nothing was done. As late as 1927 the case was still open; in that year Doyle wrote a preface for a new book, *The Truth about Oscar Slater*, by William Park, and had it published by the Psychic Press, which he was managing. At last, in the fall of 1927, Slater was released from prison, and a pardon and compensation followed. No one else was ever convicted, although researchers have blamed Francis Charteris, a relative of the victim.

Military affairs. Doyle never held a commission in the armed forces. During World War I he did insist on enlisting as a private in the Volunteer Battalion of the Royal Sussex Regiment, which drilled near his home at Crowborough, but otherwise his longstanding interest in military matters found expression through unofficial channels.

Most of his experience of warfare came in South Africa, during the curious conflict known to history as the Boer War, 1899-1902. The black population of what is now South Africa was almost incidental to this war, fought between British troops and the British settlers of the Cape Colony and Natal on the one hand, the Dutch ("Boer", i.e. farmer) settlers of the Transvaal and the Orange Free State on the other. The most dramatic events of that war included the siege of Mafeking, which led to wild excitement in the streets of London on "Mafeking Night", May 17, 1900, when the news came that British troops had reached the city, and a similar siege at Ladysmith (relieved February 28, 1900). Its less savoury contributions to civilization included the first modern concentration camps, into which British troops under Lord Kitchener (Horatio Baron Kitchener) herded some of their Boer prisoners.

Doyle saw the war as a noble enterprise and was determined to serve in it somehow, but the army would not accept him, and he volunteered instead to serve as a doctor with a private field hospital. The war had been going badly for Britain, and Doyle was interested in studying the military situation and writing about the war, as well as rendering medical help. He sailed for South Africa on the day of the relief of Ladysmith, and spent five months in hard work at the temporary hospital in Bloemfontein, chiefly battling enteric fever (typhoid) rather than battle wounds. It was a filthy, hellish experience. But he found time to observe the strategy of the war as well, and when he returned to England got them into print as *The Great Boer War* (first published in October 1900, with many subsequent editions). His suggestions were shocking, as John Dickson Carr observes in *The Life of Sir Arthur Conan Doyle*:

> First, the artillery. British guns must be concealed, as the Boers' were. . . .
>
> Second, the cavalry. The cavalry must cease to be armed with swords or lances, which belonged only in a museum. What good were swords or lances against Mauser rifles sighted up to two thousand yards? Equip your cavalry with rifles.
>
> (Here the military experts and the old gentlemen in clubs really did have an apoplectic fit.)
>
> Third and most important, the infantry. They must learn to dig trenches. . . . Teach your infantry to shoot; and for the love of heaven give them some ammunition with which to practise.

And in letters to the newspapers, Doyle called for army reform: "roughly halving their numbers, doubling their pay, and keeping them entirely for the foreign service of the Empire". Home defence would be the duty of a home guard, "civilian riflemen".

Once the war had ended, stories of the concentration camps and other alleged British atrocities swept Europe. In response, Doyle wrote a pamphlet, *The War in South Africa — Its Cause and Conduct*, which had a huge sale in England and was distributed across Europe in many translations. This propaganda service earned him a knighthood (on the day of Edward VII's coronation, August 9, 1902), making him *Sir* Arthur, although it is possible that the publication of *The Hound of the Baskervilles* eleven weeks after that of *The War*, and thus the resurrection of Sherlock Holmes, helped to gain him that honour.

For the rest of his life he broke into print at intervals on military subjects — suggesting in 1906 that motor-car owners sign up to transport riflemen to where they were needed in case of invasion, arguing in 1910 for the use of bicyclists in warfare, suggesting in 1913 and many times thereafter that a tunnel under the English Channel would protect Britain against blockade in time of war. The short story "Danger!", published in July 1914, warned of the dangers of submarines if a tunnel were not put in place, and many of its predictions came true during World War I. Once the war began (on August 3, 1914), Doyle followed it keenly and wrote constantly about it: suggesting the use of inflatable lifebelts on transport ships, calling for energetic recruitment, urging the use of body-armour, discussing air raids and ways of keeping soldiers from frequenting prostitutes.

The war, fought by Britain and France (joined in 1917 by the United States) against Germany and its eastern European allies, including Turkey, lasted four years and changed Britain's history, killing a generation of young men and destroying its class system. Most of the warfare, which killed an estimated 10 million soldiers, took place in trenches in Belgium and northern France, where shooting continued across a sea of mud and barbed wire. But it touched everyone at home. The sound of the big guns could sometimes be heard at Doyle's home on the south coast of England. Malcolm Leckie, brother of Lady Doyle, was an army doctor, killed at Mons in August 1914. Kingsley, Doyle's oldest son, was in the Royal Army Medical Corps as well; Innes, Doyle's beloved younger brother, was a lieutenant-colonel at the battlefront, then a colonel, by war's end a brigadier-general. At home, Doyle's daughter Mary did volunteer work, and he and Lady Doyle entertained Canadian troops when they had leave from their nearby camps.

Letters from the front came not only from relatives but from the generals directing the mostly ineffective British fighting. The government sent him on a tour of the battlefields in the spring of 1916, just before the terrible battle of the Somme; on his return he wrote reports in the *Daily Chronicle* which were collected as the little book *A Visit to Three Fronts*. There had been other war writing as well, and that fall appeared the first volume of *The British Campaign in France and Flanders*, which would run to six volumes, the last appearing in January 1920. *The British Campaign* is immensely detailed about tactics ("Meanwhile the enemy had made a spirited attempt to push through between the Seventh Corps and the Fifth"). The author gives credit in it to the "innumerable correspondents" who provided information for him and in some cases made suggestions about what he had drafted. The work was published in chapters in the *Strand Magazine* before appearing in book form: "I was really the only public source of supply of accurate and detailed information," Doyle said later about this project. But his work lacks historical perspective on the war, having been written while the fighting was continuing, and often omits information which later historians, drawing on official secrets, were able to use.

Public affairs. Although he twice ran for Parliament, Doyle was not generally active in party politics, except apparently during his early years in Portsmouth, when he helped to organize a local association for Liberal-Unionists — a political group favouring most of the platform of the then ruling Liberal Party, but opposing its policy of "Home Rule" for Ireland. In later years, save for those two unsuccessful appearances on the ballot, his involvement in public affairs was through pamphleteering and the newspapers, where his courteous letters were frequently to be seen.

Aside from crime and, in his later years, Spiritualism, the domestic issue that occupied him the most was reform of the laws governing divorce. By 1904, when he published "The Abbey Grange", the problem of intolerable but indissoluble marriages was clearly on his mind, probably in part because of his personal position, married to the invalid Louise while in love with Jean Leckie. In 1906 the Divorce Law Reform Union was formed; Doyle served as its president. His pamphlet *Divorce Law Reform* was published by the Union in 1909, and many letters and articles followed, as he argued that England should not "lag behind every other Protestant country in the world, and even behind Scotland, so that unions which are obviously disgusting and degrading are maintained". In Doyle's lifetime the only ground for divorce was adultery, and only a man could claim that as the sole ground; a woman had to claim something like physical abuse as well. Further, the expense of a divorce was estimated at about £700, a sum very few could find.

The atrocities practised in the Congo region (now Zaire) in the first decade of the twentieth century enraged Doyle perhaps more than any other injustice to which he turned his attention. A huge region of central Africa, nominally independent as the Congo Free State, was in effect the private property of Leopold II, King of the Belgians, who with his associates exploited it for the rubber trade, with slavery and dreadful cruelties. A Congo Reform Association was founded in Britain in 1904, and Doyle became involved in 1909. Within weeks he had *The Crime of the Congo* in print, exposing the atrocities; a frontispiece showed photographs of nine Congolese whose hands had been cut off as part of the campaign of terror that had been going on for years. Later that year Doyle was lecturing on the subject, and as late as 1912 he was still writing to the newspapers about it. Much of the information about the Congo came from Roger Casement, the British consul in the area. A few years later, at the beginning of World War I, Doyle found himself defending Casement in vain after the young adventurer, having tried to make terms with Germany on behalf of his native Ireland, was charged with treason. Casement, who may have been mentally ill, was hanged.

Doyle was keenly interested in Irish affairs. Proposals for "Home Rule" in Ireland were the central issue of British politics for much of his lifetime; he had been opposed to the idea, but by 1911 was grudgingly in favour. "There is no possible reason," he wrote in one letter, "why a man should not be a loyal Irishman and a loyal Imperialist also." He stressed his own "Irish extraction" in arguing the close ties between Ireland and the rest of the Empire. When Home Rule was finally granted, after World War I, Doyle opposed division between Ulster (northern Ireland) and the southern three-quarters of the country; he did not live to see the south become fully independent in 1937.

The word "Imperialist", which Doyle used to describe his own position, meant not loyalty to England but loyalty to a worldwide empire, which had already come to embrace a more or less independent Canada and South Africa as well as the motherland and her colonies. Ireland could become an adult member of that family, he suggested in the later years of his life. His dreams were still larger; he sympathized with, though he did not actively campaign for, the movement towards "Anglo-American Union", an eventual alliance between the British Empire and the United States. He put that idea in the mouth of Sherlock Holmes in "The Noble Bachelor" (1892), he spoke feelingly on the subject during and after his American tour of 1894, and less idealistically he speculates in *Our American Adventure* (1923) about a world in which the American revolution had not taken place:

> Then, as the most populous must always govern in any democratic system, America would quite naturally and peacefully have become the centre and chief guide to all the scattered English-speaking nations, with the four home countries as part of the huge, world-wide confederation which might have stopped all war and ushered in the millennium.

Spiritualist Interests

Enthusiasts and even biographers have been a little embarrassed by the last dozen years of Doyle's life, which he devoted to preaching the doctrine of Spiritualism. How, they have asked, can the rational doctor, the practical man of public affairs, and the creator of the purely intellectual Sherlock Holmes have let himself fall into a belief in communication with the dead, and make a laughing-stock of himself on four continents as he argued that fraudulent "mediums" were channels for communicating a vital divine message to humanity? The usual explanation is that he was somehow unhinged by the terrible experiences of World War I, in which family members and friends died so senselessly. The carnage of the war did predispose England to look for some new religious comfort and explanation, and may have directed Doyle's attention more closely to Spiritualism, but in fact he was interested in the subject long before the deaths of his brother, son, and brothers-in-law during and shortly after the war.

Doyle's life-long interest in psychic matters, as they were often called, is helpfully traced in *Conan Doyle and the Spirits* (1989) by Kelvin I. Jones. He begins with a discussion of the Roman Catholicism in which Doyle was raised as a childhood. The young Jesuit-educated doctor rejected that church, and all organized Christianity, but clearly never lost his interest in God, in the meaning of life, and in supernatural phenomena. Many of his early short stories (Jones instances "Lot No. 249") deal with the occult, often edging into the horrible. As early as the fall of 1893, he joined the Society for Psychical Research, a body which existed to investigate unexplained phenomena ranging from "automatic writing" to the manifestation of spirits at seances. Some members of the SPR (founded 1882) were convinced Spiritualists; others were rationalists, interested rather in finding a scientific explanation for hypnotism, clairvoyance and the like.

Spiritualism itself is frequently dated from March 31, 1848, when remarkable events took place in Hydesville, New York, a village in the so-called "burnt-over district" from which a series of religious revivals and creations, including the birth of Mormonism, had sprung through the early nineteenth century. On that day Kate Fox, an adolescent girl in Hydesville, established apparent contact with some entity that lived in her house. Through "rappings" the being identified itself as the spirit of a murdered man, who soon also communicated with Kate's older sister, Margaret. Interest in such communication spread; by the fall of 1849 there were enough people in touch with other spirits that a mass meeting was held in nearby Rochester. In 1852 a Mrs. Hayden brought the rapidly growing movement to England, and a British National Association of Spiritualists was organized in 1873. Among its members from an early date was Major-General Alfred W. Drayson, an astronomer and author as well as military officer, who had retired to Southsea and was a major influence on Doyle through the Portsmouth Literary and Scientific Society in the 1880's. After Doyle moved to London he continued his interest in Spiritualism, and continued to write fiction that reflected a preoccupation with the occult, although its echoes in the Sherlockian Canon are very limited. *The Hound of the Baskervilles*, seeming to promise the supernatural, proves to involve fakery instead, and "The Sussex Vampire" is almost mocking in its attitude to "ghosts".

The theory of Spiritualism took time to develop. A milestone was the 1903 publication of *Human Personality and Its Survival of Bodily Death*, by Frederick Myers, one of the founders of the SPR. This volume greatly influenced Doyle, who continued to read on psychic subjects, and to act occasionally as a member of SPR investigative teams looking at mediums or visiting allegedly haunted houses. The range of phenomena being observed by Spiritualists — or, as they put it, the range of messages being delivered to the living by spirits — now extended far beyond rapping noises. Mediums (unusually sensitive people who were able, sometimes in trances, to get in touch with spirits) often spoke with the voices of spirits, moved objects about the room without touching them, materialized unexpected items or "apports" such as foreign coins, and secreted "ectoplasm", a spirit substance that could form itself into the faces or bodies of spirit figures. Communication from the world of spirits might also come through writing, dictated to the hand of a medium, or photography, with faces that had been invisible to the human eye appearing when a picture was developed on film.

Doyle came to believe in the authenticity of these messages: not all of them, for he accepted that there were charlatans, particularly among mediums who were paid for their services, but enough of them to provide the basis for religious conviction. He made his conversion to Spiritualism public November 4, 1916, in a letter to the journal *Light*, and in 1918 he amplified his beliefs in *The New Revelation*, a little book in which he not only declared his acceptance of Spiritualist communication but set out a description of the new life in which the spirits of the dead find themselves:

> The reports from the other world are all agreed as to the pleasant conditions of life in the beyond. . . . Life is full of interest and of occupation. . . . People live in communities, as one would expect if like attracts like, and the male spirit still finds his

> true mate though there is no sexuality in the grosser sense. . . . We catch dim
> glimpses of endless circles below descending into gloom and endless circles
> above, ascending into glory, all improving, all purposeful, all intensely alive.

Certainly, he said, there was no hell, and this was a conception of heaven much
modified from the traditional picture.

The New Revelation was followed in 1919 by *The Vital Message*, with new
arguments and detailed replies to critics. Both books made a number of references to the recent war, which "brought earnestness into all our souls" and prepared the world for direct contact with the spirit messengers. In these two early
books Doyle made it clear that he saw no necessary conflict between Spiritualism and Christianity, although the new revelation would compel many changes
in the system taught by the traditional churches. The "great Christ spirit", he
wrote, clearly guides and directs the spirit world. "It is only the occultist who
can possibly understand the Scriptures as being a real exact record of events,"
and explained Jesus as a moral teacher and a powerful psychic medium — "a
supreme character in the world's history who obviously stands nearer to the
Highest than any other". But for organized Christianity he had chiefly contempt.

> Is it not time, then, for the religious bodies to discourage their own bigots and sec-
> tarians, and to seriously consider, if only for self-preservation, how they can get
> into line once more with that general level of human thought which is now so far
> in front of them? . . . They must gather fresh strength by drawing in all the new
> truth and all the new power which are afforded by this new wave of inspiration
> which has been sent into the world by God.

For the rest of his life Doyle would continue to write about his new beliefs, in
countless letters, articles, and pamphlets, and in several books, including *The
Case for Spirit Photography* (1922) and *The Edge of the Unknown* (1930). The
unusual book *Pheneas Speaks* (1927) was a report of the messages Doyle and
his family received from their designated spirit guide over a period of several
years. Doyle's largest book on the subject is the two-volume *History of Spiritualism* (1926), written with the assistance of Leslie Curnow, a researcher and
expert. As well as history, it describes Spiritualist thought and practice, and
includes a strong chapter on the compatibility of Spiritualism and Christianity,
especially in the belief in life after death that the two systems share. *The History
of Spiritualism* was dedicated to Sir Oliver Lodge (1851-1940), a friend and
prominent physicist who was keenly interested in psychic research.

Doyle travelled extensively in England and repeatedly in Europe, addressing
crowds about Spiritualism whenever he could find an audience. He also made
trips to Australia (1920-21), America (1922 and again 1923), and South Africa
(1928-29) to spread his message, and wrote four books that discussed both his
travels and his Spiritualist insights: *The Wanderings of a Spiritualist* (1921), *Our
American Adventure* (1923), *Our Second American Adventure* (1924), *Our African Winter* (1929). In 1925 he opened a Psychic Bookshop, Library and
Museum in Victoria Street, London (cables: *Ectoplasm*). He devoted much of

his energy and fortune in the last five years of his life to subsidizing its work. Doyle became the world's best-known Spiritualist, and was honoured in the movement with such titles as Honorary President of the International Spiritualist Congress. A sour note came in March 1930 when he resigned from his life-long membership in the Society for Psychical Research, crying that it had become closed-minded and hostile to genuine psychic phenomena.

In the course of his Spiritualist work Doyle came to know Harry Houdini (1873-1926), the noted American conjurer and escape artist. Conjurers were often called in to help psychic investigators detect trickery in the work of suspect mediums, and Houdini prided himself on being able to detect such fraud. He observed some mediums during a tour of England in 1920, and formed a friendship with Doyle despite their diametrically opposed views of Spiritualism. When Doyle went to America in 1922 they met for a seance in Atlantic City. Doyle believed that they had been visited by the spirit of Houdini's dead mother; Houdini thought, and wrote, that the phenomena he had seen through the mediumship of Lady Doyle were spurious. The friendship did not survive the resulting recriminations, although Doyle spoke not unkindly of Houdini in *The Edge of the Unknown*. First-hand material about the relationship appeared in *Houdini and Conan Doyle: The Story of a Strange Friendship* (1932), by Bernard Ernst and Hereward Carrington.

The oddest aspect of Doyle's psychic work is certainly the episode of the Cottingley fairies. Two girls — Elsie Wright, 15, and Frances Griffiths, 10 — reported in 1917 that they had seen fairies in their garden and been able to take photographs of them. The pictures came to Doyle's attention three years later; he accepted them as genuine, and made the news public in the December 1920 issue of the *Strand Magazine*, and more fully in a brief book, *The Coming of the Fairies* (1922). As early as 1921 there were plausible claims that the photographs had been faked, but a confession from the perpetrators came only in 1983. In old age they said they had always felt somewhat guilty for fooling Doyle and holding him up to the ridicule he suffered. The quality of the deceptive photographs (which were reproduced in Doyle's book, and frequently since) must have been very high to fool a man who was a keen amateur photographer and had written a series of essays for the *British Journal of Photography* in the 1880's (collected as *Essays on Photography*, 1982). The whole affair, including Doyle's role, is discussed in *The Case of the Cottingley Fairies* (1990) by Joe Cooper.

Posterity

Lady Doyle (née Jean Leckie) continued some of Doyle's Spiritualist work after his death; she herself died June 27, 1940, still a believer, and was buried beside Sir Arthur in the grounds at Windlesham. (When the property was sold in 1955, the bodies were reburied in the churchyard at Minstead, Sussex, where Doyle lies under a headstone with the famous inscription "Steel True, Blade Straight".) Doyle had been heard from in a number of seances, some of his messages being published in *Thy Kingdom Come* (1933), edited by Ivan Cooke (later reissued as *The Return of Arthur Conan Doyle*). Doyle's eldest son, Kingsley, had died October 28, 1918, a victim of the 1918-19 influenza epidemic. His daughter by his first marriage, Mary, long survived him, dying June 12, 1976.

Doyle was also survived by all three children of his second marriage: Denis, Adrian (known in his earlier years as Malcolm), and Lena Jean. The daughter embarked on the military career her father had always half-envied, and ended as Director of the Women's Royal Air Force, with the rank of Air Commandant; she was given the title Dame, equivalent to a knighthood, for her work. In 1965 she married Air Vice-Marshal Sir Geoffrey Bromet, thus acquiring the alternative title of Lady Bromet. He died in 1983. Dame Jean Conan Doyle now lives in London, and takes an interest in Holmesian matters as well as in the Arthur Conan Doyle Society. She controls the remaining American copyrights in Doyle's published works.

Denis and Adrian pursued other of their father's interests, including spiritualism, sport and literature. Adrian published a few books, including *Tales of Love and Hate* (1960), much in the style of his father, and was co-author of *The Exploits of Sherlock Holmes* (1954), a collection of pastiches. After Lady Doyle's death, Denis and Adrian also inherited responsibility for their father's properties, including the copyrights and papers of "the Doyle estate". Through the 1940's and 1950's, the estate was managed with vigour, if eccentricity; it licensed the use of Sherlock Holmes in the Basil Rathbone films of the 1940's and the Ronald Howard television series of the early 1950's, for example. Denis, who headed the estate, attended at least one dinner of the Baker Street Irregulars, and spoke movingly on "My Father's Friend, Mr. Sherlock Holmes", but never truly understood the Sherlockian movement. Matters worsened after Denis's death on March 9, 1955, when control of the estate passed to the temperamental Adrian (dubbed "the man with the twisted lip" by Edgar W. Smith of the BSI), and Sherlockian activities were carried on for a spell entirely without reference to the Doyle family or, for the most part, to the memory of Doyle himself.

Adrian had already made himself conspicuous by an unpleasant reaction to Hesketh Pearson's biography of his father, *Conan Doyle, His Life and Art* (1943), and wrote a tract to contradict it, *The True Conan Doyle* (1945). Fourteen years later, he had the opportunity to edit a sort of scrapbook about his father: *Sir Arthur Conan Doyle Centenary, 1859-1959*. In 1965 Adrian, who was living in Switzerland for tax reasons, opened an Arthur Conan Doyle Museum, housing many of his father's papers, curios, and works of art, in a twelfth-century castle, the Château de Lucens. Within a few years, however, he began steps to sell many of the papers and manuscripts, through the New York rare-book dealer Lew David Feldman (the House of El Dieff). In the early stages of legal proceedings involving Adrian, the Swiss government, the University of Texas (which had hoped to buy the Château with its contents), and other parties, Adrian died, on June 3, 1970.

The remaining heirs were Dame Jean Conan Doyle; Adrian's widow, Anna (married 1938); and Denis's widow, Nina Mdivani (married 1936), eldest daughter of an allegedly royal family from Asian Georgia, who was now remarried and surnamed Harwood. Nina and her husband bought the copyrights in Doyle's published works and went into business as Baskervilles Investments Ltd. That corporation was subsequently taken over by the Royal Bank of Scotland when it ran into financial difficulties, and the rights were sold to Swiss financier Andre Milos. In the late 1970's they were managed by Sheldon Reynolds of New York, who had produced the Ronald Howard television series twenty-five years earlier.

When British and world-wide copyrights on Doyle's work expired in 1980, the position also changed in the United States; remaining copyrights there (those on stories that have been published for less than seventy-five years) passed into the control of Dame Jean, rather than of the "Estate", and she has taken a direct interest in seeing that Sherlock Holmes is presented with restraint and dignity. Meanwhile, both the management of the Doyle Estate and the extent of its remaining assets has been less than clear. The most important properties are the copyrights in unpublished writings by Doyle, and the physical manuscripts that were owned by Doyle at his death, ranging from originals of the Sherlock Holmes stories to hundreds of letters to his mother. These materials continue to be sequestered while litigation involving the three heirs grinds on, but with the deaths of Nina in 1987 and Anna in 1990 it now appears possible that matters will be settled soon. Meanwhile, some previously unknown Doyle material, including his diaries from his early years of authorship, is gradually being cited by researchers as they become available from unexplained sources.

Biographical Writings

There is no definitive biography of Arthur Conan Doyle. The most comprehensive overview of his life and work can be found in *The Quest for Sir Arthur Conan Doyle: Thirteen Biographers in Search of a Life* (1987), edited by Jon Lellenberg, which is a collection of essays about the many biographical works that do exist. They include Doyle's own *Memories and Adventures* (1924, second edition 1930), as well as minor works about his travels, and several biographical novels. In the course of the reports and analysis, which discuss each biographer in turn, most of the available interpretations of Doyle's life are considered, and the story is told in greater — more balanced — detail than any single biography has so far managed to do.

After Doyle's death the first work about him to appear was *Arthur Conan Doyle: A Memoir* (1931) by John Lamond, a clergyman and Spiritualist colleague. It is an appreciation rather than a scholarly biography, and the same can be said about a number of minor books that have appeared in later years, the chief difference being that Doyle is now appreciated for his literary creations (especially that of Sherlock Holmes) rather than for his religious insights. The extreme of hagiography is Adrian Conan Doyle's *The True Conan Doyle*, written in response to Hesketh Pearson's *Conan Doyle* (1943), which treated Doyle without great respect, in particular labelling him (with no great justification) "the man in the street".

The most important biography is still the most nearly authorized of all the books about Doyle: *The Life of Sir Arthur Conan Doyle* (1949) by mystery writer John Dickson Carr (born 1905, died February 27, 1977). Carr, unlike most subsequent scholars, had access to Doyle's papers (then under the control of Adrian, with whom he would later collaborate on *The Exploits*). A brief, tantalizing appendix to his book summarizes the contents of the boxes he explored. His *Life* of Doyle is excitingly written, with long passages of conversation, including many encounters that can have had no witnesses, and the colourful language of a novel. Carr's Doyle is a chivalric hero much like his Sir Nigel, and just a little like his Sherlock Holmes, from a childhood under the nobility-minded tutelage of the Ma'am (a title Carr seems to have invented) to his defences of George Edalji and Oscar Slater. Here is Carr describing Doyle's Spiritualist campaigns:

> For eleven years his sword did not sleep. For eleven years, through a changed post-war world, all that incredible energy poured into going anywhere, speaking anywhere, challenging any opponent, working with scarcely any rest, seeming charged with an inexhaustible force and light.
> "This can't go on forever," his medical advisers told him again and again. "A man at your age —"
> At his age? To him, who somehow combined the mellowness and kindliness of a sixth decade with the driving-power of his thirties, it was not a question of his age. It was a question of what had to be done.

Carr presents a Doyle that his children could be proud to acknowledge, and a Doyle whom forty years of readers have been happy to admire. He omits the dark side of his subject: his sexual tensions, the life-long effect of watching his father's descent into alcoholism, the touchiness that led to his quarrel with Houdini. He also frequently omits dates and details, adding to his book's effectiveness as entertainment but devaluing it as a basis for further research.

Next in the series of books about Doyle came *Sir Arthur Conan Doyle, l'homme et l'oeuvre*, by Pierre Nordon (1964), with an English translation (*Conan Doyle*, 1966) in which long passages of the French original were omitted. Nordon was a Sorbonne scholar whose work betrays his approach through literary criticism rather than history. Devoted to detail, he drew extensively from the Doyle papers (and was the last researcher to have access to them). Unlike most other biographers, before and since, he gives ample attention to Doyle's non-Sherlockian writings, and he makes a serious attempt to investigate and describe Doyle's personality, something much more complex than Pearson or Carr had acknowledged.

Other biographies followed:

● *The Man Who Was Sherlock Holmes* (1964), by Michael and Mollie Hardwick, a brief narrative emphasizing the ways in which Holmes resembles his creator.

- *The Real Sherlock Holmes* (1965), by Mary Hoehling, a brief biography for young people.
- *The Man Who Hated Sherlock Holmes* (1965), by James Playsted Wood, also for young people, but with a greater attention to Doyle's fiction rather than to his life in general.
- *Conan Doyle* (1972), by Ivor Brown, a general book that breaks little new ground.
- *The Adventures of Conan Doyle* (1976), by Charles Higham, a lively book emphasizing the excitement of Doyle's life, with enthusiastic (if not always convincing) attention to psychological and sexual matters. The book contains vast numbers of factual errors that lead the reader to treat its every statement with the greatest suspicion.
- *Conan Doyle: A Biographical Solution* (1977), by Ronald Pearsall, a readable book with few new insights, but with some attempt to put Doyle into his historical and cultural context.
- *Conan Doyle: Portrait of an Artist* (1979), by Julian Symons, a brief and derivative book that provides a good general picture of Doyle. Its most useful feature is a chronological appendix, convenient for quick reference.
- *Arthur Conan Doyle* (1985), by Don Richard Cox, which is chiefly a report of Doyle's fiction, set briefly into biographical context.
- *Arthur Conan Doyle* (1987), by Jacqueline A. Jaffe, who also concentrates on describing the fiction, and who acknowledges that Carr's book has been her chief source for biographical information.
- *Arthur Conan Doyle* (1988) by James McCearney, a biography in French concentrating on Doyle's historical and literary context.

Although not separately published, a good general biography of Doyle is the 140-page Introduction to Richard Lancelyn Green's *The Uncollected Sherlock Holmes* (1983).

Biographical study of Doyle was changed dramatically by the publication of *The Quest for Sherlock Holmes* (1983), by Owen Dudley Edwards, a historian at the University of Edinburgh, who used his professional expertise and his access to Edinburgh sources to explore Doyle's early years in detail. Despite many references to the works of his later life, Doyle reaches only his early twenties in this volume. But Edwards delves deep, discussing the influences of Mary Foley Doyle, Charles Doyle, Bryan Charles Waller and other important figures on Doyle's formative period. The writing is dense and the speculation sometimes seems daring to the unacademic reader, but the amount of information unearthed by Edwards is overwhelming. For the first time a reader can be reasonably confident that at least one period of Doyle's life has been fully explored.

Since the publication of Edwards's book, several other studies have appeared concentrating only on limited periods of Doyle's life:

- *Sherlock Slept Here* (1985), by Howard Lachtman, a quick report of Doyle's American tours of 1894, 1914, 1922, and 1923.
- *A Study in Southsea* (1987), by Geoffrey Stavert, in which a prominent British Sherlockian uses his easy access to local records to reveal the details of Doyle's years as a physician in Southsea.
- *Welcome to America, Mr. Sherlock Holmes* (1987), by Christopher Redmond, a day-by-day study of Doyle's 1894 tour of America, including discussions of the

local attractions and literary folk he encountered.

Other biographical and analytical work about Doyle has appeared in forms as diverse as these:

- *Naked Is the Best Disguise* (1974), by Samuel Rosenberg, a lively and imaginative exploration of sex, violence, and perversity in Doyle's writings.
- *The Doyle Diary* (1978), by Michael Baker, presenting the life and some artistic work of Doyle's father.
- *In Bed with Sherlock Holmes* (1984), by Christopher Redmond, a study of sex and love in the Canon, with much reference to Doyle's own experiences.
- *Medical Casebook of Doctor Arthur Conan Doyle* (1984), by Alvin E. Rodin and Jack D. Key, a report on Doyle's medical practice and the appearance of medical matters in his writings.
- *Sir Arthur Conan Doyle: Interviews and Recollections* (1991), edited by Harold Orel, a collection of contemporary documents and reminiscences.

Bibliographies. *A Bibliography of A. Conan Doyle* by Richard Lancelyn Green and John Michael Gibson (1983) is definitive so far as it goes, listing first and other early editions of Doyle's books, together with a vast number of periodical articles by and about him. Extensive notes provide information which either has not been previously brought forward or has not been conveniently gathered. The book can reasonably be called indispensable for any study of Doyle. Inevitably there are errors; there are also omissions, and in particular "Green and Gibson" makes no attempt to list modern editions.

Conan Doyle Bibliography (1977) by Gaby Goldscheider was greeted as a useful checklist before the Green and Gibson bibliography existed. There are other now superseded listings as well. Many editions both early and modern are included, though sometimes with incomplete or unhelpful information, in Ronald B. DeWaal's two large bibliographies of Sherlockiana, *The World Bibliography of Sherlock Holmes and Dr. Watson* (1974) and *The International Sherlock Holmes* (1980). Other bibliographies include Jay Finley Christ's pamphlet *The Fiction of Sir Arthur Conan Doyle* (1959) and the two editions (1973 and 1977) of *A Checklist of the Arthur Conan Doyle Collection* at the Metropolitan Toronto Library, compiled by Donald Redmond. An unpublished Master of Arts thesis from the University of Minnesota (1968) is *Sir Arthur Conan Doyle in America* by Lawrence L. Reed; it lists "first English and subsequent American editions". *The Sign of the Four* has received special attention in *'Signs' of Our Times* by Nathan L. Bengis (1956) and *Sherlock Holmes Among the Pirates: Copyright and Conan Doyle* by Donald Redmond (1990), the latter also giving attention to *A Study in Scarlet*.

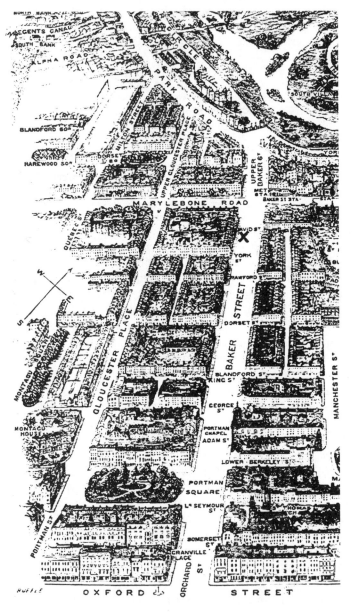

Baker Street looking northward from Oxford Street to Regent's Park. The Metropolitan Railway station at the corner of Marylebone Road, two-thirds of the way up Baker Street, made the neighbourhood accessible and popular in Holmes's day. The engraving is from Fry's "London — Illustrated", published in 1880; X marks the house that is now 111 Baker Street, identified by some scholars as Holmes's 221B.

Chapter V

The Victorian Background

The stories of Sherlock Holmes were published as late as 1927, but their setting is late Victorian and early Edwardian, the years from 1881 to about 1904. It was part of Doyle's genius that he exactly reflected his period in his writings: both its general concerns, justice and order for example, and its everyday details. Unlike many previous writers of detective fiction, he gave specific dates and referred, always plausibly, to real places and persons, from Regent Street to George Wombwell the circus proprietor. But many such allusions, and much of that atmosphere, are unfamiliar to a modern North American reader, who finds it difficult to judge whether what is strange in the world of Sherlock Holmes is so because of the century that has elapsed or because of the ocean that lies between America and Britain. Frequently the answer is that both reasons apply.

"The truth is that the Victorians had almost nothing in common with us," writes Jack Tracy in the admirable Introduction to his *Encyclopaedia Sherlockiana* (1977). He provides a brief essay about the dangers of misunderstanding the lost civilization of London circa 1895. Differences are many, from the state of technology (Victorian Britain was the great optimistic age of engineering) to the class-bound social structure. Sherlock Holmes needed precisely the environment he found, in which most men had trades (so that he could spot the weaver's tooth, the cork-cutter's hand); in which a lock could not be opened without the right key, made perhaps from an illicit wax impression; in which letters were delivered reliably enough to be, as in "The Man with the Twisted Lip", evidence.

Britain in the 1890's was still, in the satirists' phrase, Top Nation, hub of a worldwide Empire that was maintained through a vast civil service and an invincible Navy. But British domination was economic as well as political — British exports were valued at £309 million in 1891, compared to £182 million for the United States (with more than double Britain's population). Above all, however, Britons felt themselves superior in a cultural and moral sense, evident both in Holmes's amusement at his American clients and in the confidence with which British missionaries set out to civilize India and China. "Take up the White Man's burden," Kipling wrote in 1899, "Send forth the best ye breed." Britain was, and was meant to be, as Benson wrote in 1902, "mother of the free." At home, meanwhile, it was a good life for the optimistic middle classes, and a world of unsurpassed glory and delight for the rich.

So elusive is the political and social system in which Sherlock Holmes lived that it is not even easy to name his country. "England" is just one of three units that make up "Britain", the others being Scotland and Wales; Britain together with Ireland made the United Kingdom (which survives today though three-quarters of Ireland became independent in 1937). Holmes was an Englishman, though Doyle, born a Scotsman (of Irish descent), was not; both were British, but would have looked askance at being called "citizens" of anything. They were "subjects" of Her Majesty the Queen, who was not "queen of England" but Queen of the United Kingdom of Great Britain and Ireland.

Almost all of Holmes's cases are set in England, and the majority of them in London, the capital and greatest city, although Britain in the 1890s was still largely a rural nation. The population of England and Wales in 1891 was altogether 29.0 million; a further 4.0 million people lived in Scotland and 4.7 million in Ireland. London had some 4.3 million people; Glasgow in Scotland fewer than 700,000; Liverpool and Manchester in the industrialized "Midlands" each about 500,000, with nearby Birmingham a few thousand people behind.

England, Wales, Scotland, and Ireland are divided into counties, which are both geographic terms and divisions of local government. (In modern times the boundaries and names have been somewhat altered, and county governments are "local authorities".) The counties of England are as follows:

> **The home count,ies:** Middlesex, Surrey, Kent and Essex, surrounding London, which itself became a county during Holmes's active years.
> **The south:** Cornwall, Devon, Somerset, Dorset, Wiltshire, Berkshire, Sussex (where Holmes retired), and Doyle's beloved Hampshire, a principal feature of which is the New Forest.
> **The east:** Norfolk, Suffolk, Cambridgeshire, Hertfordshire, Bedfordshire, Huntingdonshire, Rutland, Buckinghamshire.
> **The central areas:** Northamptonshire, Leicestershire, Oxfordshire, Worcestershire, Gloucestershire, Herefordshire, Shropshire.
> **The midlands:** the industrial regions of Staffordshire, Derbyshire, Nottinghamshire, Warwickshire, Cheshire and Lancashire.
> **The north:** Yorkshire (largest county in England by far), Westmorland, Cumberland, Durham, and Northumbria.

Railways. It is hard to think of Holmes's England without thinking of trains. The first steam railway was built in Britain in 1825; by Holmes's time railways were the universally accepted way of travelling from one town to another (and of shipping goods, unless it was possible to send them by one of the country's many canals). Trains were frequent, fast by modern standards, and punctual most of the time. The large railway companies competed over some principal lines, with constant service between important cities, but there was less competition in the provision of periodic service to an enormous number of villages — such as Little Purlington in "The Retired Colourman". Although it was possible to make journeys in the Midlands, or along the south coast, without reference to London, much of the British network of tracks radiated from the metropolis. Each railway company had built its own station, or stations, as close to the centre of London as it could get, providing service outward in one or two directions:

> **Southeastern Railway:** To points in Kent, and (via Calais and Folkestone) to Europe, from Cannon Street Station, immediately north of the river near London Bridge, and Charing Cross Station, also just north of the river but further west, near the Houses of Parliament.

London, Brighton & South Coast Railway and **London, Chatham and Dover Railway:** To Brighton, Portsmouth, and other southern points, and (via Newhaven) to Europe, from Victoria Station, near the Houses of Parliament just north of the river, and London Bridge Station just south of the river in the east end.

London & South Western Railway: To Portsmouth, Southampton (the port from which transatlantic passenger liners embarked), Exeter, and other southern points, from Waterloo Station, south of the Thames.

Great Western Railway: To the west and southwest of England, and Wales, from Paddington Station, a little west of Baker Street in the northwest.

Great Central Railway: To Manchester and the rest of the Midlands, from Marylebone Station close to Baker Street.

London & North Western Railway: To Manchester, Liverpool and the rest of the Midlands, and to Scotland by the western route, from Euston Station, one of three clustered in the northern area.

Midland Railway: To the Midlands and by the "Waverley Route" to Scotland, from St. Pancras Station, second of the cluster on the north side of central London.

Great Northern Railway: To York and the northeast, and to Scotland by the eastern route, from King's Cross Station, a short distance from St. Pancras.

Great Eastern Railway: To the eastern counties, and (via Harwich) to Europe, from Liverpool Street Station in the northeast.

The Sherlockian today retracing Holmes's journeys outside London may go by rail or by car. Books discussing the location of Sherlockian sites include *The Game Is Afoot* (1983) and *For the Sake of the Game* (1986), both by David L. Hammer, and *Adventuring in England with Doctor Arthur Conan Doyle* (1986), by Alvin E. Rodin and Jack D. Key.

London

Samuel Johnson in 1777 is supposed to have said that "When a man is tired of London, he is tired of life; for there is in London all that life can afford." That diversity and the city's very size make nonsense of Sherlock Holmes's assertion a century later that it was his "hobby . . . to have an exact knowledge of London". It is so vast (690 square miles within the 1890's boundaries of the Metropolitan Police District) and so densely developed that one can know only selected regions of it, and even a map, or the tourist's inevitable *A to Z Atlas*, is of limited help. Certainly a Sherlockian or other scholar needs both a general map for orientation and a detailed one for close study. A reproduction of a Victorian-era street map is a virtual necessity. (Some of the small-scale Ordnance Survey maps have been reproduced in modern facsimile; an original, larger-scale one is far more useful.) For much of London has changed since 1895, through growth and development, and in key districts also through the destruction of the 1940-41 Blitz. Whole libraries of books have been written about London, including several specifically for Sherlockians, such as *On the Scent: A Visitor's Guide to Sherlock Holmes' London*, by Arthur M. Axelrad (1984); *A Tourist Guide to the London of Sherlock Holmes*, by Charles O. Merriman (originally published in the *Sherlock Holmes Journal*, 1970-73, and reprinted in pamphlet form); *Sherlock's London Today* by Gunnar Sundin (1985). *Sherlock Holmes in London* (1989) by Charles Viney is an exquisite collection of photographs of the city in which Holmes lived; *Sherlock Holmes's London* (1986, based on a 1984 edition in Japanese) by Tsukasa Kobayashi *et al.* chiefly pictures the city as it is today.

Unusual among capital cities, London is the principal commercial city of its nation as well as the seat of government. Unique among capital cities, London is built on an estuary — the tidal section of the Thames — and so the constant maritime traffic brought the world's products, people and news to its heart day and night. The docklands fell into disrepute and some decay in the twentieth century (although the 1980's have revived them), but in 1895 the warrens of streets, alleys, buildings and docks along the Thames were central to London metaphorically as well as geographically. The Canon reflects the maritime nature of London. It can be seen most graphically in *The Sign of the Four*, with its climactic scene of a boat-chase down the Thames, but it figures also in such tales as "The Man with the Twisted Lip" and "Black Peter". And constantly there are reminders of London as a city divided by water: the better-established regions north of the Thames, the Southwark slums and the new suburbs on "the Surrey shore" to the south of it.

The easternmost crossings of the Thames now are expressway tunnels and bridges. In Holmes's early years there was no crossing downstream of the ancient London Bridge, which spans the Thames at a narrow point where some 900 feet separate the City of London from Southwark. In 1894 Tower Bridge was opened, the picturesque crossing further downstream which most people think is "London Bridge". Below Tower Bridge are the entrance to the Grand Union Canal (a major commercial waterway from London north to the Midlands), the docks, Woolwich, Tilbury, Southend, and the North Sea. Blackwall Tunnel, in the dock area, was opened in 1897. Upstream of London Bridge are half a dozen crossings, including Waterloo, Westminster, and Vauxhall Bridges.

Says a guidebook prepared for the Franco-British Exhibition of 1908: "The Metropolis, as we know it, is almost entirely a creation of the Victorian Age, most of the leading thoroughfares having been widened and improved — many of them actually constructed — and the bulk of the chief public edifices remodelled, if not built, during that period." But there remained much that was very old. London became (and remains) a nineteenth-century city superimposed on a cluster of longstanding villages and two larger centres, the original City of London and the City of Westminster. Besides those two, the most important communities that became part of London by 1900 included Chelsea, Kensington, Paddington and Hampstead north of the Thames, Lambeth, Southwark ("the Borough") and Camberwell south of it. Further out lie regions that were suburban or still rural in 1895 but have since become absolutely part of the metropolis, including a few mentioned in the Canon — Norwood, Croydon, Harrow.

Most of the places known to today's tourists or would-be tourists are in either Westminster or the City of London. In Westminster are the Houses of Parliament (properly, "the Palace of Westminster") and the government offices in Whitehall and Downing Street, as well as Westminster Abbey, Trafalgar Square,

Buckingham Palace and Piccadilly Circus. To the east, in the City, are the Tower of London, St. Paul's Cathedral, the Bank of England, and the Old Bailey (Central Criminal Court). Most of these places are ancient; most of them are within a short stroll of the Thames. Not far away are such neighbourhoods as Mayfair (the "West End"), Soho and Bloomsbury, just north of Westminster, and Whitechapel (the old, sordid East End) east of the City.

It is to the north and west, however, that Sherlock Holmes country chiefly lies: in St. Marylebone, Paddington, Bayswater and Kensington, areas developed in Victorian times and demarcated by the great green stretches of Regent's Park, Hyde Park and Kensington Gardens. The principal thoroughfares here include Oxford Street, Edgware Road, Park Lane, Euston Road, Kensington High Street, Maida Vale, Regent Street, and a name that thrills every Sherlockian: Baker Street.

London roads twist, turn, and change their names at every opportunity, and in Holmes's day there was no thought of "motorways" such as those that now encircle London and in some places tunnel underground. Driving from west to east in a virtually straight line, one can travel in turn along Holland Park Avenue, Notting Hill Gate, Bayswater Road, Oxford Street, New Oxford Street, High Holborn, Holborn Viaduct, Newgate Street, Cheapside, Poultry, Cornhill and Leadenhall Street, within six miles. Those are major streets; most London streets are short and small, and it is no accident that the British idiom is to live "in" a street, rather than "on" it, for residential streets or squares often have a sense of enclosure. There were few detached houses in Victorian London; the "houses" in which middle-class people lived were what would today be called "terraced houses", in North America town houses or row houses: narrow segments of a uniform three- or four-storey structure that might stretch for a full block. Individual "freehold" ownership of such houses was rare. More common was "leasehold", by which the householder leased the land for a long period and built or bought the house standing on it. Rental was still more common: whole districts of London, recently developed from great landowners' estates, were enriching a few families through rental of street after street. Even in the suburbs rental was the norm, as for Grant Munro of "The Yellow Face", who proudly acquired a "villa" at Norbury for the characteristically modest sum of £80 a year, about $530 a month in today's currency. Mansions such as Pondicherry Lodge did exist, but were hardly typical of living conditions in London. At the other extreme were the squalid rooms in which whole families lived in Whitechapel and Southwark.

Baker Street. In the mind's eye of any reader of the Canon, Baker Street shines as if it were built of gold. For the most part, in Holmes's time the street was occupied by residences and small businesses; the streetscape is of four-storey houses (of the attached kind typical of London) built in the early decades of the nineteenth century, in "Georgian" style and largely of brown sandstone. Michael Harrison in *In the Footsteps of Sherlock Holmes* (revised edition, 1971) sets the home of Holmes in context:

> Baker Street dates from the last quarter of the eighteenth century, being named after a friend and Dorset neighbour of the Mr. Portman who developed this part of London: Sir Edward Baker, of Ranston. At the beginning, Baker Street was a fashionable street indeed, and many years were to pass before it lost its fashionable character, though it is fair to say that it has never lost its respectability. The change in character has come about through the introduction of commerce into the street: a change due principally to the building of Baker Street Station in the early 1860's. . . .
>
> In 1881, Baker Street's transition from Residential to Commercial was but half-way achieved: if there were many shop-fronts carved out of the rusticated lower-courses of the tall houses . . . there were not so many shop-fronts as there are today, and quite half of the upper portions of the houses were in private occupation: some tenanted by the shop-keepers themselves, others by lodgers of that quiet, permanent type. . . .
>
> One feels that the eminent respectability of Baker Street, no less than its convenient proximity to rail- and bus-routes, was in Holmes's mind when he picked on rooms in Baker Street.

Baker Street today is about two-thirds of a mile long, and runs north-south in the district of London known as St. Marylebone. It begins at Wigmore Street, in an intersection called Portman Square, and extends north just past Marylebone Road, to merge with Park Road at the southwest corner of Regent's Park. Until after World War I this section north of Marylebone Road was "York Place" and "Upper Baker Street"; eventually it became part of Baker Street proper, and the houses of the entire street were re-numbered in 1930. At the south end of Baker Street is Orchard Street, a brief extension reaching down to busy Oxford Street. Marble Arch, a principal London landmark, is a few yards away along Oxford Street; to the north, Madame Tussaud's waxworks and the Planetarium are in Marylebone Road just around the corner from Baker Street.

As Harrison notes, a principal influence on the street was (and is) Baker Street station. It serves not a main-line railway but the Metropolitan Line, a commuter railway which today is part of London's Underground (subway or "tube") system. Travellers from east and west of the city would connect at Baker Street to underground trains for other parts of the metropolis. Visitors to Holmes would naturally take a Metropolitan or tube train to Baker Street, then walk or take a cab from the station to 221B. Other landmarks of Baker Street, in the seven blocks (as a North American would express it) from Wigmore Street to Marylebone Road, included a post office, about halfway along the west side of the street, and the Portman Rooms, a well-known place of entertainment, slightly north of it.

The location of 221B. Tourists frequently wish to see the house in which Holmes lived, and Sherlockians dream of identifying it. Having learned that the B is a suffix indicating upstairs rooms ("first-floor" in British parlance, "second-floor" in North American), if it is not simply affectation, they go in search of a house numbered 221, and find none. The modern 221 is included in the large office building at the northern end of Baker Street that is the headquarters of the Abbey National Building Society, a major financial institution, where the public relations department takes responsibility for answering the many letters that come addressed to Holmes. The search quickly changes direction: which house on Baker Street did Watson or Doyle "disguise" with the number 221, or 221B?

The classic answer was determined in the 1930's by Dr. Gray Chandler Briggs of St. Louis, who first looked for the "empty house" that stood opposite 221B, as described in the story of that title. His success was reported by his friend Vincent Starrett in *The Private Life of Sherlock Holmes* (1933, 1960):

> Like Holmes himself he had approached the empty dwelling from the rear. He had turned into a narrow alley and passed through a wooden gate into a yard, to find himself at the rear door which had admitted the detective. Peering in, he saw the long straight hall extending through the house to a front door of solid wood, above which was a fan-shaped transom. Conclusive all of it — for already over the front door he had read the surviving placard: *Camden House....*
>
> Since Camden House stood opposite the famous lodgings, the rooms of Sherlock Holmes in Baker Street were, of necessity, those upon the second story of the building numbered 111.

Camden House survived into recent decades. The house now numbered 111, which is today a post office, was in Holmes's day not in Baker Street at all; it was 30 York Place.

An important dissenting view comes from Gavin Brend in *My Dear Holmes* (1951). He considers 111 to be too close to the railway station for plausibility (no one would take a cab for that short distance, as clients of Holmes sometimes did), and by examining other evidence carefully concludes that 61 Baker Street is the most likely candidate, with 59 and 63 also quite possible. Also suggested as the original of 221B have been such other Baker Street houses as 19, 21, 22, 27, 49, 66, 77, and 109.

Because of the "Empty House" description, it seems reasonably certain that the house was on the west side of the street. Arthur M. Axelrad in *On the Scent* (1984) shows a nice appreciation of how a candidate for the correct house might be evaluated:

> The building at 109 Baker Street, one-half block south of Marylebone Road, is certainly the most appealing choice among the traditional candidates. Expertly reconstructed by Haslemere Estates, it has what appears to be the only intact ground floor along the entire street, surmounted by three upper stories and an attic of beautiful gray-black brick. Relief is provided by three fine white-framed windows on each floor as well as the fanlighted front door painted a brilliant red and set off by a pair of slim white columns. There is also a small iron balcony across the first-floor level — very pretty but non-Canonical. The railinged area, as elsewhere on Baker Street, has been built over.

No known building meets all the criteria — bow windows are unknown in Baker Street, for example — but in any case the real location of 221B is in the mind's eye.

City transportation. Holmes and Watson are often seen walking through London — still, many experts say, the best way to see the city and the speediest way of making many trips. For longer trips the choice lay between cabs and "underground" trains. There were also horse-drawn omnibuses, such as the Brixton bus mentioned in "The Red Circle", and the "Baker Street and Pimlico" bus, which could have taken Holmes and Watson conveniently to Victoria Station.

To travel by Underground, they would have walked the short distance to Baker Street Station, where the regular trains of the Metropolitan Railway travelled clockwise and counter-clockwise around the "inner circle". The Circle Line is still an important feature of London's Underground, which has expanded hugely since Holmes's time, although trains still operate on many of the same tracks. The Metropolitan Railway, operating the northern half of the circle, is now part of London Transport's Metropolitan Line; the southern half is part of the District Line, successor to the District Railway that Holmes knew. On these tracks, a passenger from Baker Street could (and can) travel through Euston, King's Cross, Liverpool Street, Cannon Street, Charing Cross, Victoria, and Paddington before returning to Baker Street — touching, that is, most of the major railway stations, and making a twelve-mile circuit of the city. Attached to the inner circle were an extension dubbed the "middle circle", to the westward, and another called the "outer circle", across north London. Both were branches of the Metropolitan Railway; the middle circle now forms small parts of the Metropolitan and District lines, while the outer circle is part of the British Rail commuter system rather than of the Underground. A third important underground line in Holmes's time was the City and South London Electric Railway, which now forms part of the Northern Line, running north-south across the circle.

The most famous Underground passenger in the Canon is Arthur Cadogan West of "The Bruce-Partington Plans", whose body is found lying beside the Metropolitan tracks near Aldgate station. In the course of the investigation Holmes displays familiarity with the Underground — "According to my experience it is not possible to reach the platform of a Metropolitan train without exhibiting one's ticket" — and eventually finds that rather than being a legitimate passenger while alive, West was deposited, after death, on the roof of a train. It is taken for granted that the reader will understand: at various places in London the Underground actually runs through cuttings open to the sky, rather than in tunnels, and a house window could easily overlook the tracks.

Public Affairs

Government and politics touched the ordinary person less in the Victorian era than they do today. For all the growth of inspectorates during the late nineteenth century, little of daily life was subject to regulation; most of the public were hardly even touched by taxation. Income tax in the 1890's was set at sixpence in the pound, or 2.5 per cent, with incomes of less than £150 exempt. When Holmes spoke in "The Second Stain" of "another penny on the income tax", he meant an increase that would add more than £2 million to the annual collections of only £13 million, out of a total public revenue of £100 million. Ordinary people's taxation was chiefly indirect, in their contribution to the licence fees paid by publicans, tobacco manufacturers and many other merchants, and to the customs duties paid on imported goods.

It would be untrue to say that politicians attracted great respect, but Victorian society was based heavily on deference to those in positions of authority, including government. Britain is a constitutional monarchy, governed by machinery developed slowly over the centuries, with occasional discontinuities such as the "glorious revolution" of 1688, in which Parliament established its supremacy by deposing one King and choosing another. Victoria, Queen from 1837 to 1901, could trace her ancestry to Alfred the Great, not to mention bad King John, but she had considerably less power than those earlier monarchs had enjoyed. Although she retained some discretion in making government appointments, power lay chiefly with Parliament during Victoria's reign.

Parliament and government. Approval of the House of Commons, which in the twentieth century is effectively supreme, had to be coupled with that of the House of Lords and with the Queen's signature (which could not be refused, although Victoria occasionally came close), for a bill to become law. The upper house, or Lords, consisted of the entire English peerage, some 470 members from dukes to barons, as well as some bishops and Scottish and Irish peers. The lower house, or Commons, had 670 elected members. After the reform bills of 1868 and 1885, all adult men — though not women — could vote, and the old "rotten boroughs" containing only a few voters had been eliminated in favour of roughly equal constituencies.

While most peers served for life, members of the House of Commons were elected for each Parliament. The leader of whichever political party had the strongest representation in Parliament became prime minister, and could form a cabinet that might serve as long as it had the confidence of the Commons. Members of the "cabinet", frequently called "the government", today come almost entirely from the Commons, save for the Lord Chancellor, who is the presiding officer of the Lords as well as the highest-ranking appeals judge, but in Victorian times they could come from either Lords or Commons. Several Canonical stories refer to members of the government. In "The Second Stain", Holmes is visited by the prime minister, Lord Bellinger, and by the "Secretary of State for European Affairs", whose title does not correspond to reality; substitute "Foreign" for "European", however, and one has the Foreign Secretary. Lord Holdhurst in "The Naval Treaty" holds the same office. In "The Mazarin Stone", the prime minister and the Home Secretary appeal to Holmes; the latter is the cabinet officer in charge of internal affairs, particularly the police. Other leading members of the cabinet included the Chancellor of the Exchequer, in charge of finances, and the Colonial Secretary.

There is no appeal from the decisions of Parliament, which are, so long as the government maintains confidence, really the decisions of the prime minister and cabinet. Britain still has no written bill of rights, and no judicial review by which laws can be set aside as unconstitutional. A respectable middle-class Briton of the Victorian era might, however, have felt well-armed with what are now called civil rights, for unwritten provisions of the constitution clearly protect freedom of speech and other such activities. A prohibition against unreasonable search and seizure is expressed in the ancient saying that "An Englishman's home is his castle." Such rights were less reliably applied to members of the lower classes, against whom abuses were not unknown.

Local government depended on a mixture of tradition and centrally managed bureaucracy. Many local matters were in the hands of "vestry councils", still, as the term suggests, not fully divorced from the local parish churches. (Holmes refers to a vestry council with some amusement in *The Hound of the Baskervilles*.) Cities and boroughs were individually incorporated, with responsibilities conferred on councillors and mayors; the office of Lord Mayor of London had existed since 1189. The entire country was divided into counties, each headed by a Lord-Lieutenant and other officers (Arthur Conan Doyle was Deputy-Lieutenant of Surrey from 1902 to 1921). The vast area surrounding London became an "administrative county", governed by a London County Council, in 1888, in a change which nearly obliterated the old county of Middlesex. The ancient City of London, though geographically a mere district of the metropolis, retained its historic self-government.

Political history. "From 1868 to 1881 English politics were dominated by the rivalry between Disraeli and Gladstone," says R. J. Evans, introducing a chapter of his handy book *The Victorian Age 1815-1914*. Disraeli (later Lord Beaconsfield) was the leader of the Conservative Party; Gladstone, "the Grand Old Man", was leader of the Liberal Party. Both parties had been lately formed, from the old "Tories" and "Whigs", after a Reform Bill in 1866 which greatly expanded the number of voters, and it would be dangerous to assume that they had rigid principles or the sort of structure associated with modern political parties. They did have general philosophies — the Liberals emphasizing social reform and meritocratic institutions on behalf of the middle classes, the Conservatives extolling the benefits of tradition for the squires and landowners, but also for the working classes. Such politics are entertainingly reflected in the novels of Anthony Trollope (1815-1882), including *The Prime Minister* (1876). But, as Evans points out, the rivalry between Gladstone and Disraeli was as much personal, or a consequence of social origins, as political. The parties alternated in office:

> 1868: Gladstone, Liberal.
> 1874: Disraeli, Conservative.
> 1880: Gladstone, Liberal.
> 1885: Lord Salisbury, Conservative (Disraeli died 1881, shortly after yielding the party leadership).
> 1886: Gladstone, Liberal.
> 1886: Salisbury, Conservative.
> 1892: Gladstone, Liberal (died in office 1894, succeeded by Lord Rosebery).
> 1895: Salisbury, Conservative (retired 1902, succeeded by Arthur Balfour).

Within a few years, the Liberal Party would be in difficulties, eventually to be eclipsed by the Labour Party further to the political left, which was not even imagined in Holmes's time.

The public issues of the Victorian era are often incomprehensible to modern readers. But many dramatic changes, now seen as inevitable steps forward, had been introduced in the 1870's, chiefly by Gladstone: reform of the notoriously corrupt and disorganized army; an overhaul of the ancient, complicated judicial system; the Trade Unions Act of 1875, which gave such organizations their rights and legalized collective bargaining; a Public Health Act to provide for "drains" (sewers, a British fascination ever since) and water supply; perhaps most important, the Education Act of 1870, which established across England the "board schools" which Holmes praises in "The Naval Treaty". Until that time, such elementary education as existed had been in private hands or those of the Church of England. Gladstone had also made unsuccessful attempts to regulate licensing hours (the times when pubs could be open) and the liquor trade. But after 1880, through his second and subsequent governments, alternating with those of Salisbury, little was done save for the 1888 reform of local governments. There was considerable social unrest, reflected in the Trafalgar Square riots of 1887 and the London dockers' strike of 1889, during the depressions of the 1880's and 1893, but in the later 1890's the economy was healthier again. It was another age of optimism.

The chief issue of the period, however, was the complicated and tragic question of Ireland, which had been an organic part of the United Kingdom since 1800, electing Members of Parliament just as England, Scotland, and Wales did, although local laws and customs were different. From time to time attempts were made to introduce reforms in Ireland, particularly to change the rules under which landlords (often living in England) were able to oppress their tenants. Sir Robert Peel, prime minister 1834-35 and 1841-46, was a leader in promoting such reforms, and Gladstone, his disciple, continued in the same direction, but gradually came to recognize that reforms (the Irish Church Act of 1869, the Land Act of 1870) were not working.

While England was almost entirely Anglican (in nineteenth-century terms, Protestant), Ireland had a Roman Catholic majority. The census of 1861 reported an Irish population of 5.8 million; twenty years earlier, before the massive starvation and emigration prompted by the potato famine of 1845-47, it had been more than eight million. The number continued to fall, reaching 4.6 million by the turn of the century. The census also revealed, to some astonishment in England, that three-quarters of the population of Ireland were Roman Catholic, a fraction that was not falling. This anomaly, in a supposedly united country with an active and legally "established" Anglican church, led to tensions, particularly as the Roman Catholic Church sought greater control of educational and social institutions. As concessions and reforms were introduced, more were demanded; Ireland was, says historian D. G. Boyce, "handed over to the priest and the farmer". Inevitably there were proposals for self-government, known in the language of the day as Home Rule.

By 1885 a Home Rule party led by Charles Stewart Parnell (1846-1891) was able to win a sizeable number of Parliamentary seats. After some wavering, Parnell chose to support the Liberals, and in April 1886 Gladstone, accepting the inevitable, introduced a Home Rule bill. By a narrow margin it failed, largely because it was not seen to provide adequate protection for the Protestant minority in Ireland, concentrated in the northeastern counties that made up the province of Ulster. From that point, positions hardened, the Protestant "Unionists", as they became called, forming a long-lasting alliance with the Conservatives.

A second Home Rule bill in February 1892 was also defeated, and thereafter there was as little progress on the "Irish Question" as on any other important issue during the 1890's. It returned to the agenda in the tumultuous first decade of the twentieth century, and a tentative Home Rule bill was finally approved, but its implementation was delayed by World War I. Von Bork speaks in "His Last Bow" about "Irish civil war", something of an exaggeration by 1914, although there had been isolated outbreaks of violence; his suggestion of a close connection between Irish agitation and German subversion seems authentic. The Easter Rising of 1916 was a more serious affair, and finally, after the war, a Liberal coalition government under David Lloyd George passed the Government of Ireland Act of 1920. It was a compromise that pleased neither the Home Rule faction under John Redmond nor the Ulster Unionists, but after a fashion it worked, conceding autonomy separately to a six-county region in Ulster and to the remainder of Ireland. The southern, chiefly Roman Catholic region quickly moved from Home Rule to independence as the Irish Free State (later Eire or simply "Ireland"). After much violence in the early 1920's, relations between Eire and a self-governing Ulster were stable for a generation. The Ulster violence with which contemporary newspaper readers are familiar can be seen as a continuation of the Irish unrest that delighted Von Bork as a destabilizing influence in Victorian and Edwardian England.

Of politics in the usual sense, there is nothing in the Sherlock Holmes stories. Leaders of the government are seen a few times, in connection with international crises, and the occasional Member of Parliament is mentioned, including Reginald Musgrave. In "The Bruce-Partington Plans", Watson reads in the newspaper of "an impending change of government", probably the 1895 cataclysm in which the Liberals, split over Home Rule, lost power to Salisbury's Conservatives; but there is no hint of how (or whether) Watson and Holmes intended to vote. Five years later, Arthur Conan Doyle was in no doubt, standing for an Edinburgh seat in Parliament on the ticket of the "Liberal-Unionists", a splinter group supporting the Conservatives. He lost narrowly to a Liberal, but Salisbury's Conservatives were returned to office. In 1906, when Sir Henry Campbell-Bannerman led the Liberals to a landslide victory, Doyle tried again, this time in a rural district of Scotland, and lost decisively.

Money and Social Class

Holmes, visiting the Queen in one story, is able to pass as a young plumber in another; the unique profession of consulting detective made him as nearly class-less, it seems, as any man in Victorian England. His finances are similarly indeterminate, and it is not even clear whether he earned enough by his profession to support himself. But the society in which he moves is depicted with deadly accuracy in terms of its wealth or poverty and its exact gradations of status.

Money. The British unit of currency is the pound, or pound sterling, so called because its value was once based on the weight of silver; its symbol is £. The pound was divided into 20 shillings and the shilling (symbol s) into 12 pence (symbol d); shillings were abolished in 1971 and the pound re-divided into 100 new pence, so that 5p corresponds to one shilling. Paper money was rare in the Victorian era, and began with the £5 note — a single pound was represented by a gold coin called a sovereign. Silver coins in general use included the half-crown (2/6, that is, two shillings and sixpence), the florin (two shillings), the shilling, the sixpence (half a shilling), and the threepenny bit; bronze coins were the penny (a giant coin weighing one-third of an ounce), the halfpenny and the farthing (a quarter of a penny). Other coins, such as the crown, existed but were less often used. The "guinea" of 21 shillings (one pound and one shilling) was mentioned in some business transactions, but there was no coin corresponding to it.

International exchange rates, based on silver and gold, valued the pound at $4.87 American, not far from the old rule of thumb that £1 was five dollars, and thus a shilling equalled a quarter. More important as a measure of the currency, however, was its buying power, enormously greater than twentieth-century inflation has left it. There was no net inflation in Britain from 1815, when the Napoleonic Wars ended, until World War I. The 3 per cent interest typically paid on solid investments was thus a fair return. Judging from prices reported in the Canon and elsewhere, it seems possible to estimate that £1 in 1895 bought about as much as $80 in the North America of 1990. A shilling, the daily wage of a Baker Street Irregular, thus corresponds to $4, and the eightpence for an "expensive" glass of sherry in "The Noble Bachelor" to about $2.65. Henry Baker's goose in "The Blue Carbuncle" cost 12 shillings, which thus amounts to $48 — a plump, pricy bird which would indeed have hampered him as he carried it. The same formula makes it clear that John Clay had his eye on $2.8 million in gold, and that the cost of going round the world in style (£5,000 in "The Three Gables") was $400,000. Less lavishly, the dress John Straker of "Silver Blaze" bought for his mistress was worth $1,850.

This conversion formula is based chiefly on price indices between 1900 and the present. Translations of incomes will tend to look low; in fact, incomes were low, which is to say that the standard of living has risen since 1900. Watson's wound pension of 11/6 a day works out to $16,800 a year; Neville St. Clair of "The Man with the Twisted Lip" earned $160 a week as a journalist, $105 a day as a beggar. The beleaguered St. Clair could not, even in an era without income taxes on the middle class, afford the middle-class villa of Grant Munro ("The Yellow Face") at £80 a year ($530 a month), but a beggar's life gave him a living wage.

For a few Victorians, of whom the most striking Canonical example is the Duke of Holdernesse in "The Priory School", money was never an issue. He could write a cheque for £6,000 with hardly a wince. The wealthy had their country houses, their tenants (land, not capital, was still the principal form of wealth) and their London clubs — and the less than wealthy often tried to keep up with them; Holmes notes in "The Second Stain" that a prominent politician has "many calls" on his resources and has been forced to get his boots re-soled. In an era before credit cards (and cheques were chiefly a recourse of the rich) nearly everyone lived strictly on a cash basis, a constraint one sees in — for example — Henry Baker's difficulty: when he lost his hat, he had to make shift, for he had no immediate funds to buy a new one.

Social classes. "Class" in Britain in Victorian times was not chiefly a matter of wealth. More important to a Victorian was "birth" or ancestry, and there were also such factors as education, the experience of an elite public (boarding) school and perhaps university days at Oxford or Cambridge. For gentlemen and ladies thus defined, expectations could be rigid. Karl Krejci-Graf, writing in the *Sherlock Holmes Journal* in 1973, explained some of the constraints, citing Canonical stories by their four-letter abbreviations:

> A nobleman might discard a mistress when about to marry money (Nobl), but he might not wear ostentatious clothes or jewels (Scan). A foreigner could be a lady (Houn, Danc, Suss) or become one by marriage (Nobl), but a man would remain a foreigner, whether he was well liked (Gold) or not (Thor). A gentleman might become a burglar (Reig, Seco, Chas, Bruc, Vall, Illu, Last . . .) or a murderer (Abbe, Devi); as might a lady (Chas). A nobleman might shield a criminal (Prio); there was respect even for a noble spy (Last). But a man who had been a criminal was left in the lurch even if innocent (Blue), unless he had become wealthy and a member of society in the meantime (Glor, Bosc, Illu).

A full analysis of class-bound Britain, in the Victorian period or today, is work for a sociologist, but one can at least define some of the categories of "gentlemen" and "ladies" with whom Holmes came into contact — and can note that those terms may, by and large, define their manners, but say nothing about their morals.

At the peak of society came royalty, the large family of Victoria, who had been Queen since 1837. She figures indirectly in the Canon as "a certain gracious lady" honouring Holmes after his success in "The Bruce-Partington Plans". Her oldest son, "Bertie" — more formally Edward, Prince of Wales, later to be Edward VII — may have been the "illustrious" client in the story of that name. About Victoria's eight other children, the Canon is silent. Royal families of several other nations — Scandinavia and the Netherlands, in particular — do figure, however. European royalty was heavily interrelated at the end of the nineteenth century, members of all its families tracing their ancestry to the aged Victoria and to Christian IX of Denmark.

"Nobility" means the families of the members of the House of Lords, or "peers" — the dukes, marquesses, earls, viscounts and barons, altogether a few thousand men and women. The Canon presents a few dukes, such as the Duke of Holdernesse in "The Priory School", and a number of noblemen with the title "Lord", usually attached to marquesses and earls. The etiquette of such matters is complicated (and well set out in Jack Tracy's *Encyclopaedia Sherlockiana*). It is helpful to know, for example, that "The Noble Bachelor" commits a solecism in identifying Lord Robert St. Simon as "Lord St. Simon"; the first form suggests correctly that he is the son or grandson of a peer, the second form suggesting incorrectly that he is a peer himself. "Lady" indicates the wife or daughter of a peer, but it may also indicate the wife of a knight, such as Arthur Conan Doyle himself, and knights are not peers but commoners. (Doyle's wife was Lady Doyle; his daughter is Dame Jean Conan Doyle not because of her relationship to him but to honour her own military career, "Dame" being the female equivalent of "Sir" as a knight's title.)

Ranking below the nobility were, and are, the aristocracy, a less rigidly defined category of distinguished persons who might be knights or baronets (holders, like the Baskervilles, of a hereditary but not noble title) or merely members of what were recognized as "good families". This stratum of society is seen occasionally in Holmes's cases, though aristocratic clients are less conspicuous than the few who came from the nobility. Reginald Musgrave perhaps qualifies, as does Lady Brackenstall of "The Abbey Grange"; their cases are both set in the ancient, sprawling country houses one identifies with the propertied English classes. But the likes of Hilton Cubitt in "The Dancing Men" and Dr. Grimesby Roylott in "The Speckled Band" are, at best, gentry, respectable persons with country property but hardly aristocratic. Professors — Coram in "The Golden Pince-Nez", Presbury in "The Creeping Man" — barely qualify even for that category, having achieved their reputations through merit rather than social origins.

All these distinctions were of great importance to those who held them, or aspired to them, at the turn of the century, and studied *Debrett's Peerage* or *Burke's Peerage, Baronetage and Knightage* assiduously. Some social mobility was possible, but within limits. A rear-admiral earning as much as £2,737 did not associate with an able seaman making £18 to £29 a year. The riches Nathan Garrideb saw within his grasp would have bought him treasures, but not social acceptance, and even Neil Gibson of "Thor Bridge", probably the richest man in the Canon, was not the social equal of someone with "Lord" in front of his name. Of course, Gibson was an American, and thus condemned to be an outsider in a generally closed social system; entry to it was chiefly, as in "The Noble Bachelor", through marriage.

Holmes moved only rarely in such circles, despite his own descent from "country squires", that is, landed (land-owning) gentry. The majority of his cases involve him with the middle classes of professional, commercial and trading people, for whom money was indeed, the paramount source of position. One sees in *Whitaker's Almanack*, which published pages of government appointments and salaries, the range of their incomes, from £2,000 for the President of the Board of Agriculture (a Member of Parliament) to £150 for his private secretary, £700 for the Chief Inspector and £400 for his deputy, to "£70 to £250" for the second-division clerks. That at least was secure income, enough to permit luxuries like magazines, travel, and antimacassars in the parlour. More than one case mentions the new and glamorous profession of engineering; other cases involve lawyers, doctors, clerks, civil servants of varying status, military officers, a tea merchant, a schoolmaster, and a newspaperman. Such people were the readers of the Holmes stories as well as their characters; they were a new phenomenon in England with the nineteenth century increase in literacy, and they made the *Strand Magazine* possible and necessary. Lower on the social scale, in turn, come such clients as landladies, governesses (though they might move, on carefully limited terms, in the households of the gentry and even nobility), pawnbrokers and policemen.

But many in Victorian England were much poorer, although the desperately poor and the underclass are seldom seen in the Canon; it is a novelty when Henry Baker falls among "a little knot of roughs" in the Tottenham Court Road. Donald Rumbelow, setting the social stage for the strange crimes of Jack the Ripper, describes how people lived in the poorer districts, as analysed by a contemporary, Charles Booth:

> At the bottom were the occasional labourers, loafers and semi-criminals. Above them were the "very poor" and the "poor". The word "poor" he defined as those who had a meagre but regular income of between 18 shillings and 21 shillings a week, and the "very poor" were those whose income fell below this level. The former struggled to make both ends meet and the latter lived in a state of chronic want. The condition of the lowest class of all, which doesn't get a rating, can be imagined. At a rough guess there were about 11,000 of them. . . . This figure includes the "dossers" and the homeless outcasts who slept on staircases, in doorways and even in dustbins and lavatories for warmth. Their lives, Booth said, were the lives of savages, "with vicissitudes of extreme hardship and the occasional excess".

And about the slightly less desperate classes:

> The commonest work was sweat shop tailoring. For trouser finishing (sewing) linings, making button holes and stitching on the buttons a woman might get twopence ha'penny a pair and have to buy her own thread. . . . Fifty-five per cent of East End children died before they were five. . . . *The Lancet* . . . had estimated that in 1857 one house in every sixty in London was a brothel and one woman in every sixteen a whore. . . . [In lodging-houses] a double bed was eightpence a night and a single bed fourpence.

After the horribly cold winter of 1886-87 came massive demonstrations about dockyard pay and standards of living in general, leading to riots in Trafalgar

Square in November 1887; but little changed. Steps to introduce any form of relief for the poor were not quick in coming.

It perhaps goes without saying that women's class was determined by that of their fathers or husbands, save for the few (Irene Adler, Mrs. Hudson) who managed to make independent lives. The Canon presents a number of them, again representing the middle class: Mary Sutherland with her £100 a year from blue-chip investments (more than enough for a single lady living at home), Violet Hunter unsure why an employer should offer her £100 in addition to room and board, and Mrs. Warren for whom 50s. (two and a half pounds a week) would have been generous for board and lodging, although her mysterious lodger was willing to pay twice that.

Servants. The modern impression of domestic servants in the Victorian period depends heavily on the picture given in "Upstairs, Downstairs" on television in the 1970's (a serial largely written by those good Sherlockians Michael and Mollie Hardwick). There, one saw an affluent upper-class household with a large staff of servants, headed by a strict, efficient butler and a jolly, competent cook. Such establishments are found in a few places in the Canon — Reginald Musgrave, living at Hurlstone, kept thirteen servants, and Charles Augustus Milverton at Appledore Towers probably had a similar number.

But less ambitious households are far more common in the Canon, and they too had their servants — eight at Birlstone in *The Valley of Fear*, four maids and presumably a few other servants in Alexander Holder's house in "The Beryl Coronet". Smaller households might have only a single servant, generally a maid ("housemaid" or "maid-of-all-work"). Hilton and Elsie Cubitt had but one maid, as did Grant and Effie Munro in their far from ostentatious suburban cottage. Watson himself, in his married days, had a maid, Mary Jane. Still less impressive was the household of Jabez Wilson, the pawnbroker in "The Red-Headed League": he had "a girl of fourteen" to do a little of the domestic work.

The Canon is, in fact, pervaded with servants; Jack Tracy's *Encyclopaedia Sherlockiana* devotes six columns to listing them in their various categories. "Domestic service" is a calling now almost extinct, but in Victorian England it was both universal and respectable, if hardly enviable. Vast numbers of people earned their living in that way, being sometimes little better than slaves, sometimes virtually members of the family that employed them, albeit members who knew and kept their place. Far more women than men were in service; there were a few positions for gardeners and grooms (those in charge of horses), and the wealthiest households needed butlers and footmen, but every respectable household needed its maid, or maids. Their brothers and suitors were likely to be labourers ("navvies"), although a maid like Agatha, in Charles Augustus Milverton's household, would naturally choose Escott, the rising young plumber, as a suitor if she could get one. The soldiers "flirting with a nurse-girl" in "A Scandal in Bohemia" are similarly very plausible. A maid, certainly in a less wealthy household, would be presumed to be as uncouth as Isadora Klein's Susan in "The Three Gables". More intelligent and skillful maids naturally looked to places in more comfortable households, where nevertheless they might be exploited economically and even sexually. Enoch Drebber made himself "disgustingly free and familiar" with the maids in his boarding-house, *A Study in Scarlet* notes.

In a quite different category from housemaids came ladies' maids such as Theresa Wright, who attended Lady Brackenstall in "The Abbey Grange". The status of Irene Adler's maid is unclear, but a maid who travelled with the mistress, as one did with Lady Frances Carfax, was a maid whose functions involved clothes, toilette and correspondence rather than the stereotypical feather-duster. Maids in large households did not cook, although the single maid in a smaller household (to say nothing of Jabez Wilson's "girl") probably had kitchen duties as well as the responsibilities of serving meals, sweeping, answering the door and building the parlour fire. Other miscellaneous categories of servant ranged from gardeners through coachmen to pageboys.

Governesses were different altogether. They were employees rather than servants, and ate their meals with the children in the "nursery" rather than with the servants (in the kitchen or, in grander houses, the "servants' hall"). Such Canonical stories as "The Copper Beeches" deal touchingly with the position of governesses, dependent on the income they could earn with "a little French, a little German, music, and drawing". Those were middle-class, even upper-class, achievements, but the governess's sex and financial need condemned her to precarious social position and vulnerability to every sort of danger. A "nurse", or nanny to younger children, had still lower status.

Daily Life

The popular idea of the "Victorian" period as dull, stifling and prudish is hardly borne out by the Canon, which shows people engaging in a full range of normal human activity — bicycling, attending the theatre, buying children's toys, drinking in pubs, collecting butterflies, betting on horse-races. No doubt Mary Sutherland of "A Case of Identity" spent many hours in a narrow drawing-room, pasting cuttings in an album and singing to the piano, but she escaped by taking paid work as a "type-writer", and insisted on having a social life as well, insisted on attending the gas-fitters' ball so she could show off her purple plush dress. On every page of the Canon are people whose lives are full and complicated. In the case of the aristocracy who populate a few of the stories that richness is perhaps not surprising, but the fact is that the reader will find it also in the majority of stories that are about the middle classes.

Of course it is true that the Victorian period gave far more liberty to men than to women. The Canon shows a few women earning their living as governesses (like Arthur Conan Doyle's sisters), a couple of type-writers, and a few landladies, but otherwise women confine their activity to the household circle or, like Nancy Barclay in "The Crooked Man", to charitable activity. The Canon hardly deals with the immense lower class, in which women, like men, had to earn a living or starve: as factory operatives, in piece-work manufacture of matchboxes and other little articles, or as prostitutes. Women of the classes chiefly encountered by Sherlock Holmes function primarily as wives, mothers and sisters. Watson gives some loving descriptions of the elaborate clothes they wore about their daily activities, but of course does not refer to that unmentionable and ambiguous garment the corset, somewhere underneath the mousseline-de-soie, a garment at once confining (it is impossible to slouch, and hard to breathe, in a corset) and provocative (giving Mrs. St. Clair of "The Man with the Twisted Lip", for example, her notable "figure"). The corset is also a more likely cause than modesty for the fainting spells that characterized Victorian women at moments of stress.

The legendary sexual repression that required Victorians to veil the legs of their pianos, and to refer to men's trousers as "inexpressibles", is a feature not of the 1890's but of two generations earlier. By the 1860's, indeed, English society enjoyed a good deal of sexual freedom, and the "pretty horse-breakers", or high-society prostitutes, attracted great admiration in the press and imitation in their style and fashion. (Michael Harrison, well known as a Sherlockian author, deals with them at length in *Fanfare of Strumpets* [1971].) Prostitution was commonplace at less exalted social levels as well, and there were, quite apart from brothels, many places of amusement where men and women mixed familiarly. This of course is not to say that everyone engaged in lascivious behaviour, but the possibility was certainly there. Pornography, too, was a sizeable industry throughout the Victorian period. Repression, indeed prudery, returned to society in the latter part of the century; in 1877 the closing of the merry and notorious Cremorne Gardens amusement-rooms in London marked the end of an era. The "social evil" that was lower-class prostitution continued, providing the context for Jack the Ripper's bloody work in 1888, but the newspapers spoke more about the need for social reform, and less about the stylish carriages of aristocratic men's mistresses. Middle-class late Victorians were supposed to be respectable, even if there were fewer constraints on their daily and hourly behaviour than their grandparents had known.

The crinoline that was fashionable in the 1860's, a rigid framework giving support and shape to a woman's petticoats, was a coquettish rather than modest garment, for it allowed glimpses of the "ankle" — a Victorian enthusiasm — and frequently of a great deal more. Extremely low necklines were also in fashion at that period. In the 1870's, the crinoline having passed out of fashion, women wore bustles, an artificial augmentation of the derrière, and longer skirts. The fashion of the 1890's was for an hourglass figure, with wide shoulders, puffed sleeves and long flared skirts, supported by multiple petticoats. There was plenty of lace, and there was plenty of variety, as a woman might change her costume several times in a day: breakfast-gown, morning dress, walking costume, at-home dress, tea-gown, and finally dinner dress (much barer, especially about the shoulders, than anything worn during daylight hours). Men wore narrow, tight trousers, and shirts with detachable, starched, upright collars. Hats were essential for both sexes when out of doors: elaborate millinery for women, bowlers or top-hats for men (certainly not, except in the countryside, deerstalkers). Sherlockians occasionally plan costume-parties that require impassioned hunting through Victorian magazines for the details of clothing appropriate to an exact social station and circumstance.

Many attempts to imitate the Watsonian (or Doylean) style have come to grief over details of daily life and etiquette. It is useful, for example, to understand the Victorian obsession with death — hardly surprising in an era before antibiotics, when women often died in childbirth and children did not survive infancy. The annual death rate in London was about 29 per thousand, four times the modern figure. The Canon makes casual mention of mourning-stationery with its black border, of mourning-bands on men's arms, of black veils and undertakers' wreaths; the proper use of these articles amounted to a cult. Less concretely, one has to understand the degree to which social respectability depended on an arbitrary conception of "honour", involving not so much morality as responsibility for one's debts. Such considerations lie behind the seriousness of "the Tankerville Club scandal" and other incidents throughout the Canon. One might rise above many kinds of misbehaviour, but money was of central importance to Victorian society.

Lacking television, Victorians entertained themselves, and if the results could be ghastly hours of parlour games, it could also be a level of articulate conversation that sounds artificial to the modern ear, although the Canon may well be reporting it accurately. Lacking the telephone, they relied on frequent postal service, and wrote readable, grammatical letters with pens that had to be dipped in liquid ink. Lacking airplanes (or funds) to take them to distant holiday destinations, they made occasional excursions by rail to see the sights of London or to attend the races at Winchester. Lacking movie stars to admire, they bought souvenir photographs (like the one Watson spots in "Charles Augustus Milverton") of society beauties, and they read with interest about the doings of royalty. Lacking citrus fruit and, for part of the year, green vegetables, they ate meat and potatoes, and made much of green peas when spring provided them. Lacking the disillusionment and disorientation that would come with the World Wars of the twentieth century, and be expressed by its philosophers and artists, they lived (if one overlooks the desperation of the poorest classes) a comfortable and satisfied life.

Many books describe life in Holmes's day, especially in bustling London and among the wealthier classes. For Sherlockians a particularly useful volume is *Oscar Wilde's London* (1987), by Wolf Von Eckardt and others, which begins with Wilde and his literary circle but extends to every aspect of life in the great city between 1880 and 1900. On specifically sexual matters there is *The Girl with the Swansdown Seat* (1955) by Cyril Pearl. Books about Holmes's later years include *The Edwardians: The Remaking of British Society* (1975) by Paul Thompson, and *Edwardian Life and Leisure* (1973) by Ronald Pearsall. The life of little villages, into which Holmes occasionally penetrated, is lovingly reported in *Lark Rise to Candleford* (1945) by Flora Thompson.

Newspapers. Local and regional newspapers existed throughout England — in *The Hound of the Baskervilles* Holmes speaks of the *Leeds Mercury* and the *Western Morning News* — but the more important part of the press for Holmes was the London newspapers. He read them chiefly for the crime news and the "agony column", more formally known as the personal advertisements. The papers varied in social standing, political position (many of them regularly conducting crusades for reforms of one kind or another), and quality, descending to the "garbage papers" for which Langdale Pike of "The Three Gables" wrote.

The morning papers of London were, and are, "national", being distributed throughout England, as one sees for example in "The Stock-Broker's Clerk". Most famous of these is *The Times*, founded in 1788, known for its extensive political coverage (in Victorian times it published virtually verbatim reports of Parliamentary proceedings) and for its role as a newspaper of record, with the Court Circular detailing the engagements of royalty, and its Births column listing the offspring of everyone of importance across the land. *The Times*, however, is a minority, highbrow taste, the general reading public being catered to by other newspapers. "The Blue Carbuncle" provides a nice illustration: the Countess of Morcar advertised for her missing gem in *The Times*, which cost 3d when most of the other morning newspapers (*Daily Telegraph, Standard, Morning Post, Daily Mirror* and others) were a penny or a halfpenny. In the same case Holmes advertises the hat and goose in the evening papers, which were more local (and which are now extinct): " . . . the *Globe, Star, Pall Mall, St. James's Gazette, Evening News, Standard, Echo,* and any others that occur to you." In addition to the daily papers there were weeklies that ranged from the political and satirical *Punch* to *The Sporting Times*, known as "the Pink 'Un" for the distinctive colour of its paper, and the *Illustrated London News.*

Telegraph and Posts. A telegram is a message put in writing by its sender, transmitted over wires in an electrical code, and reduced to writing again at the other end of the wire, where a messenger from a telegraph-office delivers it to the recipient. Introduced in the 1840's, telegrams became the first means of communication that eliminated distance as a consideration; the Post Office could deliver a message from London to Edinburgh as quickly as from one part of London to another, and for the same basic charge of sixpence for the first twelve words and a halfpenny for each additional word. To France the charge was 2d a word; to Canada one shilling. Telegrams pervade the Canon as an idiosyncrasy of the nervous and impulsive Holmes, who can be terse ("telegraphic") in one message, expensively chatty in another, such as the two-shilling-and-threepence telegram that introduces "The Boscombe Valley Mystery". Telegrams serve also as a device to emphasize the period quality of the tales, for Holmes is seen to use the telegraph even when telephones (introduced in London in the early 1880's) would have served better. He does have a telephone by the turn of the century, but it seems an anomaly.

Watson observes that Holmes "never wrote when he could telegraph", but he did frequently write, as did everyone who wanted to communicate in Victorian

England. A one-penny postage stamp would take a letter (weighing up to one ounce) anywhere in the United Kingdom, while the parcel Holmes examines in "The Cardboard Box" probably cost 3d to convey from Belfast to Croydon. At these prices a vast number of items passed through the post office: some 1.8 billion letters, and 50 million parcels, each year. Modern North Americans accustomed to thinking of the mail as a leisurely means of communication must remember that it was both reliable and rapid in Victorian England. Says *Whitaker's Almanack:*

> In the E.C. or City district [of London] there are twelve deliveries daily. . . . In the other districts there are from six to eleven collections and deliveries. Letters properly directed, and properly posted, should be delivered within from two to four hours.

Still more urgent messages could be designated for "express delivery" at an additional 2d, or the "district messenger service" for 3d per half-mile. For letters outside London, overnight delivery was the standard.

Literature. To posterity, the great Victorian writers are Charles Dickens (who died when Doyle was a child) and Alfred Lord Tennyson (whose important work had all been written by the 1870's, though he lived to 1892). The writers Doyle loved best were similarly out of date by the 1890's: Sir Walter Scott (1771-1832) and James Fenimore Cooper (1789-1851), whose historical novels he tried to emulate. Of modern authors, he probably admired Robert Louis Stevenson most. Stevenson was in the Scott and Cooper tradition, and so was Rudyard Kipling, whose friendship Doyle acquired in 1894. The Canon never mentions Kipling, or another author of romantic adventures, H. Rider Haggard (1856-1925). But it does portray Watson, the man of action but hardly of intellect, as a reader of the now almost forgotten sea stories of William Clark Russell (1844-1911), whom Doyle also admitted to enjoying. Other objects of his admiration, and also friends, were Robert Barr and Jerome K. Jerome.

Yet Doyle, a more complex man than Watson, also admired Thomas Hardy (1840-1928), whose *Tess of the D'Urbervilles* (1891) is about sex and complex human relationships; like all his work it is realistic with a grimness that emerges only occasionally in Doyle. "Nearer to nature in his writing than any other contemporary writer," Doyle said of Hardy. And he spoke with enthusiasm of a figure now almost forgotten, Olive Schreiner (1855-1920), South African author of *The Story of an African Farm* (1883) and other works about emotion, sex and progressive social themes. Much better known now, and less understood in his own time, was George Meredith (1828-1909), who by the 1890's had progressed from radical crank to grand old man. Doyle lectured on his work as early as 1888, but confessed that he admired him more for his ideas than for "artificial" characters and "grotesque" language.

By the 1890's, readers were looking for such modern stuff, and finding it in the pages of the *Strand* and competing magazines: stories and novels by H. G. Wells, Grant Allen, and soon W. Somerset Maugham (1874-1965), more readily thought of as a twentieth-century figure. The old-fashioned three-decker novel was dead, and modern novelists were writing slimmer books on racier topics. Doyle complained that too many of them concentrated on love and sex, which indeed was one reason he admired Stevenson: only a modest representation of women among his characters. "In British fiction," he once told an audience, "nine books out of ten have held up love and marriage as the be-all and end-all of life. Yet we know in actual practice this is not so." Still, he admired skill where he found it, even saying complimentary things about Oscar Wilde. For success in presenting male friendship rather than conventional love, Doyle might also have cited George du Maurier (1834-1896), whose *Trilby* (1894) is as much about men's friendship as is Doyle's own saga of Holmes and Watson.

Religion. England has an "established" religion, a branch of Christianity called the Church of England, enjoying certain privileges, as well as obligations to provide its services to the whole population. In the Victorian period the majority of the people of England were nominally Anglican — adherents of the Church of England — although only a minority attended services regularly or followed the teachings of the church. In 1893 it was estimated that in England and Wales there was seating-room for 6,255,000 people in Church of England establishments; "the Church population" was estimated at twice that. The Roman Catholic Church had about two million adherents in England, many of them probably of Irish extraction. Methodist bodies accounted for about a million, other Nonconformists such as Presbyterians and Baptists fewer than a million. The rest (with small exceptions such as an estimated 80,000 Jews) clearly had no religion at all, and much of "the church population" obviously did not sit down in church on a typical Sunday.

The origin of the Church of England, in the sixteenth-century rift between King Henry VIII and the Pope, is well known. From that time, the buildings, clergy, bishops and appurtenances of the traditional Roman Catholic establishment were instead "Anglican"; the language of the Church of England, however, was English, in which the Bible was read (the King James translation of 1611) and the liturgy was conducted (according to the Book of Common Prayer, finally revised in 1662). As a national institution, the Church of England became what is known as a "broad church", tolerating considerable variations in belief and practice. In the eighteenth century a liberal Protestant style was dominant, without great rigour in social or moral teaching and also without great elegance in the liturgy. One response to that laxity was an evangelical revival leading to the "Methodist" movement of John Wesley, eventually to separate from the Church of England altogether. Then in the 1850's came the "Oxford Movement", associated with John Henry Newman, which urged the church in an opposite, Catholic direction, towards formal liturgy and mediaeval piety. Some priests and some bishops sympathized with the Oxford party, in a few cases to the point of leaving the Church of England and becoming Roman Catholics; some were closer to the Methodists in their emphasis on individual salvation and social reform. Vast numbers stayed somewhere in the middle.

The "supreme governor" of the Church of England was the Queen. Its "primates" were the Archbishop of Canterbury, in southern England, and the Archbishop of York, in the north. But the archbishops had very little authority over the bishops, the unchallenged ecclesiastical rulers of their dioceses. In Victorian times England and Wales were divided into thirty-four dioceses, each divided into parishes in charge of a "rector" or "vicar", who might prefer to be styled "minister" if he were very Protestant in taste, or "priest" if he were very Catholic. Every person living in England was in a parish, whether the humble Little Purlington, mentioned in "The Retired Colourman", or the elegant St. Monica's, London ("A Scandal in Bohemia"). The parish was still for some purposes a unit of local government, and at least in small communities the vicar was an important figure in local society. Vicars and other clergy were all listed in *Crockford's Clerical Directory*, which Holmes consults in "The Retired Colourman".

Science. The chief discoveries that are the foundation of modern science had been made before Holmes's time: the second law of thermodynamics was formulated in 1850, the speed of light measured in 1862, Mendel's law of heredity articulated in 1865, the periodic table devised in 1869. Similarly, the great technological innovations had been made: the internal combustion engine was first made to work in 1860 (though it would be decades before it began to supplant steam power), pasteurization (the basis of biotechnology) was introduced in 1864, Bell invented his telephone in 1876. By 1895 there were bicycles, phonographs, vaccines, machine guns, photographs, dynamite, and primitive radio. Bridge-building, still seen as the central activity of civil engineering, had achieved such triumphs as the Brooklyn Bridge in 1874, the enormous Forth Bridge in 1890.

The luckless Victor Hatherley in "The Engineer's Thumb" is a hydraulic engineer; Violet Smith of "The Solitary Cyclist" is engaged to a man with an even more modern profession, an electrical engineer. Pure or applied scientists are thin on the ground in the Canon, however, unless one counts Sherlock Holmes himself, who is first glimpsed conducting research in the pathological laboratory at St. Bartholomew's Hospital. Time and again he is presented as doing chemical work, sometimes for very practical ends ("If this paper turns red, it means a man's life"), sometimes out of sheer curiosity or for recreation. Donald A. Redmond, writing in the *Baker Street Journal* in 1964, suggested that many of the experiments and analyses Holmes is seen conducting are part of "a consistent pattern of investigation" begun by his work into the chemical definition of bloodstains. The Canon does include a number of amateur scientific enthusiasts of a kind who were common in the Victorian period, and who did much to advance science in the nineteenth century through collection of data and through taxonomic work in botany, zoology, and geology. Stapleton in *The Hound of the Baskervilles*, Nathan Garrideb in the story that bears his name, even Holmes himself in "Wisteria Lodge" with "a spud, a tin box, and an elementary book on botany" are in various degrees scientists of this kind.

Finally, there are theorists like Dr. Mortimer, again of *The Hound of the Baskervilles*, with a keen interest in what would now be called anthropology — "the comparative anatomy of the Bushman and the Hottentot", and Sherlock Holmes's own skull. One of Mortimer's monographs is titled "Is Disease a Reversion?", a theme that must have drawn interest from Holmes, who also expressed opinions about the relationship between individual development and the evolution of the species. Charles Darwin had published *The Origin of Species* in 1859, four years after the essentials of evolution had been set out in Herbert Spencer's *Principles of Psychology*. The general principle of evolution was accepted by scientists, and indeed by educated people in general, in Holmes's generation, but many of the specifics were (as to some degree they remain) matters of debate and uncertainty, and echoes of the issue can be heard whenever men of science get talking as Dr. Mortimer and Sir Charles Baskerville did.

As distinguished from science, medicine plays a considerable part in the Canon, as one might expect from stories written by an able and curious physician. In Holmes's day medicine had only a modest number of drugs in its armamentarium; antibiotics, to combat infection, were as yet unknown, but anaesthetics were generally used. Watson's enthusiastic use of brandy in almost every circumstance, including accidental amputation ("The Engineer's Thumb"), should perhaps not be taken as typical of Victorian medicine, which however relied strongly on common sense and a belief in cleanliness and fresh air. Medical matters in the Canon and in Doyle's other works are dealt with exhaustively in *Medical Casebook of Doctor Arthur Conan Doyle* (1984) by Alvin E. Rodin and Jack D. Key.

The Empire and the World

Sherlock Holmes's London was not merely the capital of England and of the United Kingdom; by the later Victorian era it had also become the heart of the British Empire, which extended over 9.8 million square miles (about a sixth of the earth's surface) and 305 million people. Territories of the Empire were ruled through the Colonial Office and the India Office, to which local governors reported. Among those territories were Canada, India, Ceylon (now Sri Lanka), Hong Kong, Natal and the Cape Colony (later to be South Africa), the Gold Coast (Ghana), many Caribbean islands, the Australian territories, and New Zealand. Large areas of East Africa which were later to be British colonies, and eventually such independent nations as Zambia, Tanzania, Kenya and Zimbabwe, were still in the private hands of the Imperial British East Africa Company (chartered 1888, with Cecil Rhodes as its leading figure) and the British South Africa Company (chartered 1889). Canada, an early colony, had achieved a measure of self-government in 1867; Australia acquired a similar status in 1901, and other colonies and territories would follow.

Canada. Until World War I, when Canadian troops earned national pride with their blood at Vimy and other scenes of carnage, most English-speaking Canadians still thought of themselves as British. The "Union Jack" still waved, despite the one-third of the population who were French-speaking Québecois rather than in any sense English (their representation has fallen to about one-quarter of the population in the late twentieth century), and despite a tide of immigration from eastern Europe into the opening farmlands of the prairies. "Confederation" in 1867 had meant a large measure of self-government for the newly united British colonies in North America, but the government at Ottawa still looked to Britain to conduct its foreign affairs. Full independence came only with the Statute of Westminster, 1931. In Holmes's time Canada was still, in British eyes at least, a colony; young Henry Baskerville went there to farm, but had no hesitation about returning to the motherland when his time came. And British troops were stationed at such garrisons as Halifax, as "The Copper Beeches" reflects.

America. The United States, on the other hand, was self-consciously independent of Britain, dating its freedom from July 4, 1776, and actively recalling the battles that had been fought to maintain it. Arthur Conan Doyle addressed the subject in a letter to *The Times* in 1896:

> To understand the American's view of Great Britain one must read such an American history as would be used in the schools. . . . American history, as far as its foreign policy is concerned, resolves itself almost entirely into a series of wrangles with Great Britain, in many of which we must now ourselves confess that we were absolutely in the wrong. . . . This war of 1812 would possibly only occupy two pages out of 500 in an English history, but it bulks very large in an American one, and has left many bitter memories behind it. . . .

As recently as 1895 there were threats of war over the boundaries of Venezuela, in which both countries had interested themselves.

In the 1890s the United States had not yet become the world's dominant nation economically, although its primacy in the western hemisphere, asserted in the Monroe Doctrine of 1823, was widely accepted. The need to exert force in support of that doctrine produced America's first foreign war, against Spain, in 1898. The country was growing (by some 1,000 immigrants every day through New York) and developing its industry and confidence. But in spite of popular resentment against Britain, and in spite of the notoriously high American tariffs, the cultured classes of America looked to the mother country for much of their literature, art, and furnishings. Audiences were eager, even fawning, to hear Doyle speak about authorship when he toured the country's major cities in 1894.

The Canon is thickly sprinkled with Americans who come to England for things they could not find at home, from Hatty Doran of "The Noble Bachelor" in search of a husband to Neil Gibson of "Thor Bridge" looking for respectability on an old-country estate. The presence of so many Americans reveals Doyle's enthusiastic interest in the United States; indeed, he favoured Anglo-American union some day. It reveals, as well, the close links that existed between the two great English-speaking lands regardless of their periodic political differences. Americans were sometimes figures of fun — not least "Altamont", the Irish-American who proves to be Holmes himself in "His Last Bow"

— and many of the Canonical allusions suggest a British understanding of America as a place where the inhabitants shot first and asked questions later. But casual references to points from Long Island to Texas, and Holmes's insights into the fraudulent American in "The Three Garridebs", make clear how thoroughly American visitors were a part of the British scene.

American government in the 1890's was weaker than American business; it was the heyday of the "robber barons" and their powerful companies, led by John D. Rockefeller's Standard Oil and (from 1901) Carnegie's United States Steel. Neil Gibson of "Thor Bridge" is in the mould of these industrial giants, at whom the Sherman Antitrust Act of 1890 was aimed. After the Civil War (1861-1865) government was in some disrepute, and presidents were weak: Grover Cleveland (served 1885-1889 and 1893-1897), Benjamin Harrison (1889-1893), William McKinley (1897-1901, assassinated at Buffalo). Then came Theodore Roosevelt (born 1858, president 1901-1909, died 1919), whose energy as frontiersman and war hero was translated into active public service not just in antitrust efforts but in world affairs, helping to lead the United States into the international community.

European affairs. "The whole of Europe is an armed camp," says the prime minister to Holmes in "The Second Stain", a story published in 1904 and set in a "nameless" decade slightly earlier. He goes on:

> There is a double league which makes a fair balance of military power. Great Britain holds the scales. If Britain were driven into war with one confederacy, it would assure the supremacy of the other confederacy, whether they joined in the war or not.

That is a fair statement of the position in Europe after 1893, when France and Russia signed a treaty creating the "Dual Alliance" as a counterbalance to the "Triple Alliance", formed in 1882, of Germany, Italy and Austria-Hungary. Britain remained neutral between these two blocs throughout Holmes's day, even seeking, especially under Gladstone, to arrange a solution of the remaining border disputes and irritants. As an island power, Britain felt little threat of the kind of war that had repeatedly swept over continental Europe. Its protection was not an army but its unchallenged Navy ("Britannia rules the waves"), and its chief geopolitical interest was maintenance of communication with such distant points as India. For that reason, if any major power was a threat it was Russia, menacing the Indian sub-continent from the north. Britain had fought the Crimean War of the 1850's against Russia, and Russia was the unseen opponent in what Rudyard Kipling called "the Great Game", Britain's continuing troubles in southern Asia, including the Afghan Wars of the 1870's.

It had also done much to weaken Turkey, the dominant power in southeastern Europe, in a war in 1877-78. Britain was instrumental in arranging a peace settlement that included the loss of many of Turkey's European territories. Bulgaria became largely independent, its Christian population free from the "atrocities" attributed to the rulers of Muslim Turkey; Bosnia and Herzegovina remained officially part of the Turkish empire but were placed under Austro-Hungarian "administration". Other Balkan states — Serbia, Montenegro, and the rest — were similarly unstable, to the point that "the Eastern Question" was the accepted political name for the uncertainties of power in that whole region of Europe. In that area would begin the conflict that eventually became World War I and that continues, little altered, in the 1990's.

The British tactic was to keep Russia and Austria in balance in the east, as it did with Germany and France in the west. But in the end neutrality proved impossible, as Britain came to recognize German expansionism as the central fact of European politics. By 1891 the population of Germany was 49 million, while France had 38 million, only slightly more than Britain. Bismarck tried in 1889 to bring Britain into the Triple Alliance, but solving the western question without the eastern — that is, holding France in check without protection against Russia as well — was inadequate, and the plan fell through. Eventually Britain would instead find itself allied with France, and led the combat against Germany when European war came in 1914-1918.

These were the principal countries of Europe in the 1890's:

• France had been Britain's historic enemy, against which the long Napoleonic wars (1798-1815) were fought. After those wars France had endured two monarchies, a republic and the Second Empire before the disaster of the Franco-Prussian War, 1870-1871. Largely instigated by Germany's "iron chancellor", Otto von Bismarck (1815-1898), that war saw the grim siege of Paris and eventually a humiliating treaty of peace under which the rich lands of Alsace and Lorraine were turned over to German control. The Third Republic, which followed, saw France much weakened, but still perceived as a threat by Germany, and also by Britain, especially where colonial claims came into conflict, as in Egypt. Harmony between Britain and France — the liberal powers of Europe, as distinguished from the conservative empires further east — grew only slowly. But numerous references to France in the Canon indicate the close cultural and commercial relations that inevitably existed between the two countries separated only by the narrow strip of water that is the English Channel.

• Germany came into existence in 1871 as a confederation of German-speaking states under the leadership of Prussia, whose king (Wilhelm I 1871-1888; briefly Frederick; Wilhelm II 1888-1918) was also Emperor of Germany. The power lay with Bismarck, as chancellor, until his retirement in 1890. Germany at this period was the world's leading industrial nation, drawing on iron and coal resources and a growing chemical industry. At the same time it was developing a huge military machine with the barely disguised purposes of further damaging France in the west and extending its influence in the Balkan countries of southeast Europe.

• Italy was also a new country, a kingdom created in 1870 from a collection of variously ruled little states. Its king (Umberto I from 1878 to 1900) reigned over some 30 million people, and had some territorial and naval pretensions; the treaty stolen in the Canonical tale titled "The Naval Treaty" was between Britain and Italy. Surrounded by Italy, but not part of it, was the Vatican State, an enclave in Rome ruled by a Pope who resented the loss of his temporal kingdom, the "Papal States", to a united Italy, and as a result refused to recognize the Italian king. Leo XIII, pope 1878-1903, appears to have consulted Sherlock Holmes professionally more than once.

• Austria-Hungary was a curious hybrid in southeastern Europe: a German-speaking empire and a Hungarian-speaking kingdom united under one ruler, Franz Joseph, who ruled Austria from 1848, added Hungary to his domain in 1867, and continued on the throne to 1916. Its population was some 45 million; its chief political interest, competing with Turkey for influence in the Balkan states. At the other side of the Austro-Hungarian Empire was the German-speaking province of Bohemia; the title "King of Bohemia", assigned in the story "A Scandal in Bohemia" to a flamboyant princeling named Wilhelm, in fact belonged to the Emperor.

• Turkey, or the Ottoman Empire, was the great Muslim power of the world, its domain extending over northwest Asia, Arabia including Mecca, and a corner of Africa, with total population of 32 million people. A small corner of Europe remained of what had once been large Turkish territories. Abdul Hamid II, sultan 1876-1908, was noted for cleverness and cruelty, shown particularly to the non-Muslim populations of the empire, such as the Armenians (and, earlier, the Bulgarians). For cruelty, corruption, and the gradual disintegration of the empire, Turkey became known as "the sick man of Europe". Britain found it difficult to support the sultan, even for the sake of holding Russia at bay, but Holmes was not above accepting a "commission" from him, mentioned in "The Blanched Soldier".

• Russia was a vast empire stretching over half of Europe, the plains where Napoléon's army had come to grief in 1812, and the full width of Asia as well. The Emperor or Czar (Alexander II ruled 1855-1881, Alexander III 1881-1894, Nicholas II 1894-1917) presided over a court at St. Petersburg with a strongly French flavour, but the population of some 109 million included 17 million Asians. While facing Germany, Austria-Hungary and Turkey in the west, Russia also had to consider Japan in the east. When war in the Pacific came in 1904-05, Japan was easily victorious (the peace settlement was mediated by Theodore Roosevelt). There remained constant fear of a Russian menace in Europe.

• The Netherlands and Belgium had been a single country until 1830, when a division took place: Belgium, largely Roman Catholic, becoming a kingdom in the southern districts (Leopold II reigned 1865-1909), and the Netherlands, with a Protestant majority, becoming a kingdom in the north (William III reigned 1849-1890, Wilhelmina 1890-1948). Belgium had 6 million people, the Netherlands 5 million. Formerly a world power, and indeed a rival to Britain on the seas, the Netherlands maintained large colonies in the East Indies (including Sumatra) and elsewhere. As the Protestant country nearest England, the Netherlands ("Holland") had traditionally had a sizeable population of expatriate English, and close trade links with Britain.

• Norway, one of the two countries making up the peninsula called Scandinavia, had since 1814 been governed in a joint monarchy with its neighbour, Sweden. Oscar II (reigned 1872-1907) is mentioned as "the King of Scandinavia" in two Canonical adventures. Sweden had about 5 million people, Norway 2 million. In 1905 the union was dissolved and a Danish prince became King Haakon VII of an independent Norway. The third Scandinavian country, Denmark, had a population of 2 million; its king was Christian IX, the grand old man of European royalty (reigned 1863-1906).

Relations among these countries — as well as Spain (population 17 million, but much weakened by the loss of its colonies in the course of the nineteenth century) and other nations — were conducted through private diplomacy and secret treaties, of the kind reflected in "The Bruce-Partington Plans", "The Naval Treaty" and other Canonical tales. No country knew exactly what any other country was bound to do by its treaties with third and fourth countries, and diplomatic and military action could be highly arbitrary and dramatic in an age of autocratic governments not directly answerable to the public will. Individual relationships counted for much, not least the family connections formed as the children and grandchildren of Christian IX of Denmark and Victoria of Britain married and intermarried. Wilhelm II of Germany, who would lead his country to war against Britain in 1914, was Victoria's grandson.

The geopolitics of Europe was the chief consideration for most of the powerful nations. Russia had to consider its Pacific rim, Germany had colonies in Africa, Belgium had the rubber-rich Congo, France had some overseas possessions, but the mother country and the security of borders was in each case the central concern. The case of Britain was more complicated: first because of its ties with the United States, second because of its island position (enabling it to think first of the seas while other nations had to think of land frontiers), and third because of its colonies scattered around the world, above all India.

India. India (including present-day Pakistan, Burma, Sri Lanka and Bangladesh) is as large as Europe and had in Holmes's day something like 288 million people, all under British rule in a bewildering variety of provinces, native states, princedoms, and other arrangements. The British presence in India had begun as a commercial venture, becoming military and governmental in the course of the eighteenth century. By Holmes's day power was wielded by a huge bureaucracy, headed in Calcutta by the Viceroy and Governor-General, in London by the officials of the India Office. There was also a large military presence. A number of British regiments had a presence in India, under a system by which one battalion of a regiment would be stationed abroad and the other at home in Britain for enlistment and training; on this principle one battalion of Watson's regiment, the Northumberland Fusiliers, was in the 1890's based near Rawalpindi. In addition there was a much larger Indian Army, made up of native soldiers though largely with British officers.

The great traumatic event in the history of British India was the Mutiny by some of the native soldiers, chiefly in Bengal, in the summer months of 1857.

Set off by religious passions on top of a general discontent with the scope of the changes British rulers were making to Indian customs (a threat to the caste system, in particular), the Mutiny was the occasion for many dramatic incidents of the kind reflected in *The Sign of the Four* and "The Crooked Man", the most famous being the massacre at Cawnpore and the siege of Lucknow. Women as well as men had the opportunity to show heroism or to be butchered, or to experience horrors that were a familiar background for the early readers of the Canon. When order was restored there were ugly reprisals, followed by reforms in the government of the army and of India in general. In 1877 Victoria was proclaimed Empress of India, and gradually some self-government was introduced. (Full independence came in 1947.)

Every Victorian knew a good deal about India. Its principal cities (Madras, Bombay, Calcutta) were well-known names, and a staple of daily life was the tea that was India's most familiar export. Other Indian trade included wheat, rice, cotton, and opium. Tales of rajahs, tiger-shooting and fabulous gems were familiar — it seems a little odd that a landlady in "The Crooked Man" should have seen a rupee coin and identified it only as "a bad florin". India was a source of drama and colour for the British of the 1890's, and it is little wonder that it appears in the Canon as the source of swamp adders, cheetahs, cigars and colonels.

Who's Who

Notable people in Holmes's world ranged from Henry Edward (Cardinal) Manning, head of the Roman Catholic Church in England at a time when it was still under popular suspicion, to Beatrice Webb, young socialist agitator and writer who, with her husband Sidney, helped to found the London School of Economics. A modest selection of other names:

Grant Allen (1848-1899) was the Canadian-born author of philosophy and journalism on many subjects, as well as some thirty novels, the most famous being *The Woman Who Did* (1895). This book shocked many readers with its depiction of a woman who, in protest against the subjection of her sex in conventional marriage, had a child with her lover. He was acquainted with Doyle, and asked him to write the final chapters of the novel *Hilda Wade*, then being serialized, when he realized he would not live to complete it.

Robert Barr (1850-1912) was an author with Scots and Canadian roots who by 1892 was well enough established in the English literary world to be co-founder (with Jerome K. Jerome) of *The Idler*. He was at least an acquaintance of Doyle, and wrote an interview profile in *The Idler* in 1894 which is an important source about the author's literary opinions and style of life at that period.

James M. Barrie (1860-1937), who became Sir James, is best known as the creator of Peter Pan. Like Doyle, he was originally Scots, and some of his important writings deal with village life in Scotland. He collaborated with Doyle on the comic opera "Jane Annie" (1893).

Henry Ward Beecher (1813-1887) was the most prominent of the Protestant preachers who were important figures in American cultural and political life in the late nineteenth century. He used his oratory in support of the Union (the north) during the American Civil War, and subsequently became a fashionable Congregational pastor in Brooklyn. In 1874 a scandal and divorce case in which Beecher was cited as co-respondent tarnished his image but did not end his career; surely this incident was not the reason Watson admired Beecher, as "The Cardboard Box" indicates. Beecher's sister, **Harriet Beecher Stowe**, was author of *Uncle Tom's Cabin* and "The Battle Hymn of the Republic".

Isambard Kingdom Brunel (1806-1859) was the first of Britain's great engineers, constructing much of the Great Western Railway as well as the colossal steamships *Great Eastern* and *Great Britain*.

Lewis Carroll was the pen-name of Charles Lutwidge Dodgson (1832-1898), Cambridge mathematician and in his spare hours author of *Alice's Adventures in Wonderland* (1865) and *Through the Looking-Glass* (1871). Modern commentators have noted with raised eyebrows his hobby of taking photographs of little girls, sometimes unclad, including Alice Liddell, a colleague's daughter and the apparent original of his fictional Alice.

Joseph Chamberlain (1836-1914) was a shopkeeper's son who made a fortune in manufacturing and entered municipal politics. In a three-year term as mayor of Birmingham (one of the large Midland cities, grown quickly on the proceeds of textile manufacture) he built parks, roads, courts, markets, gas lines, sewers and water pipes, adopting policies of activism unlike anything Britain had previously seen, including extensive slum clearance. He then became the first of the prominent "radicals" sent to Parliament from the Midlands, and served in important Cabinet posts in the Liberal governments of Gladstone and Balfour. Neville Chamberlain, prime minister in the 1930's, was his son.

Lord Randolph Churchill (1849-1895) was a prominent Conservative politician and hot debater in the late 1870's and 1880's, briefly serving as leader of the House of Commons while the prime minister, Lord Salisbury, was in the House of Lords. (His own title was an honorary one, his father being the Duke of Marlborough.) His son **Winston Churchill** (1874-1965), who became Sir Winston, was a soldier and war correspondent in the 1890's, followed him into politics and served as prime minister and Britain's saviour in World War II.

Charles Darwin (1809-1882) developed his theory of "evolution through natural selection" as the result of observations, most famously in the Galapagos Islands, during the voyage of the *Beagle* in the early 1830's. *The Origin of Species* (1859), followed by *The Descent of Man* (1871), dealt with physical evolution; their author can hardly be blamed for the "social Darwinism" developed by enthusiasts to justify unrestrained competition, regressive politics, even racism. The belief that Christianity opposed Darwinism is largely untrue for Britain, where religious leaders accepted Darwin's theories within a generation.

Benjamin Disraeli (1804-1881), who became Lord Beaconsfield, was a novelist and orator who made a mark as politician and prime minister (1868,

1874-1880) through flamboyant style as well as reformist policies and adroit diplomacy. Although a Conservative, he was no Tory, believing in a traditional England in which all classes would share the benefits. And he was an enthusiastic supporter of the monarchy, as well as a genius at flattering the elderly Victoria and attracting her endorsement and affection.

Charles Dickens (1812-1870) was Britain's greatest novelist, the master of satire and emotion-wrenching language. *David Copperfield* and *Oliver Twist* draw on his own wretched boyhood, while other works demonstrate the range of his genius — *A Tale of Two Cities* is about the French revolution, and *A Christmas Carol* is virtually a morality play. All English novelists are influenced by Dickens's candid portraiture, though many, including Doyle, have revolted from his undisciplined wordiness. Dickens left unfinished *The Mystery of Edwin Drood*, an excellent puzzle that has attracted many Sherlockian speculations.

Charles Dilke (1843-1911), who became Sir Charles, was a prominent figure in the "radical" wing of the Liberal party who could well have become prime minister, leading his party from strength to strength and changing the course of history, had he not been accused in 1885 of dalliance in the bed of young Virginia Crawford. The resulting scandal and divorce case destroyed his career.

Edward, Prince of Wales (1841-1910), originally Albert Edward ("Bertie" to intimates), later King Edward VII (reigned 1901-1910), was the oldest son of Queen Victoria. Although he became a dignified, popular, and successful king, particularly effective as "Edward the Peacemaker" in managing the squabbles among European nations, his reputation as Prince of Wales (heir to the throne) was for spendthrift luxury, gambling, and womanizing. Occasionally, as in the Tranby Croft gambling scandal of 1891, he came close to serious trouble. His most prominent mistress was **Lillie Langtry**, "the Jersey Lily"; there were numerous others, probably including the sensational actress **Sarah Bernhardt** (1845-1923). As the host *par excellence* of weekend house-parties he also had many opportunities for dalliance with society ladies. The Prince has been seen as the "illustrious client" who employs Holmes in the story of that title, and his career is well reflected also in the events of "A Scandal in Bohemia".

Sigmund Freud (1856-1939), a physician in Vienna, became the founder of psychoanalysis, which he maintained was an entirely scientific technique for understanding and changing feelings and behaviour. Freud in fact was as much artist as scientist, basing his theories on only a small number of patients. He treated them in the 1880's; *Studies in Hysteria* was published in 1895, to be followed by more speculative works such as *Totem and Taboo* (1913). The Freudian ideas now part of general knowledge, such as phallic symbolism and the "Oedipus complex", acquired their influence somewhat after Holmes's day.

William Schwenck Gilbert (1836-1911), who became Sir William, was a dramatic and comic writer whose chief works are the operettas on which he collaborated with **Arthur Sullivan** (1842-1900), who became Sir Arthur. Gilbert wrote the comic, often satiric, verse and largely devised the plots; Sullivan composed the music (he also achieved some distinction with more serious choral music, operas and even hymns). There were thirteen Gilbert and Sullivan operettas, from *Trial by Jury* (1875) to *The Grand Duke* (1896), with *H. M. S. Pinafore*, *The Pirates of Penzance*, and *The Mikado* the best known, *The Yeomen of the Guard* probably the finest.

William Ewart Gladstone (1809-1898) was known as "the Grand Old Man" by the end of his long career as leader of the Liberal Party, and prime minister 1868-74, 1880-85, 1886, 1892-94. The social reforms introduced by his first government were not equalled by any later accomplishments, and he was eventually trapped in the quagmire of Irish Home Rule, which he could not get Parliament to approve. One reference work describes Gladstone as "a good classical scholar and an earnest high churchman". His moral uprightness, coupled with personal quirks, gave him a keen interest in the rehabilitation of prostitutes, and he sometimes walked London's streets himself, seeking soiled doves to rescue.

Charles George Gordon (1833-1885) served in the army in several parts of the Empire, earning the nickname "Chinese" for his role in suppressing a rebellion in China, and in the 1870's went to Egypt as a colonial governor having reached the rank of major-general. In 1885 he went to Khartoum in the course of dealing with another rebellion, this one more substantial, and was killed by the forces of the Mahdi, predecessor of the charismatic Khalifa. His death outraged Britain and made an impression on Dr. Watson, who subsequently displayed his portrait in the Baker Street rooms.

William Gilbert Grace (1848-1915) was the greatest cricket player of all time, as well as a physician. His broad figure and flamboyant beard attracted attention to his skill with the bat (126 times in his career he scored a "century", 100 runs or more in a match) and he was a hero to children and sportsmen alike, reputedly the best-known man in England in 1895.

Oliver Wendell Holmes (1809-1894) was a medical professor at Harvard University for most of his life, and the author of such humane volumes as *The Autocrat of the Breakfast-Table* (1858) and its sequels, as well as poetry and novels. He was much admired by Doyle, who visited his fresh grave when he came to Boston late in 1894, and repeatedly praised him in his writings about literature. Whether he took the genial doctor's surname for that of his great detective seems an unanswerable question. The doctor's son, Oliver Wendell Holmes Jr. (1841-1935), became a justice of the United States Supreme Court.

Ernest William Hornung (1866-1921) was a novelist who became Doyle's brother-in-law. Hornung dedicated his book *The Amateur Cracksman* (1899), in which he introduced the "gentleman burglar" A. J. Raffles, "To A. C. D. — this form of flattery."

Harry Houdini (1873-1926), real name Ehrich Weiss, was an American escape artist and conjurer whose flamboyance made him world-famous. Having flirted with Spiritualism, he chose to devote his energy to exposing fraudulent mediums, of whom there were many; his friendship with Doyle dissolved because of their differences on this issue.

Henry Irving (1838-1905), who became Sir Henry, original name John Henry Brodribb, was a prominent actor who reached fame in *The Bells* in 1871-72 and went on to be the best-known Shakespearean leading man of his period, often playing opposite **Ellen Terry** (1847-1928) at the popular Lyceum Theatre in London. In 1894 Irving performed in Doyle's play "Waterloo" as half of a double bill with a revival of "The Bells"; he played it again from time to time until his 1905 retirement. Irving's secretary was **Bram Stoker** (1847-1912), the author of *Dracula* (1897), a novel about vampirism in eastern Europe and London.

Jerome K. Jerome (1859-1927) was an actor and humorist whose most enduring work is *Three Men in a Boat* (1889). In 1892 he was part of the small group that founded the literary magazine *The Idler*. Jerome was a good friend of Doyle, having courted his sister Connie and shared many literary conversations with him.

Rudyard Kipling (1865-1936) is the poet of Empire, although also well known for children's stories, most importantly *The Jungle Book* (1894). His "Recessional" was published in *The Times* June 22, 1897, the day of Queen Victoria's diamond jubilee, and was hailed by some as the greatest poem in English:

> God of our fathers, known of old,
>   Lord of our far-flung battle-line,
> Beneath whose awful Hand we hold
>   Dominion over palm and pine —
> Lord God of Hosts, be with us yet,
> Lest we forget — lest we forget!

These sentiments are less jingoistic than they at first appear. But there was a ruthless, even sadistic, tone to Kipling's work, and his patriotism and vulgarity went out of fashion. Doyle visited Kipling in 1894 while the latter was living in Vermont.

Charles Stewart Parnell (1846-1891) was a leader of the movement for Irish Home Rule both in Parliament (converting Gladstone to the cause) and outside it (inventing the tactic of boycotts, and organizing other forms of pressure). His public career was ruined in 1890 when his private life became an issue for the courts: he had been living for some years with Kitty O'Shea, with whom he had three children, and finally the lady's husband sought a divorce and created a scandal.

Robert Cecil, third **Marquess of Salisbury** (1830-1903), was the last prime minister to be a member of the House of Lords rather than of the Commons. He held that office 1885-86, 1886-92, 1895-1902 and for much of the time was his own foreign secretary as well, his interests being more in diplomacy than in domestic affairs. Lord Bellinger of "The Second Stain" is in large part a portrait of Salisbury.

Leslie Stephen (1832-1904), who became Sir Leslie, was a prominent writer, editor and biographer. He edited the *Cornhill* magazine (which would later publish some of Doyle's early fiction) in the 1870s, and was creator and editor of the *Dictionary of National Biography*, a landmark of British historical scholarship and self-consciousness, in the following decade. His wife, Harriet, was the daughter of the novelist **William Makepeace Thackeray** (1811-1863). His daughter was feminist author **Virginia Woolf** (1882-1941).

Alfred Tennyson (1809-1892), who became Lord Tennyson, was the leading poet of the Victorian period. His work first appeared in the 1830s, and in 1850 he became Poet Laureate, an honour that obliged him to write verses for national occasions. His *Idylls of the King*, blank-verse poems of the Arthurian age, which began appearing in 1859, express the nobility of the Victorian age as well. They were much admired by Queen Victoria and Albert, the Prince Consort. Other important works include "Locksley Hall" and "In Memoriam".

Victoria (born May 24, 1819, died January 22, 1901), became Queen on the death of her uncle, William IV. She wore the crown longer than any other British sovereign and gave her name to an age that lasted from the end of the Napoleonic wars in 1815 until the opening of World War I in 1914. Social and economic changes during her reign were accompanied by the development of a constitutional monarchy, made possible by her long stable reign and frequently wise interventions in public affairs. She was stubborn, eccentric, and middle-class in habit, but well aware of her role as mother of her far-flung peoples. She came to be much loved (and by Sherlockians is frequently alluded to as "A Certain Gracious Lady"). Through the royal marriages of her nine children, Victoria was also mother of most of Europe's rulers — her oldest daughter, also named Victoria, married Frederick, Crown Prince of Prussia, who became Emperor of Germany. **Albert** (1819-1861), prince of Saxe-Coburg and Gotha, became Prince Consort when he married Victoria in 1840. He took a keen interest in promoting industry and culture, his works including the Exhibition of 1851 with its "Crystal Palace". The Queen never recovered from his death, living in seclusion as "the Widow of Windsor" for most of her last four decades. A Golden Jubilee in 1887 and Diamond Jubilee in 1897 celebrated the fiftieth and sixtieth anniversaries of her accession to the throne (June 20, 1837).

Herbert George Wells (1866-1946) was a struggling teacher, an undoctrinaire socialist, and the author of a vast body of literature, much of it classifiable as science fiction, including *The War of the Worlds* (1898). He also wrote social commentary and the very successful (and weighty) *Outline of History* (1920).

Oscar Wilde (1854-1900) was an Irish-born author who emerged from youthful "aesthetic" posturing to win critical success with plays such as "The Importance of Being Earnest" (1895). His one novel was *The Picture of Dorian Gray* (1890). Wilde, who was bisexual, conducted a passionate friendship with **Lord Alfred Douglas** (1870-1945), son of the Marquess of Queensberry, who created a scandal that destroyed the writer. Wilde served two years (1895-97) in prison for violating a clause prohibiting "gross indecency" that had been made law, almost by accident, in the Criminal Law Amendment Act of 1885.

Chapter VI

Crime and Punishment

As a detective, Sherlock Holmes seeks to solve mysteries, which for the most part involve crimes. (A few of the stories present exceptions, puzzles in which no crime has been committed, although it is not always clear until the mystery is cleared up that that is so.) He traces the event to its origin and brings a malefactor to justice.

But of course "justice" is a philosophical, even theological, idea, distinct from "law" as it is, at the other extreme, distinct from revenge. Sherlock Holmes takes pains in more than one story to make clear that he is neither a police agent nor in any sense an officer of the law; on several occasions he lets malefactors go free either because their deeds were justifiable or because, as in "The Blue Carbuncle", pity takes precedence. In "The Abbey Grange" he constitutes himself judge, and appoints Watson jury, to make the acquittal orderly. In "The Blue Carbuncle" he simply flings the door open and throws the criminal out. "I suppose that I am commuting a felony," he tells Watson, "but it is just possible that I am saving a soul." That too is justice.

The earliest forms of law, barely holding private vengeance in check, prescribed terrible punishments for crimes and what would now be called torts. The principle associated with the ancient Hebrews of "an eye for an eye and a tooth for a tooth" was intended to limit the penalties that could be extracted, and even that stern *lex talionis* has been much limited not only by the mild teachings of Jesus of Nazareth (and the rabbis before him) but by subsequent legal codes. Although the death penalty applied to dozens of crimes in Victorian Britain, it was rarely imposed, as juries refused to convict in cases where hanging seemed disproportionate. More important, however, is the principle that the punishment for crime was being imposed according to written laws, and by an impartial state rather than by representatives of the victim. Such was the system of law under which Holmes, his clients, and the criminals he pursued all lived.

British Law

Underlying the specific "laws" or Acts passed by Parliament, and the "by-laws" of cities, was and is a great body of "common law", law in the form of traditions and court judgements (precedents) dating back to the year 1189, and still in use not only in Britain but in the United States, most of Canada, and many other lands. The best-known use of the phrase is in "common-law marriage", the principle that a partner has the rights of a spouse because of cohabitation rather than a marriage certificate. Sherlockians may be less aware of common-law property rights, which for example give a creator some control over invented characters, quite apart from copyright. Then there are the common-law rights of way over which old Frankland, in *The Hound of the Baskervilles*, loved to dispute:

Sometimes he will shut up a right of way and defy the parish to make him open it. At others he will with his own hands tear down some other man's gate and declare that a path has existed there from time immemorial, defying the owner to prosecute him for trespass. He is learned in old manorial and communal rights.

Other aspects of the common law deal with contracts and commercial transactions; inheritances; "torts" or personal wrongs such as slander or trespass; civil rights ("an Englishman's home is his castle"); and crime. The common law changes only gradually, through court rulings on specific cases, unless Parliament intervenes. The ancient distinction between two classes of crime, "felonies" and "misdemeanours", was abolished in 1967 in Britain, for example. Holmes is said (in *A Study in Scarlet*) to have "a good practical knowledge of British law", but surely did not have time to rival the knowledge of a solicitor (a lawyer who advises a client) or a barrister (one who, having been "briefed" by a solicitor, conducts a case in court). His knowledge was "practical" for the purposes of a detective.

British legal procedure, satirized in Charles Dickens's novels in the middle of the nineteenth century, was being gradually reformed by Holmes's day, although even now the system remains complicated, especially in civil law (matters concerned with contracts or private lawsuits rather than with crime). As a detective Holmes was more concerned with the disposition of accused criminals, who usually came, except in London, to a Justice of the Peace. Minor matters would be handled there; more serious cases would be referred to the "quarter sessions", more formal proceedings under a panel of JP's, or to the Assizes, court sessions held in the chief town of each county. In London, accused criminals came first to a police-court, such as the one at Bow Street, and matters too serious for disposition there would go to the Central Criminal Court at the "Old Bailey", established in 1834.

There was no court of criminal appeal until 1907, when such a body was created, largely because of pressure from Doyle after his investigation of the George Edalji case. In Holmes's day, the verdict of a court was final, and put immediately into effect, a convicted criminal being carried off to prison. The chief prisons in London were Newgate (the old horror near the Old Bailey), Pentonville, Wandsworth, and Wormwood Scrubs. Elsewhere, there were important prisons at Portsmouth, Portland, and several other places, including the most famous of them all, Dartmoor Prison near Princetown, built in 1809 for French prisoners of war, which plays an important role in *The Hound of the Baskervilles*. There were also many local prisons, including Reading Gaol, made famous by Oscar Wilde's "Ballad" about his imprisonment there (1895-97). Prison treatment was, by twentieth-century standards, desperately cruel, depending on isolation, boredom, and (frequently) hard labour, to say nothing of deliberate tortures such as whipping or the treadmill which could be part of a man's sentence. The convict uniform made of coarse cloth stamped with the government's "broad arrow" is familiar to readers of the Canon from a Sidney Paget drawing of Jack Prendergast in "The 'Gloria Scott'". Women convicts were sent to Holloway, in London. The criminally insane could be imprisoned at Broadmoor, in Berkshire. Executions (by hanging) took place inside the prisons; public hanging at Tyburn Tree, where London's Marble Arch now stands, had been abolished in 1783, and the last public execution anywhere in London was in 1868.

Policing and Detection

Police officers are persons who enforce public order. They are usually paid by the government (although there can also be private police, such as the Coal and Iron Police who figure in *The Valley of Fear*), and their character varies with that of the authority they serve. The police in a dictatorship, or "police state", can be cruel, partial, and arbitrary, as the narrative in "The Golden Pince-Nez" suggests. In a relatively free country, such as Britain, the police generally act according to accepted rules of law and decency. There may be individual instances of corruption or brutality, and of course the police cannot do much to make the law they enforce more enlightened than legislators have decreed, but there is a strong tradition of fairness and independence. No one, not even the authorities responsible for prosecuting an alleged criminal, can tell the police what lines of inquiry to pursue or to overlook when a crime appears to have been committed. British police are under the guidance of government authorities — the county councils, or in the case of London's police the Home Secretary, one of the senior members of the central government. But legislation and tradition give local police officials, and even individual constables, both the right and the duty to proceed as seems best to them. Policing is independent of prosecution — the arm of the government which argues the case against alleged offenders in court — and that in turn is independent of the judges and the prisons. Individuals are protected against police mistreatment by, among other things, the Judges' Rules, a codification of longstanding prohibitions against torture, trickery and other improper ways of obtaining evidence.

Scotland Yard. Police headquarters in London has been called "Scotland Yard" since 1829, when the newly established Metropolitan Police built its headquarters in a little street by that name, just off Whitehall. In 1890 the police moved to a nearby site which immediately became "New Scotland Yard". Headquarters was moved again in 1967 (to a nearby street called Broadway), and the building that was Scotland Yard in Holmes's day is now the Norman Shaw Building, still housing police offices.

Policing in London long predates 1829, but consisted chiefly of local constables and "thief-takers", criminals themselves who would finger their associates for money. The Bow Street Runners, created in the middle of the eighteenth century, were the first uniformed force, attached to one busy police-court. The Police Act of 1829, creating a Metropolitan Police under the central government's auspices, was the work of Robert Peel, then Home Secretary and later to be prime minister; in his honour constables became known as "Peelers" and later "Bobbies". They were outfitted in understated uniforms, to emphasize their civilian rather than military character, and equipped with rattles (replaced by whistles, after earlier experiments, in 1886) and truncheons. London constables did not carry firearms in Holmes's day, and most still do not; police guns were brought out only in case of need, as for the notorious Sidney Street shoot-out in 1911. A volume of *General Instruction for the Police*, issued in the early months of the force, remains the basis for its work today. For historical reasons, the Metropolitan Police do not have jurisdiction in the old City of London. It has its own force, which figures in the Canon only once, in "The Stockbroker's Clerk".

Most police work was — and remains — the tedious duty of patrolling the streets, preventing crime rather than investigating offences. But by about 1840 there were officers assigned to the duty of watching "habitual criminals", and in 1842 a Detective Branch was created, with two inspectors and half a dozen sergeants. It took the name Criminal Investigation Department — CID — in 1878, and was the parent of the later anti-terrorist Special Branch and of the famous Flying Squad ("the Sweeney"). Jack Tracy in the *Encyclopaedia Sherlockiana* sums up the workings of the CID as it figures in the Holmes tales:

> Plain-clothes detectives are distributed throughout the divisions ... as well as assigned to the central office at Scotland Yard. The headquarters staff investigate cases of an imperial or national character ...; and cases in which inquiries may have to be pursued in several districts ... or otherwise can best be handled by them ..., including those referred from provincial forces ... or foreign ones ...; and often those involving special investigative expertise, such as murder cases. ...
>
> While the C.I.D. has no jurisdiction beyond the Metropolitan Police District, upon occasion it may be called upon by the Chief Constable of provincial forces who wish to avail themselves of the Yard's experience and resources in the investigation of certain cases. Such instances are rare and usually involve murder. ...
>
> The Metropolitan Police Act of 1839 permits the hiring of official police personnel by private firms or individuals, for private purposes, provided the entire cost of the policeman's maintenance is borne.

The Metropolitan Police are headed by a Commissioner. Occupants of that office during Holmes's era were Sir Edmund Henderson (1869-1886), Sir Charles Warren (1886-1888), James Monro (1888-1890), and Sir Edward Bradford (1890-1903), none of them professional police.

Many histories of Scotland Yard have been written, including *The Rise of Scotland Yard* (1956) by Douglas G. Browne, *Scotland Yard and the Metropolitan Police* (1929) by John F. Moylan, and *The Story of Scotland Yard* (1936) by Basil Thomson. More modern is *Bloody Business* (1992) by H. Paul Jeffers. *The King's Peace* (1895) by F. A. Inderwick remains a classic. Several volumes deal with the pioneering work of Sir Bernard Spilsbury in forensic pathology, though it came too late to illuminate Holmes's career.

Most of the police with whom Sherlock Holmes came in contact were from the CID, although he also encountered Metropolitan Police constables (such as the luckless John Rance in *A Study in Scarlet*) and representatives of other forces, from the county constabulary in Berkshire, Kent, Hallamshire, and elsewhere to the police in such foreign cities as New York and Cleveland. Most prominent of the Scotland Yard detectives in the Canon is Lestrade (initial G., first name not known), who appears in some fifteen cases and is praised by Holmes as "the pick of a bad lot", for the Baker Street opinion of the professionals was not high. From *A Study in Scarlet* to "The Three Garridebs" he is seen, sometimes consulting Holmes voluntarily (or under pressure to wrap up a case that is baffling him), sometimes being summoned when Holmes needs the resources of the official force or has a criminal to hand over. Second to Lestrade stands Tobias Gregson, who also receives praise from Holmes ("the smartest of the Scotland Yarders") and turns up in five cases. Other CID men in the Canon include Athelney Jones, Gregory, Merivale *et al.* They are generally pictured as well-meaning and energetic, but unimaginative, hence contemptuous of Holmes's theorizing and unorthodox methods.

Victorian crime. The police of the nineteenth century struggled to control petty theft (in an era when coins were the only money) and drunken violence, and although proof is near impossible, it seems clear that England, London in particular, became more orderly through the early decades of organized policing. At times the police were also involved in maintaining order against political demonstrations, the most dramatic case being the battle in Trafalgar Square on "Bloody Sunday", November 13, 1887, against a vaguely Socialist mob. More interesting to the modern reader than routine police work are the occasional dramatic cases, usually of murder, with which the police dealt. A few examples:

● Poisonings in 1856 attributed to Dr. William Palmer of Rugeley. He was hanged for one of them, never tried for the other deaths including that of his wife. Then in 1865 came the poisonings of a wife and mother-in-law by Dr. Edward William Pritchard of Glasgow. Holmes refers to both cases in "The Speckled Band".
● The arrest of Arthur Orton, unsuccessful claimant to the Tichborne fortune, in 1866.
● A murder (1876) and a long series of burglaries committed by a clever little man described by Holmes as "my old friend Charlie Peace". As Peace was hanged in 1879, Holmes must be referring to his reading in criminal literature rather than to a personal encounter.
● Arrests beginning in 1886 in connection with a male brothel in Cleveland Street, London, where some of the patrons had close connections with aristocracy and royalty.
● A series of strychnine poisonings of women committed by Neill Cream, hanged in 1892.
● The imprisonment of Adolf Beck for fraud in 1896; he was released in 1901 when it became clear that there had been a case of mistaken identity. He was prosecuted again in 1904 but eventually let go.

Continental (and American) crime was also of interest to Holmes. It is a pity that the theft of the "Mona Lisa" from the Louvre came too late (August 22, 1911) for his professional attention, and that he was in Tibet, or perhaps Mecca, while Lizzie Borden was being tried for the August 4, 1892, murders of her father and stepmother in Fall River, Massachusetts (she was acquitted). The theft of the Irish Crown Jewels from Dublin Castle in July 1907 is also outside the purview of the Canon.

Jack the Ripper. Most dramatic of all Victorian crime stories is that of Jack the Ripper. Unlike other monsters of popular culture, the Ripper did exist, though no one was ever identified as the monster ("Saucy Jack", he called himself in one taunting letter to the police) or charged with the killings attributed to him in London in 1888. Five victims — all prostitutes in the east end of London — are definitely considered the Ripper's work:

- Mary Ann (Polly) Nichols — Bucks Row, August 31.
- Eliza Ann Chapman — Hanbury Street, September 8.
- Elizabeth Stride — Berner Street, September 30.
- Catharine Eddowes — Mitre Square, September 30.
- Mary Jeannette Kelly — Dorset Street, November 9.

Several other cases (notably the August 7 murder of Martha Tabram, or Turner, in George Yard Buildings) are sometimes associated with the Ripper, but do not entirely fit the pattern, which included gruesome and increasingly elaborate disembowelling.

Several features of the Ripper case are peculiarly interesting:

- The taunting letters to the police and the press, including one signed "Jack the Ripper" (origin of the enduring name), and one in which the author claimed to have eaten part of the kidney of one victim.
- A chalked message, "The Juwes are not the men who will be blamed for nothing," erased by police commissioner Sir Charles Warren because it might lead to violence against the large Jewish population in the East End. Some later analysts have seen a Masonic meaning in this message and in the details of the atrocities.
- Incompetent police work, under Warren's direction, and general hysteria from the population, leading to many false arrests.
- A plethora of suggestions about the killer's identity, from Prince Albert Victor, Duke of Clarence (who, however, was in Scotland at the time of some of the killings) to barrister Montague John Druitt. The most plausible suggestions involve not celebrities but local residents, such as "Kosminski, a Polish Jew", referred to in contemporary police files.

For the literal-minded Sherlockian, the important question is why Holmes did not solve the Ripper case. Several parodies and films have him doing so, notably *A Study in Terror* (novel by Ellery Queen, published in England as *Sherlock Holmes Versus Jack the Ripper*, 1966; film the same year) and "Murder by Decree" (film 1979). The most recent effort of this kind is *The Whitechapel Horrors* (1992), a novel by C. Douglas Baker. The *Baker Street Journal* published a "Ninetieth Anniversary Jack the Ripper Memorial Issue" in 1978, with a number of articles dealing with aspects of the case from a Sherlockian viewpoint, and *Canadian Holmes* had a similar issue in 1988. Other such articles have appeared from time to time.

Useful books about the Ripper case include *The Ripper File* (1975) by Elwyn Jones and John Lloyd; *The Complete Jack the Ripper* (1975) by Donald Rumbelow; *Jack the Ripper, One Hundred Years of Mystery* (1987) by Peter Underwood. A summary of sources and data is *Jack the Ripper: A Bibliography and Review of the Literature*, by Alexander Kelly (1984).

Forensic sciences. Holmes insisted that his detective work was "scientific", and indeed is first glimpsed in the pathology laboratory at St. Bartholomew's Hospital, working on a chemical test for bloodstains. "It is the most practical medico-legal discovery for years," he declares — this in a story published in 1887 and supposed to have taken place in 1881. Later he is seen examining metal filings through a microscope as part of one investigation, testing some liquid with litmus-paper in another, and comparing the idiosyncrasies of typewriters, to say nothing of his work with tobacco ashes, footprints, bicycle tires, and anything else that might be examined through a high-powered lens. Meanwhile, not until the 1930s did the Metropolitan Police set up a laboratory, although the police did rely on the borrowed assistance of outside experts for some years before that. Ballistic evidence (the examination of bullets to identify the gun that fired them) came into use in the 1920s, for example.

Of course the most familiar aspect of forensic science (the application of science to legal and police matters) is fingerprinting. It is reflected in the Canon in several references to "thumb-prints", particularly in "The Norwood Builder", where Lestrade over-casually asks Holmes, "You are aware that no two thumb-marks are alike?" He intends to use a bloody print — faked, it later proves — as evidence against Holmes's client. If the story took place in or about 1895, this reference is a slight anachronism; when it was published in 1903, fingerprinting was still novel in Britain. (Its public acceptance followed the dramatic 1905 conviction of the Stratton brothers for a pair of brutal murders.) In fact the technique had been used elsewhere for decades: it was first introduced in India by Sir William Herschel as a means of proving identity in a largely illiterate society, and had been introduced for law enforcement in the United States in the 1880's. (Mark Twain's *Pudd'nhead Wilson*, 1894, takes the uniqueness of fingerprints for granted.) A Home Office committee struck in 1899 heard about fingerprinting from Herschel's successor in Bengal, Sir Edward Henry. Not only was the system adopted, but Henry was brought home to introduce it, as assistant commissioner of the Metropolitan Police in charge of the CID.

Although modern methods involve lasers and photography, the classic fingerprinting techniques are straightforward: fine powder is scattered across a fingerprint found at the scene of a crime (a black powder such as lampblack for light surfaces, a light powder such as flour for dark surfaces). The print can then be lifted up with transparent sticky tape, and kept for comparison with known prints that have been collected from suspects using a stamp-pad, or filed at police headquarters from previous crimes.

Fingerprinting replaced the earlier technology of "Bertillonnage" or body measurement, developed by the French forensic scientist Alphonse Bertillon. His ingenious idea, which in turn replaced mere verbal descriptions, was first used in France, and adopted at Scotland Yard and British prisons in the 1880's, as Sir Basil Thomson records:

> The measurements were the length and breadth of the skull, the length of the foot and the cubit, the length of the middle finger. He distributed them as belonging to one or other of three equally numerous classes — small, medium, and large. Each of these primary headings is successively subdivided according to height, span, length and breadth of the ear, height of the bust, and colour of the eyes, this last providing seven divisions.

Although Holmes in "The Naval Treaty" expresses "enthusiastic admiration" for Bertillon, the system was imperfect in practice. As Thomson also notes, "One prison warder would press the caliper closer home than another, and one mistake of this kind threw the system out of gear."

Detective Stories

In the words of P. D. James, who ought to know, detective stories are about "the restoration of order out of disorder". More obviously, detective stories are about a detective, someone attempting to identify (and, usually, capture) a criminal. The limits of the genre are not absolutely clear, for all the vast analysis they have received. David Skene Melvin and Ann Skene Melvin compiled a bibliography of such analysis in 1980 — not a bibliography of detective stories themselves, only of the secondary writings about them — and gave it the long but descriptive title *Crime, Detective, Espionage, Mystery, and Thriller Fiction and Film: A Comprehensive Bibliography of Critical Writing through 1979.* Obviously there is much to be said.

Precursors of Sherlock Holmes. Doyle did not invent the detective story, though he did much to define its form. A number of earlier authors not only anticipated his work, but influenced it. "The puzzle is vital to the detective story but is not a detective story in itself," writes Julian Symons in *Bloody Murder: From the Detective Story to the Crime Novel* (1972), denying that — for example — the Biblical book of *Susanna and the Elders* is a detective story. On the other hand, he continues, not all crime literature can be called detective stories. (One thinks of the "sensational literature" with which Holmes was said to be familiar: writings about real crimes and criminals, however fancifully recorded, as in Henry Fielding's biography of the eighteenth-century master thief Jonathan Wild.) Says Symons: "The characteristic note of crime literature is first struck in *Caleb Williams* by William Godwin (1756-1836), which appeared in 1794."

In the work of Edgar Allan Poe (1809-1849), his detective stories are of small importance, but they figure large in the history of crime fiction, and Poe may even be said to have written the first detective story (in 1841). Three of his tales present the work of a Parisian reasoner, C. Auguste Dupin: "The Murders in the rue Morgue", a "locked-room" mystery in which particularly bloody killings are found to be the work of a wild beast; "The Mystery of Marie Roget", based on the actual murder of Mary Rogers in New York in 1841; and "The Purloined Letter", where the brilliantly simple principle is that the safest place to hide an object is in plain sight. Two other Poe stories are also recognizable as detective tales — "The Gold Bug", which offers a cipher suggestive of that in "The Dancing Men", and "Thou Art the Man", a murder story about guilt and vengeance.

Doyle always acknowledged a great debt to Poe, and called him "the world's supreme short story writer". "Mental acuteness," he wrote, "is the one quality which can be ascribed to the ideal detective, and when that has once been admirably done, succeeding writers must necessarily be content for all time to follow in the same track." Besides creating the essentially acute detective in Dupin, Poe created his dull companion, and teams of that kind remained the pattern of detective stories for decades.

A friend of Charles Dickens who wrote somewhat in his style, William Wilkie Collins (1824-1889) is lauded by the *Oxford Companion to English Literature* as a highly successful novelist: "Collins wrote the first full-length detective stories in English, and set a mould for the genre which has lasted for a century. He excelled at constructing ingenious and meticulous plots." Of Collins's many novels, the most prominent are *The Woman in White* (1860) and *The Moonstone* (1868). The latter was identified by Dorothy Sayers, no mean Sherlockian, as the finest detective story ever written. It uses a background of Indian idols and intrigue to set a story of jewel theft, drug use, respectable love, and below-stairs intrigue, in which the detective, Sergeant Cuff, is solid, plodding and more or less plausible. Its complex construction (an example of what the *Oxford* calls "interesting experiments in narrative technique") leads to confusion and inconsistency in details, but the story-telling is first-rate.

A pioneer of what is now recognized as the detective story was Emile Gaboriau (1833-1873), author of five novels about Monsieur Lecoq of the Sureté of Paris, most importantly *Le Dossier 113* (1867). Although Holmes in *A Study in Scarlet* calls Lecoq "a miserable bungler", the insult is mostly for effect — Gaboriau was in fact the first to make his detective a master of disguise, an observer of trifles, a preserver of footprints in plaster of paris. His achievement is the greater because the police were even less well respected in France than in England at the middle of the nineteenth century.

"A curiosity because of the enormous sale it inexplicably achieved", in the words of Julian Symons in *Bloody Murder*, was the 1886 novel *The Mystery of a Hansom Cab*, by Fergus Hume (1859-1932). Symons calls it "a reasonably good imitation of Gaboriau"; it is set in the lower quarters of the then new, teeming city of Melbourne, Australia. Other detective novels were appearing in the decade before Doyle produced *A Study in Scarlet*, including *The Leavenworth Case* by Anna Katherine Green (1846-1935) of the United States. But they were imperfect — Doyle a dozen years later spoke contemptuously of "the idea that seemed to prevail in all detective stories that the hero reached his result by chance, and not by any special sharpness of his own". He was determined that he could do better, and soon managed to turn away from the "sensational" novels of the 1870's to what became the mature form of the detective story, depending largely on character and deductive technique.

Modern authors. The usual discussion of detective stories divides them into two chief kinds: the British, emphasizing reason and plot, and the American, emphasizing violence and often sex. The stereotypes are Michael Innes and

Agatha Christie for the British, Dashiell Hammett and Mickey Spillane for the Americans. As a broad generalization it has some truth, but there are plenty of American detective stories that depend on reasoning, and there can hardly be a bloodier, grittier author than the very British P. D. James. As with any novel, the style and emphasis are up to the author. Only people who have not read detective stories think that they all follow the same formula.

Although Doyle is acknowledged to have set the standard, even invented the genre, one important change came later. He wrote chiefly short stories, and (although there are dissenting opinions) his four detective novels are generally thought to be weaker than the short stories about Holmes. But the novel is now the norm, and while detective novels sell by the millions, short stories are a specialized taste found chiefly in *Ellery Queen's Mystery Magazine*. The development of the detective novel is usually dated from *Trent's Last Case* (1913) by Edmund Clerihew Bentley.

Bibliographies of detective fiction make long and exhausting reading, even if fringe genres such as thrillers and crime novels, as distinguished from true stories of detection, are excluded. Among the most honoured classic authors are these:

* Mary Roberts Rinehart, for *The Circular Staircase* (1908) and similar stories of the had-I-but-known school.
* G. K. Chesterton, for his Father Brown short stories: *The Innocence of Father Brown* (1911) and four subsequent collections.
* R. Austin Freeman, for the cases of that humourless polymath Dr. Thorndyke, told in short stories that appeared in *The Singing Bone* (1912) and other collections.
* Agatha Christie, for dozens of enjoyable but forgettable novels, many of them presenting Hercule Poirot or (Miss) Jane Marple as the detectives. She was first published in *The Mysterious Affair at Styles* (1920). Her most original accomplishments are *The Murder of Roger Ackroyd* (1926) and *Murder in the Calais Coach* (1934).
* S. S. Van Dine (Willard Huntington Wright), for his wordy, affected novels presenting Philo Vance, the earliest detective in this genre to work in New York. Best of the lot is probably *The Canary Murder Case* (1927).
* Ellery Queen (Frederic Dannay and Manfred B. Lee) for many books, in which the detective is also named Ellery Queen: *The Roman Hat Mystery* (1929), *The Glass Village* (1954), and such exceptions to all the rules as *And on the Eighth Day* (1963).
* Erle Stanley Gardner for Perry Mason, in interchangeable mysteries that began with *The Case of the Velvet Claws* (1933).
* Dorothy Sayers (1893-1957), for a series of books presenting Lord Peter Wimsey, notably *Murder Must Advertise* (1933) and *Gaudy Night* (1935). Sayers was also an early scholar of Sherlock Holmes.
* Michael Innes for John Appleby in *Lament for a Murder* (1939), *Appleby's End* (1945) and many other coolly-plotted books.
* Ngaio Marsh, for Roderick Alleyn in *Surfeit of Lampreys* (1941) and other novels.
* Josephine Tey for Alan Grant in *The Franchise Affair* (1947) and her best, quirkiest book, *The Daughter of Time* (1951).

• Margery Allingham, for Albert Campion and later Inspector Charles Luke in such books as *The Tiger in the Smoke* (1952).
• P. D. James, for Adam Dalgliesh in realistic novels that are also detective stories, such as *Shroud for a Nightingale* (1971).

At the other extreme from the amateur reasoners of these tales come the so-called "hard-boiled" detective stories, originating in the 1940s. Prominent in this category are Dashiell Hammett with his "Continental Op" (*Red Harvest* [1929], *The Maltese Falcon* [1930]), and Raymond Chandler with Philip Marlowe (*The Big Sleep* [1939]). There is detection in such books, but primarily there is violence, usually accompanied by sex.

Deserving special attention is Rex Stout (born December 1, 1886; died October 27, 1975), not only a Sherlockian from the earliest days, but creator of Nero Wolfe, the literary detective who most completely follows in Sherlock Holmes's footsteps. Wolfe appeared first in *Fer-de-Lance* (1934) and continued through more than forty books narrated by his smart-aleck Watson, Archie Goodwin. Some readers grumbled that their quality declined over the decades, but the possibility of a late tour-de-force such as *The Doorbell Rang* (1965), in which J. Edgar Hoover himself is made the goat, kept them turning the pages. Wolfe lives in the heart of New York, in a bachelor establishment where he raises orchids, drinks prodigious quantities of beer, and growls at clients. He rarely leaves the premises himself, sending Goodwin out to do the legwork while he eats, drinks, and cogitates, finally announcing his solution to a gathering of protesting witnesses and sceptical police officers in his study. These eccentricities are enough to suggest a Holmesian influence, but Sherlockians prefer to see more. John D. Clark made it explicit in an article in the *Baker Street Journal* in 1956: Wolfe is the son of Holmes and Irene Adler, conceived in Montenegro in 1892. It is a pleasant enough speculation, given something like definitive status by William S. Baring-Gould in his mock biography *Nero Wolfe of West Thirty-Fifth Street* (1969). Readers without the patience for such fancies may prefer the suggestion of D. F. Rauber in the *Journal of Popular Culture* in 1973: "Because Rex Stout so completely reproduced the Doyle formulas and characteristics, it is possible to claim, with only slight exaggeration, that Wolfe *is* Holmes in modern dress." His fans, including a number of Sherlockians, have organized The Wolfe Pack (PO Box 822, Ansonia Station, New York, New York 10023), which publishes a journal, the *Gazette*.

Rules and conventions. Detective stories are a sort of game, rather like crossword puzzles, as well as a form of literature. Their rules have been set out by several commentators, most famously by Ronald Knox in an Introduction to a collection of *Best Detective Stories of the Year* for 1928. Those were short stories, but what he said applies equally to novels:

I. The criminal must be someone mentioned in the early part of the story, but must not be anyone whose thoughts the reader has been allowed to follow.
II. All supernatural or preternatural agencies are ruled out as a matter of course.
III. Not more than one secret room or passage is allowable.

IV. No hitherto undiscovered poisons may be used, nor any appliance which will need a long scientific explanation at the end.

V. No Chinaman must figure in the story.

VI. No accident must ever help the detective, nor must he ever have an unaccountable intuition which proves to be right.

VII. The detective must not himself commit the crime.

VIII. The detective must not light on any clues which are not instantly produced for the inspection of the reader.

IX. The stupid friend of the detective, the Watson, must not conceal any thoughts which pass through his mind; his intelligence must be slightly, but very slightly, below that of the average reader.

X. Twin brothers, and doubles generally, must not appear unless we have been duly prepared for them.

Most of these rules are still generally accepted; indeed, so stylized is the detective story that they seem inevitable. (Number V may appear a little arbitrary, and is perhaps a reaction against the fashions of the 1920's.) Yet most respected authors have violated one or another of the rules now and again, and certainly Doyle did so repeatedly; Sherlock Holmes is a habitual offender as regards rule VIII.

Knox takes for granted the existence of a "Watson", a convention that is still widely followed (though less widely than in the era of Hercule Poirot's Captain Hastings, Philo Vance's S. S. Van Dine, and Dr. Thorndyke's Christopher Jervis). A similar innovation on Doyle's part is the amateur status of the detective, who is independent of the official police and frequently in active rivalry with them. That distinction, as commentators on detective stories have pointed out, seems to require that the police be taken for granted as honest, but not bright. It may not transfer well to other cultures — the great detective of French fiction is an official policeman, George Simenon's Maigret, and in French detective stories are *romans policiers*, police novels. Even in English, an increasing number of detective stories do centre on police detectives, such as the many best-sellers of Ed McBain; such books are often classified as "procedurals" because they emphasize routine procedure, not amateur brilliance. But the classic detective story, directly derived from Doyle, is most often about a detective who seems to be Holmes's descendant.

And yet modern authors have found ways of bending the rules, stretching the limits. Writes Erik Routley in *The Puritan Pleasures of the Detective Story* (1972):

> We have seen the detective story as romantic and thrilling; we have seen it as moralism; we have seen it as a kind of novel, exploring human and social situations and attempting to reveal character as well as solution. We have pursued it to the point at which some of its authors suddenly found that the solution was as unimportant as their literary ancestors had held it to be indispensable.

Perhaps few Sherlockians would want to go that far.

Good and evil. A detective story is not simply a puzzle, but specifically a puzzle about the commission of a crime. Sherlock Holmes speaks once or twice of "sin", but much more often of "crime", which is more easily identified. Although there are some detective stories from cultures in which it cannot be taken for granted that law is the same thing as justice — one thinks of Joseph Skvorecky's short stories about Lieutenant Boruvka of Prague — that equation is usually assumed, and most detective fiction does come from the free countries. The detective represents justice (not merely vengeance) in pursuit of offence (not merely nonconformity), or one might even say good in pursuit of evil. The detective story is in this sense utterly moral: the good guy wins, and the wages of sin is death on the gallows. But of course this is a very mechanical morality. Says Erik Routley:

> The reader of detective stories probably does read them partly because of the curious property they have of providing relaxation from anxiety. If the reader identifies himself with the successful detective, and to some extent with the forces of law and order, he gets some satisfaction from seeing crime brought home to the right culprit, honesty vindicated, and the law protecting society, including himself, from the consequences that would come if the crime were allowed to run free. He gets satisfaction from this precisely because he is worried by the extent to which, in real life, crime does run free.

Generally — as frequently in the Holmes tales — the situation is somewhat muddied. The victim may have deserved killing, and the criminal may thus be a hero. Several times Holmes pardons criminals, once (in "Charles Augustus Milverton") positively glorying in seeing a murder committed. Holmes, the agent of justice, is also the agent of mercy in "The Boscombe Valley Mystery", "The Blue Carbuncle", and several other tales. Sometimes he justifies himself explicitly with reference to a higher law, noting in the latter story that "it is the season of forgiveness" and in "The Abbey Grange" that *vox populi, vox Dei*, the voice of the people (in this case of Dr. Watson) is the voice of God. One does not expect to find God in a detective story, but when extreme moral questions are at issue, the Almighty is apt to be nearby, and to suggest judgements that go beyond simple-minded human justice.

The Valley of Fear illustrates how Doyle was able to transcend the requirements of simple morality, but first he had to meet them. He caused Holmes to investigate a murder, work out the truth, and locate the murderer — not only the murderer, but the mastermind behind him, the incarnated evil that is Professor Moriarty. As the murderer's story is told, it becomes clear that the victim deserved to die, not only because the struggle amounted to self-defence but because of dark deeds some twenty years in the past. Then, in turn, the story of those dark deeds is told, in the second half of the long novel, and the reader loses track of Sherlock Holmes and John Douglas in reading about the wickednesses of the Scowrers. It is perhaps easier for a modern reader than it was for the reader of 1915 to wonder whether the Scowrers, or Mollie Maguires as they were really called, were as utterly black as the story paints them. Were they not, in part, defenders of the working man against the institutionalized violence of the Pennsylvania mine-owners? The detective story is better designed to raise such uncomfortable questions than to answer them; and yet the final paragraphs of *The Valley of Fear* do bring ambiguities forward, as Moriarty manages to have John Douglas killed after all, and Holmes is left muttering that "You must give me time!"

If Sherlock Holmes can go against the law, or rise above it, he has greater difficulty going against convention, against custom. Sociologist Bonnie Menes:

> Sherlock Holmes is the defender of social norms; he enters a case not when a law, but when a norm, has been broken. . . . An exorbitant wage is cause for investigation. There should be no secrets between a husband and wife, yet one spouse in a marriage is acting mysteriously. Two people are scheduled to marry, but one fails to show up at the altar. No public crime has been committed, no private transgression even, but an unspoken social rule has been broken.

And much the same is true of other detectives on the printed page; their business is to investigate what seems odd, as well as to take obvious murders in hand. Holmes is in this way, as well as in his defence of the moral law, profoundly conservative. His personal eccentricities hardly cancel that continuing truth. The title of Routley's book, *The Puritan Pleasures of the Detective Story*, has something to do with these traits, which are not so much limitations as accommodations of the hero and his adventures to the needs of the *Strand Magazine*'s readers:

> Holmes satisfied a craving which had emerged from the puritan background. . . . The positive principle in the English puritan tradition (which is, as I believe, not wholly or even primarily a religious movement) has three basic constituents: intellectualism, moralism, and the acceptance of the values of the city.

In short, Holmes — like other detectives — is a middle-class figure, whatever his own style. Again and again he is seen acting for the respectable classes and the established authorities — the Queen herself, the "Illustrious Client", the contemptible King of Bohemia, the Czarist authorities in the unpublished "case of the Trepoff murder". He has no sympathy with the Scowrers, none with the revolutionaries of "The Golden Pince-Nez", none even with "the British workman" whom he mentions in tones of contempt. The reader does see him mixing on cordial terms with boxers, publicans and sinners when it suits him, and he can be scathing about the boring society of the idle rich, but Holmes is a man who clearly likes his comforts and respects the well-established. Such attitudes are in the mainstream of detective stories, which can hardly exist save in the context of a middle-class order waiting to be disrupted by an untidy murder. A long and illuminating article about these points is "Sherlock Holmes, Order, and the Late-Victorian Mind" by Christopher Clausen, published in 1984 in the *Georgia Review* and reprinted in *Baker Street Miscellanea*. David S. Payne in *Myth and Modern Man in Sherlock Holmes* (1992) explores such aspects of Holmes in detail, observing for example that

Holmes's solutions are solutions of individual crimes and serve only to restore the imbalance caused by that crime. He never brings the original balance into question.

Bibliography. Countless books have been written about detective fiction, of which perhaps the most important is *Murder for Pleasure* (1941), by Howard Haycraft (1905-1991), himself a Sherlockian. Routley's *The Puritan Pleasures* contains many insights and many facts, as does *Bloody Murder* (1972, third edition 1992) by Julian Symons, also published as *Mortal Consequences*. Holding a special place in the hearts of many mystery readers is *Murder Ink* (1977, 1984) by Dilys Wynn, for all its idiosyncrasies.

The definitive reference book in the field is *Encyclopedia of Mystery and Detection* (1976), edited by Chris Steinbrunner and Otto Penzler. A smaller work in the same vein is *Whodunit?* (1982), edited by H. R. F. Keating. A continuing source of information about detective fiction of every kind is the quarterly journal *The Armchair Detective*, published by The Mysterious Bookshop (129 West 56 Street, New York, New York 10019).

The two best-known actors to portray Sherlock Holmes. Left, Basil Rathbone at the Tower of London for "The Adventures of Sherlock Holmes", 1939. Right, Jeremy Brett on the Granada Television sound-stage, 1985.

Chapter VII

Holmes in Modern Media

Reading the original sixty stories has never been enough for enthusiasts of Sherlock Holmes. From early days, they have insisted on seeing the great detective on the stage or the screen, and to the present day they continue to demand new adventures, although few, if any, can fitly be compared with the originals. A few films and dramas, perhaps, may claim to be works of art in their own right, somehow rising above the taint of being "derivative". Others achieve dignity by making no attempt to be anything but straightforward representations of the Canonical stories.

Other appearances of Holmes in the media, from print to television, are less admirable, including irreverent attempts to put him in contact with Karl Marx, portray him as a duck or a 'dog, give him explicit sexual experiences, or send him travelling through time and hyperspace. Harpo Marx has played Holmes (successfully) for laughs; other less talented artists have been embarrassing failures. In print, such efforts may deserve the name of "parody", although some are serious and even moderately successful. All new tales of Holmes are known to Sherlockians as "pastiches". A history of the genre is *The Sincerest Form of Flattery* (1983) by Paul D. Herbert, which includes a long bibliography in tiny print.

Pastiches and Parodies

Sherlock Holmes was being mocked and imitated in print within a year after *The Adventures* first appeared. Robert Barr — who may have been quietly encouraged by Doyle, a personal friend — published "Detective Stories Gone Wrong: The Adventures of Sherlaw Kombs" in *The Idler* in May 1892, and a sequel came in 1894. John Kendrick Bangs in the United States was doing similar things within a few years, and made Holmes a major character in his comic novel *The Pursuit of the House-Boat* (1897). That and other stories by Bangs are surveyed in an article by Jon Lellenberg, published in *Baker Street Miscellanea* in 1984.

Other parodies in the early years appeared as parts of such series as "Lost Diaries" and "As They Would Have Told It". Bret Harte produced one ("The Stolen Cigar Case") as part of his 1902 collection *Condensed Novels*, and other authors did their best to mock Holmes under such names as Shamrock Jolnes, Kerlock Shomes and Oilock Combs. Humour was the intent of all the early parodies, including Stephen Leacock's "Maddened by Mystery" in *Nonsense Novels* (1911):

> The Great Detective sat in his office. He wore a long green gown and half a dozen secret badges pinned to the outside of it.
> Three or four pairs of false whiskers hung on a whisker-stand beside him.

> Goggles, blue spectacles, and motor glasses lay within easy reach.
> He could completely disguise himself at a second's notice.
> Half a bucket of cocaine and a dipper stood on a chair at his elbow.

Mark Twain had done much the same thing in "A Double-Barrelled Detective Story" (1902). Nor were these early parodies limited to English. In 1907 Maurice Leblanc included "Herlock Sholmès arrive trop tard" in *Arsène Lupin, Gentleman-Cambrioleur*, the first book about that master-criminal. The following year appeared *Arsène Lupin contre Herlock Sholmès*, first translated into English as *The Fair-Haired Lady* (and subsequently published under various other titles). All these efforts were good fun, and Doyle did not entirely disapprove, for he wrote two pastiches himself — "The Field Bazaar" (1896) and "How Watson Learned the Trick" (1924). He is reported to have said that "The Adventure of the Two Collaborators", by Sir James Barrie, in which one of the collaborators is Barrie and the other is Doyle, was the best pastiche he had ever seen.

Serious attempts to imitate the Canonical stories may have begun with Vincent Starrett, whose sensitive and convincing "Adventure of the Unique *Hamlet*" was privately printed in 1920, but not given general distribution until twenty years later. In 1944 Little, Brown published *The Misadventures of Sherlock Holmes*, an anthology edited by Ellery Queen that included dozens of parodies including works by Barr, Leblanc, Twain, Leacock, O. Henry, and others. Sherlockians greeted it with enthusiasm, but the heirs of Doyle were outraged, and before long the book was withdrawn from circulation. It is a cherished item in many Sherlockian collections, one printing in particular being a rarity.

In a category all its own is *A Taste for Honey* (1941), by H. F. Heard, a gentle and horrifying story about "Mr. Mycroft" the beekeeper. Heard wrote two sequels — *Reply Paid* (1942) and *The Notched Hairpin* (1949).

The Man Who Was Wanted. A Sherlock Holmes short story entitled "The Case of the Man Who Was Wanted" appeared in *Cosmopolitan* magazine in the United States in August 1948, and in the *Sunday Dispatch* newspaper in England early in 1949, as the work of Doyle, a long-lost sixty-first story for the Canon. It is, as the story suggests, the tale of how Holmes manages to locate a fugitive; the detection is mostly conducted at a distance, for the man himself is aboard a transatlantic liner.

Jon Lellenberg in his little book *Nova 57 Minor* (1990), which also contains the full text of "TMWWW", as it has been abbreviated, tells the full story of this tale. He writes:

> In 1942, the typescript of an unpublished Sherlock Holmes story was discovered among Sir Arthur Conan Doyle's papers. Despite statements by his sons Denis and Adrian that the story was not up to their father's standard, there was great clamor to have it published; and no doubt the financial potential of an unpublished Sherlock Holmes story was not lost upon the Conan Doyle Estate. In due course, it did appear — only to have its authorship quickly claimed by an unknown, retired English architect named Arthur Whitaker (born 1882). Whitaker said that he had written it in 1910 and sold it for ten guineas to Sir Arthur, who had declined any col-

laboration but was willing to pay for the possible use of the story idea. When this claim surfaced, the reaction of the Conan Doyle Estate was immediate, direct, and vitriolic. It was also premature; Whitaker was able to prove that the story was his work. And so it became known that "The Man Who Was Wanted," instead of being the sixty-first Canonical adventure, was only a pastiche.

It may, however, have introduced the fashion of writing new adventures that would attempt to rival the authentic ones in tone and length; pastiches were becoming imitation rather than parody.

The Exploits of Sherlock Holmes. The most successful imitators of the tales were Doyle's son Adrian and a collaborator, John Dickson Carr, who had written many detective stories of his own, as well as the authorized biography of Doyle. In 1952-53 a dozen stories, the first six by the two collaborators, the latter six by Doyle alone, were published in *Collier's* magazine, where many of the original tales had appeared forty years earlier. Book editions appeared in 1954 and several times thereafter, under the title *The Exploits of Sherlock Holmes*.

These are the story titles, in the order in which they appear in the collected edition (slightly rearranged from their magazine publication):

"The Adventure of the Seven Clocks"
"The Adventure of the Gold Hunter"
"The Adventure of the Wax Gamblers"
"The Adventure of the Highgate Miracle"
"The Adventure of the Black Baronet"
"The Adventure of the Sealed Room"
"The Adventure of Foulkes Rath"
"The Adventure of the Abbas Ruby"
"The Adventure of the Two Women"
"The Adventure of the Dark Angels" (previously, "Demon Angels")
"The Adventure of the Deptford Horror"
"The Adventure of the Red Widow"

Reaction naturally varied, although it is clear in retrospect that these stories, whether or not of Canonical quality, are much better than most pastiches that have followed them. E. T. Buxton Jr. reviewed them for the *Baker Street Journal* and was not uncomplimentary:

> At least two and possibly three of these are of very fine quality. "The Sealed Room" is the perfect story. There is not one false note in it, and the plot is good, a logical, concealed key and a keenly deduced solution by Holmes. It is certainly above average, a better story, for instance, than as good ones as "The Cardboard Box" or "The Golden Pince-Nez". The other first-rate tale is "The Black Baronet".... The third story of high merit is "The Deptford Horror." In suspense, danger and horror it is exceeded only by "The Speckled Band"....
>
> It is the first four stories in the book that are defective — they are just *not* Sherlock Holmes.... All four stories suffer from out-of-tune use of words and character attitude.

August Derleth. Shortly after the publication of the Canon came to an end, a student at the University of Wisconsin, August Derleth, wrote to ask Doyle whether there would be more tales. Learning that there were not, he determined to write substitutes himself, and choosing a page at random from his desk calendar, he scribbled the note, "In re: Sherlock Holmes". When the date thus selected arrived, he sat down and wrote "The Adventure of the Black Narcissus", which was subsequently published in *Dragnet* magazine for February 1929. More stories followed, enough to make a book, which was inevitably titled *In Re: Sherlock Holmes* (1945).

Derleth did not venture to use the names of Holmes and Watson in his stories. He called his hero Solar Pons, the companion Dr. Lyndon Parker, the arch-villain Baron Ennesfred Kroll, the venue Praed Street. No reader can be deceived. Wrote Vincent Starrett later: "Solar Pons is not a caricature of Sherlock Holmes. He is, rather, a clever impersonator, with a twinkle in his eye, which tells us that he knows he is not Sherlock Holmes, and knows that *we* know it, but that he hopes we will like him anyway for what he symbolizes."

In Re: Sherlock Holmes was retitled *The Adventures of Solar Pons* in some later editions. It was followed by other collections of stories: *The Memoirs of Solar Pons* (1951), *The Return* (1958), *The Reminiscences* (1961), *The Casebook* (1965), and *The Chronicles* (1973). There is also a novel, *Mr. Fairlie's Final Journey* (1968). Derleth had at one time intended to duplicate the Sherlockian Canon, and ended up with more stories than the sixty required. Miscellaneous Pontine material appeared in *Praed Street Papers* (1965) and *A Praed Street Dossier* (1968). Sherlockians welcomed the tales of Solar Pons with enthusiasm. A society of "Praed Street Irregulars" was organized by Luther Norris, a noted Sherlockian collector in Los Angeles, and flourished for a few years, publishing *The Pontine Dossier* as its journal, 1967-71.

August Derleth (born February 24, 1909; died July 4, 1971) was a prolific writer in many branches of fiction, with a special interest in books that reflected and interpreted rural Wisconsin. For Sherlockians, he continues to be acknowledged as, in Julian Wolff's words, "the greatest serious imitator of the Master". He is also the first writer to create a novel, as opposed to a short story, in the Canonical tradition. Derleth's work is unique in having inspired the publication of pastiches of its own, tales by Basil Copper, beginning with *The Dossier of Solar Pons* (1979).

Nicholas Meyer. A new kind of pastiche became instantly popular with the publication of Nicholas Meyer's *The Seven-Per-Cent Solution* in 1974. Although its Foreword speaks of "a surfeit of forgeries" already in existence, there had been nothing like it — a novel-length serious text presented as an authentic Canonical tale, one of Watson's manuscripts newly discovered and committed to print. (A possible exception: *A Study in Terror*, Ellery Queen's 1966 novel connecting Holmes with the Jack the Ripper murders.) This one was a sensation, achieving success both in hardback and in paperback, and then becoming a well-received film.

The Seven-Per-Cent Solution purports to tell the true story of the events of 1891, the period of Holmes's obsession with Professor Moriarty, which in this interpretation is not his successful investigation and defeat of the master-criminal's gang, but his descent into drug-induced paranoia, Moriarty being an innocent mathematics teacher and Holmes's childhood tutor:

> "Dr. Watson, your friend is persuaded that I am some sort of —" he groped for the words — "criminal mastermind. Of the most depraved order," he added with a helpless shrug, throwing up his hands. "Now I ask you, sir: in all honesty — can you see in me the remotest trappings of such an individual?"

Watson takes Holmes under his care and entices him to Vienna, where the young Dr. Sigmund Freud is gaining renown for his cures of cocaine addicts. So much of the story is quite plausible: Freud did himself use cocaine, break the habit, and become interested in the treatment of addiction. Meyer's narrative continues: Holmes, weaned from his drugs, stumbles into a mystery and of course solves it, averting "a European war". Final revelations follow as Freud hypnotizes Holmes to find out about the traumas of his childhood.

Meyer (born 1945) already had one minor movie script to his credit. He told interviewers that he had always enjoyed Sherlock Holmes in a casual way, but became seriously interested while he was working in New York as a film industry publicist: "There was this little bar I used to go to after work; one evening I saw a young lady there whose acquaintance I sought to make. We got onto the subject of Holmes, and I was astounded by how much this young woman knew about those stories. After that I went back and reread the entire canon." He wrote *The Seven-Per-Cent Solution* when the screen-writers' strike of 1973 deprived him of more immediate work, and it made him an immediate success. After the book, and the film that followed, he became a director as well as a writer, delivering "Time After Time" (1979), a film about H. G. Wells and Jack the Ripper that intrigued many Sherlockians, and "Star Trek II: The Wrath of Khan", among other successes.

A sequel to Meyer's remarkable work was *The West End Horror* (1976), in which he brings Holmes and Watson into contact with George Bernard Shaw, Bram Stoker, and Gilbert and Sullivan.

Modern pastiche novels. Many imitators followed, none of them as successful, or as well written, as the original; some were workmanlike, others appallingly bad. These novel-length pastiches, mostly in trade paperback format, make up a body of material many times longer than the original Canon. In a few cases these books have been convincing, well-told mystery stories involving Holmes — an outstanding example being *The Quallsford Inheritance* (1986) by Lloyd Biggle, Jr. Also receiving much acclaim from Sherlockians have been three titles by Canadian author Beth Greenwood: *Sherlock Holmes and the Case of the Raleigh Legacy* (1986), *Sherlock Holmes and the Case of Sabina Hall* (1988), *Sherlock Holmes and the Thistle of Scotland* (1989).

But there are many other books about which the complaints jostle one another for priority. To begin with, the Watsonian style is not so easy to imitate, especially for American writers who put American slang and idiom into his mouth, and make a hopeless muddle of British titles of nobility. Watson's (that is to say, Doyle's) prose is invariably clear; sentences like these, not difficult to find in pastiches, make the sensitive reader wince:

- I was aware of what he spoke.
- "Let me disagree on that point," stated Holmes.
- I can only say, with medical retrospect, that it was like the sensation in the *glans penis* at the moment of *ejaculatio*, only it rapidly spread throughout my entire body in one hot glorious wave of molton [*sic*] pleasure.

Watson also knows the subtleties of the usage of "shall" and "will", and can spell. He is also, as Sherlockians have enjoyed pointing out, unreliable about dates, train times and other such details, but perhaps not so unreliable as authors who have their Victorian characters send telegrams from a railway station, mention "blocks" as a unit of distance, or imagine that Holmes might eat waffles for breakfast. Still more important, Watson's stories have a dignity which the pastiches frequently lack, presenting as they do riots in the streets of Cambridge, explicit sexual encounters of various kinds, and astonishing behaviour on Holmes's part. In one he plays his violin to entertain the patrons of an Italian restaurant, in another he rides a horse. Nicholas Meyer started this trend by compelling the Holmes of *The Seven-Per-Cent Solution* to wield a coal-shovel as he helps propel a rushing railway train. Dramatic physical action is not unknown to the Holmes of the Canon, who wields a screwdriver in "Lady Frances Carfax" and wrestles in the grass in "The Naval Treaty", but for the authors of pastiches it is his daily routine.

They also portray him rubbing shoulders with every possible figure of history or fiction. Among the characters who have been introduced into pastiches of the past two decades are these, and many others:

Prince Albert of Monaco	W. G. Grace
Annie Besant	Adolf Hitler
Professor Challenger	Dr. Jekyll
Aleister Crowley	Karl Marx
Benjamin Disraeli	Hiram Maxim
Arthur Conan Doyle	Hercule Poirot
Count Dracula	Ramanujan
Edwin Drood	Rasputin
Alfred Dreyfus	Theodore Roosevelt
Edward VII	Baron Rothschild
Friedrich Engels	Rupert of Hentzau
Sigmund Freud	Tarzan
Fu Manchu	Oscar Wilde
William Ewart Gladstone	Virginia Woolf

In story after story, as the fame of these characters perhaps suggests, Holmes finds himself required to solve mysteries on which the fate of the civilized world depends. The outcome of World War I turns on his actions, or the black arts of a master-magician will enable him to rule the world, or the huge gold reserves that

stabilize international economics may disappear. In *The Earthquake Machine* (1976), by Austin Mitchelson and Nicholas Utechin, Holmes is cabled to come at once: "Your country at stake." In several of the books, as he did in Meyer's *The Seven-Per-Cent Solution*, Holmes averts a war. Such a motif was still being used at the end of the 1980's, in *Sherlock Holmes and the Mark of the Beast* (1989) by Ronald C. Weyman. The extreme is reached in the frankly parodic *The Strange Case of the End of Civilisation as We Know It*, the published script of a British television film (1977). Even when an author cannot possibly twist his plot to include international spies, assassinations, wars, statesmen and Armageddon, he may at least have Holmes call the case "the most serious I have yet encountered" or make equally extravagant mutterings.

A disproportionate number of the novel-length pastiches involve Irene Adler or Mycroft Holmes; a disproportionate number follow Nicholas Meyer's lead in reinterpreting the relationship between Holmes and Moriarty, or in shedding new, if somewhat questionable, light on Holmes's character and origins. (Meyer attributed his introduction of adultery and murder into Holmes's childhood memories to the speculations of that solid Sherlockian scholar Trevor S. Hall in *Sherlock Holmes: Ten Literary Studies* [1969].) A book whose title is *Exit Sherlock Holmes* (1977, by Robert Lee Hall) can hardly do otherwise than end with Holmes's departure from the scene, and in a thoroughly unexpected way; *The Last Sherlock Holmes Story* (1978, by Michael Dibdin) makes and keeps a similar promise. *The Adventure of Sherlock Holmes' Smarter Brother* (1975, by Gilbert Pearlman, based on a Gene Wilder film of the same year) also delivers what its title promises, and reveals Moriarty behind the villainy into the bargain.

Some of these works, including *Smarter Brother*, are intended strictly for laughs, but others are apparent attempts at serious fiction using Holmes and Watson. By and large, they lack the complexity and verbal texture of the originals, as well as the modest (but achievable) ambitions in plot and social significance. By 1980, many Sherlockians had come to dread any work ostensibly about Holmes that included an author's note explaining the origin of the manuscript in a battered tin dispatch-box inherited from a great-uncle or bought by a friend at an estate auction. At the end of the 1980's, Dame Jean Conan Doyle made it known that she wanted the appearance of pastiches to stop — it seemed best, she suggested, that authors should invent their own characters. In the United States, where most such material was published, she still controlled some copyrights on the Canonical stories, and was able to enforce that preference, so that publication of commercial pastiches ceased. Elsewhere, some have continued to appear, but the vast stream that flowed from 1975 to about 1985 has dried up.

Variations on a theme. Of special interest have been a few novels that look at Holmes and his milieu from a less familiar viewpoint. The earliest of these were a pair of sensitive and brilliant novels by John Gardner (not the American novelist of the same name, but a British author of detective fiction). They are *The Return of Moriarty* (1974, British edition titled simply *Moriarty*) and *The*

Revenge of Moriarty (1975). Their premise is that, like Holmes, Moriarty escaped death at the falls of the Reichenbach. *The Return of Moriarty* thus tells in a new way the events of "The Empty House", in April 1894; its strength is the portrayal, exciting but not melodramatic, of Moriarty's underworld empire, where sophisticated ingenuity is coupled with the rough work of thugs and whores. *The Revenge of Moriarty* is set two years later, as the Napoleon of Crime, having escaped to America when London was made too hot to hold him, returns, and incidentally plans the theft of the Mona Lisa from the Louvre. Holmes figures in both books, though their chief detective is Inspector Angus McCready Crow of Scotland Yard. Even at the end of the second volume, Moriarty escapes his clutches; the scene is thus set for a third Gardner epic, which however has not appeared.

Other attempts in that genre included these:

- *Enter the Lion: A Posthumous Memoir of Mycroft Holmes* (1979) by Michael P. Hodel and Sean M. Wright.
- *I, Sherlock Holmes* (1977), ostensibly Holmes's own memoirs, by Michael Harrison.
- *The Supreme Adventure of Inspector Lestrade* (1985), by M. J. Trow, who subsequently wrote several other increasingly surrealistic novels about the life and work of Inspector Sholto Lestrade of Scotland Yard.
- *The Private Life of Dr. Watson* (1983), by Michael Hardwick.
- *Good Night, Mr. Holmes* (1990) and *Good Morning, Irene* (1991), by Carole Nelson Douglas, in which Irene Adler finally receives a convincing and sympathetic treatment.

Beyond all these works are a multitude of exceptions and special treatments, from *Sherlock Holmes, Bridge Detective* (1973, by George Gooden and Frank Thomas) to *Trouble in Bugland* (1983, by William Kotzwinkle), in which Inspector Mantis, an insect in Sherlockian garb, solves mysteries in a world of Victorian insects. Especially popular with Sherlockians have been the comic works of Robert L. Fish, short stories appearing in *Ellery Queen's Mystery Magazine* and collected in *The Incredible Schlock Homes* (1966) and its sequels. In the likes of "The Adventure of the Spectacled Band" and "The Adventure of the Snared Drummer", Schlock Homes of Bagel Street indulges in puns and slapstick:

> "You have arrived at a crucial moment, Watney!" said he, his keen eyes glittering. "If this litmus paper remains blue, then all is well. If it turns red — then I am afraid we shall have to depend upon store-bought whiskey for our afternoon libations!"

Theatre

The stage adaptations of the Canon that can be presumed to be closest to Doyle's ideal are his own plays of *The Speckled Band* (1910) and *The Crown Diamond* (1921). The former was a success in the original production with H. A. Saintsbury as Holmes; Charles Millward took over when the play was brought to

New York after almost five months on the London stage, but Saintsbury returned in a 1921 revival. The script was published (by Samuel French) in 1912. As for *The Crown Diamond*, its run was short, its revivals have been few, and the script has never been published; it became the short story "The Mazarin Stone" just a few months after its first performance, in Bristol, with Dennis Neilson-Terry as Holmes. Neither play was as successful as the much greater play, loosely based on a draft by Doyle, that had established Holmes's image on the stage before the turn of the century.

William Gillette. For two generations of Americans, the face of Sherlock Holmes was the face of William Gillette, who played Holmes from 1899 through 1932, to unvarying acclaim. His principal vehicle was *Sherlock Holmes*, a play he wrote himself, in circumstances described by P. M. Stone in a special supplement to the *Baker Street Journal* in 1953:

> Some enterprising reporter for a New York newspaper . . . had reported that A. Conan Doyle had stated that, should anyone ever suggest a play based on the Sherlock Holmes stories, his own choice would be William Gillette for the leading role. Doyle had, in fact, said nothing of the kind, and at that time had not even met the actor. Later, however, Charles Frohman, the famous theatrical producer, saw the newspaper paragraph, and, realizing its potential, turned it over to Gillette. . . . A year or more later, Gillette received a second and more urgent message from Frohman requesting him to prepare at once a stage version of the great detective's career, the producer having meanwhile secured Doyle's permission. . . .
>
> Following an exhaustive study of the renowned detective's achievements, as set forth by the indefatigable Dr. Watson, Gillette wrote to Conan Doyle, inquiring as to how many liberties he could take with his famous literary character. Doyle is reported to have replied that Gillette could "marry the detective — murder him — or do anything he pleased."

Any qualms Doyle may have had about Gillette were apparently stilled when the two men met in May 1899, and the author found the actor "the living image of Sherlock Holmes", as biographer John Dickson Carr puts it.

The resulting playscript, though publicly described as being by Doyle and Gillette jointly, was entirely Gillette's work. The play had its premiere October 23, 1899, at the Star Theatre in Buffalo, and then moved to New York for a run of seven months at the Garrick Theatre. From September through April it ran at the Lyceum Theatre in London, where Dr. Watson had met Mary Morstan in *The Sign of the Four* fourteen years previously. Productions were numerous, if not continuous, over the next few years, sometimes in New York and sometimes in other cities across North America. Gillette returned to the role in 1915 and again in 1923, and beginning in the fall of 1929 a "Farewell Tour" took him to dozens of communities. Gillette's last recorded appearance in his great play came March 19, 1932, in Princeton, New Jersey.

The play is melodramatic to a modern audience, its dramatic climax — in which a lighted cigar glows in a darkened dungeon, tricking the villainous Moriarty into believing that Holmes is still in the room — likely to draw snickers. The heroine, Alice Faulkner, gets Holmes at the end. In a plot largely drawn from "A Scandal in Bohemia" and "The Final Problem", though with echoes from several other Canonical tales skillfully woven into the story, the subsidiary villain, James Larrabee, is as thoroughly foiled as Moriarty himself. Gillette did not carry even the principal members of his company with him through his career, so that many Dr. Watsons and many Miss Faulkners were seen; on the farewell tour Wallis Clark and Peg Entwistle played those roles. The play was revived occasionally after Gillette's death, but returned to general favour in 1974, when the Royal Shakespeare Company mounted a production in England (brought to America 1974-76) starring John Wood. It is now frequently seen, the text being in print from Samuel French, Inc., the chief publishers of playscripts, who first issued it in 1922. The published text carries copyright notices and declares that the play "is subject to a royalty", payable to Samuel French. A text was also published by Doubleday in 1935. Gillette recorded an adaptation of his play for ABC radio in 1935, having done a half-hour version of "The Speckled Band" in 1930. Carleton Hobbs starred in it on BBC radio in 1953.

A lesser play by Gillette is *The Painful Predicament of Sherlock Holmes*, a brief comedy in which the great detective has no lines whatsoever to speak. He presented it first in 1905, and occasionally thereafter; its chief claim to historical fame is that a very young Charlie Chaplin played Billy, the page, at the London production in October 1905. The text was published in 1955.

William Hooker Gillette, the actor who started this branch of the Holmes industry, was born July 24, 1853, in Connecticut, which remained his home. The mansion (with a working railroad in its grounds) that he built with his vast earnings from the stage is near Hadlyme, Connecticut, and is now operated as Gillette Castle State Park. Gillette made his professional debut in 1875, and reached fame in 1896 when he wrote and starred in a play about the American Civil War, *Secret Service*. It was not long after that triumph that he began work on *Sherlock Holmes*, and *Secret Service* remained in his repertoire for the next three decades. He was still playing Holmes as he neared eighty, P. M. Stone recalls:

> On Gillette's first entrance, as he slowly removed his overcoat and seated himself at the foot of the staircase before sending up his card to Miss Faulkner, the entire house stood up, and, after an impressive moment of silence, extended to the distinguished actor a tumultuous greeting in tribute to the genuine affection and admiration in which he was held. No doubt his thoughts drifted back to that auspicious evening of September 13th, in 1875, when he had made his first important theatrical appearance at the old Globe Theatre in Washington Street [in Boston].

If enthusiasts of Holmes admired Gillette, he returned their respect, attending the 1934 dinner of the Baker Street Irregulars and being listed as a BSI member in 1935. He died April 29, 1937. An exhibition in his memory was staged in 1970-71 at the Nook Farm Visitors' Center in Hartford, Connecticut, and the published catalogue includes photographs of him in various plays, as well as fragments of valuable information. Also informative is *Molding the Image*, a brochure produced to accompany a 1983 exhibition of Gillette material at the University of Minnesota. The best-known image of Gillette is the cartoon by

"Spy" (Leslie Ward) that appeared in *Vanity Fair* magazine. That fully coloured drawing has been reproduced at least twice as a print for modern Sherlockians' walls. Gillette is also acknowledged to have been Frederic Dorr Steele's ideal Holmes, though not directly the model for his illustrations. It is generally thought that the curved pipe now associated with Holmes, but not mentioned in the Canon or seen in early illustrations, was introduced by Gillette, who found that his speeches were more audible over it, and his face more visible, than through a straight pipe.

Modern plays. The only important Sherlockian play for several decades after William Gillette was *The Return of Sherlock Holmes* by Harold Terry and Arthur Rose, produced in Cardiff and London in 1923-24 (starring Eille Norwood) and revived in 1930 and 1953. It was largely based on "Lady Frances Carfax", "Charles Augustus Milverton" and "The Empty House". A number of minor productions can also be unearthed, including *Sherlock Holmes* by Ouida Rathbone, which had just four performances (one in Boston and three in New York) in 1953.

Also in 1953, Holmes came to the stage of the Sadler's Wells Ballet Theatre, London, in the production *The Great Detective*, choreographed by Margaret Dale and with music by Richard Arnell. Kenneth Macmillan danced both the Great Detective, in deerstalker and inverness, and "The Infamous Professor", i.e. Moriarty; Stanley Holden was "His Friend, the Doctor", i.e. Watson. Such a *jeu d'esprit* was not seen again until the National Tap-Dance Company of Canada staged *The Hound of the Baskervilles* in 1987.

A landmark production was *Baker Street*, a musical which opened on New York's Broadway February 16, 1965, after tryouts in Boston and Toronto. The music and lyrics were by Marian Grudeff and Raymond Jessel; the book, taken chiefly from "A Scandal in Bohemia" and "The Final Problem", was by Jerome Coopersmith. Fritz Weaver appeared as Holmes, Peter Sallis as Watson, Martin Gabel as Moriarty, and Inga Swenson as Irene Adler. *Baker Street* is a beautiful piece of entertainment, if no more plausible than any other work in which a love interest must be balanced with a heart-stopping Sherlockian plot. Not surprisingly, some of the best songs are put in the mouth of Irene Adler — "Letters" and "Finding Words for Spring" — and one can forgive the authors for giving her a duet with Holmes, "What a Night This Is Going to Be". More unexpected, and perhaps the most touching moment of the play, is the song given to Watson, "A Married Man". And Holmes does not lose his dignity when he sings his solo in Act I, scene 7:

> I have waited in vain
> For someone to explain
> What love conceivably can offer
> The cerebral type of man,
> But no one ever has
> And no one ever will
> For no one ever can —
> But, ah!

The cold, clear world of the intellect
Is the world that I revere.
In the pure, dry air of the scientist
I am in my proper sphere. . . .

Baker Street ran on Broadway for 311 performances
 there have been a few revivals. The book and lyrics were published in 1966
(*Baker Street: A Musical Adventure of Sherlock Holmes*), and several 33-rpm
records were released with some or all of the music, including the original cast
album from MGM Records in 1965.

During the Sherlock Holmes boom that followed the 1974 revival of Gillette's *Sherlock Holmes*, dozens of minor plays took the stage. There were also a
few major productions in the 1970's and 1980's:

* *Sherlock's Last Case*, by Matthew Lang, first produced in London in the summer
of 1974, and subsequently staged in several other British cities. It came to Broadway in the summer of 1987 with Frank Langella in the title role.
* *The Incredible Murder of Cardinal Tosca*, by Alden Nowlan and Walter
Learning, first produced by Theatre New Brunswick (Fredericton) in January
1978. Later that year it was seen in Toronto and elsewhere in Canada, and the
script was published by Learning Productions of Fredericton.
* *The Crucifer of Blood*, by Paul Giovanni, first staged on Broadway in
1978-79 with Paxton Whitehead as Holmes and Glenn Close as the heroine, Irene
St. Claire. A television production in 1991 starred Charlton Heston (who had also
appeared in *Crucifer* in Los Angeles in 1981, with Jeremy Brett as Watson).
* *The Secret of Sherlock Holmes*, by Jeremy Paul, starring the Holmes and
Watson made familiar by Granada Television in the 1980's: Jeremy Brett and
Edward Hardwicke. It opened in London September 22, 1988, and played for a
long run amid constant rumours of a North American tour.

Film

It is plausibly said that Sherlock Holmes has appeared in more films, and been
represented by more actors, than any other character. Ronald DeWaal in his
World Bibliography estimates the number of films as "over 150" as of 1974.
They range from early, ephemeral pieces and long-lost comedies to modern feature films, as well as the classic Basil Rathbone movies of the 1940's which for
four decades defined the public image of Holmes. Two large-format volumes
deal exclusively with the subject: *Sherlock Holmes on the Screen* (1977), by
Robert W. Pohle Jr. and Douglas C. Hart, and *The Films of Sherlock Holmes*
(1978), by Chris Steinbrunner and Norman Michaels.

The earliest such work is a mere eighteen feet of 16-millimetre film titled
Sherlock Holmes Baffled — "clearly made for viewing on a mutoscope or peep-
show machine", according to Michael Pointer, who discovered it. It was filmed
April 26, 1900. The films of the following two decades — several from Denmark, others from Italy and Germany, as well as England and the United States
— were mostly short and, as DeWaal puts it, "pseudo-Sherlockian", treating
Holmes as a figure of fun. Comic actor Mack Sennett made several Holmes
comedies in 1911-1912, directed by film pioneer D. W. Griffith.

After the 1916 film of William Gillette's play was released, however, other serious films followed, including forty-seven starring Eille Norwood. All but one of his films co-starred Hubert Willis as Watson. They began with a full-length "Hound of the Baskervilles" in 1921 and went on with forty-five two-reelers (length about 35 minutes apiece) based on individual cases, chosen in an unusual order. The first series (1921) began with *The Dying Detective* and *The Devil's Foot* before continuing with the inevitable *A Scandal in Bohemia. The Final Problem* was held until last of all, concluding the third series of films (1923). Later that year Norwood co-starred with Arthur Cullin as Watson in a full-length *Sign of the Four.* Eille Norwood (real name Anthony Brett; born October 11, 1861; died December 24, 1948) also had a career as a stage actor, and did play Holmes on the stage in 1923 in *The Return of Sherlock Holmes.* Arthur Conan Doyle — who had no opportunity to see most of the great Holmesian actors — thought very highly of Norwood, paying this tribute in *Memories and Adventures*:

> He has that rare quality which can only be described as glamour, which compels you to watch an actor eagerly even when he is doing nothing. He has the brooding eye which excites expectation and he has also a quite unrivalled power of disguise. My only criticism of the films is that they introduce telephones, motor cars and other luxuries of which the Victorian Holmes never dreamed.

Norwood was succeeded on screen by Arthur Wontner, who made *TheSleeping Cardinal* (retitled *Sherlock Holmes' Fatal Hour* for an American audience) in 1930, *The Missing Rembrandts* in 1932, *The Sign of Four* in 1932, *The Triumph of Sherlock Holmes* (*The Valley of Fear*) in 1934, and *The Silver Blaze* (*Murder at the Baskervilles*) in 1936. Wontner (1875-1960) maintained an interest in Holmesian matters, accepting an honorary membership in the Sherlock Holmes Society of London, and was judged by some as the finest portrayer Holmes ever had — "the veritable fathomer of Baker Street in person", said Vincent Starrett.

Among the other portrayers of Holmes in the early film period were these:

- John Barrymore in *Sherlock Holmes* (retitled *Moriarty* in England), 1922.
- Clive Brook in *The Return of Sherlock Holmes*, 1929, and *Sherlock Holmes*, 1932.
- Raymond Massey in *The Speckled Band*, 1931.

Basil Rathbone. Steinbrunner and Michaels in *The Films of Sherlock Holmes* explain how the screen's most influential Holmes came to be:

> In 1939, at a Hollywood cocktail party — so legend has it — Twentieth Century-Fox studio head Darryl Zanuck suddenly turned to a fellow guest, British actor Basil Rathbone, and declared he would make a perfect Sherlock Holmes. . . .
> "Hi there, Sherlock, how's Watson?" Variants of the chant were to haunt Rathbone the rest of his career. In his autobiography, *In and Out of Character,* Rathbone laments at "being 'typed,' more completely 'typed' than any other classic actor has ever been or ever will be again. . . ."

The films that star Rathbone as Sherlock Holmes — fourteen of them, made in two brief bursts — were successes when they first appeared and have been perennials ever since. It is difficult to find a week when one of them is not being shown on some television station's late movie, and video rental has given them a whole new audience. A full study of them is *Ready When You Are, Mr. Rathbone* (1992), by Roger Johnson.

Only two of the fourteen films were made by Twentieth Century-Fox; they are the two generally considered best, and certainly the two most faithful to to Holmes's late-Victorian environment. Steinbrunner and Michaels again:

> Here, quite innovatively, Holmes was sent back some fifty years and more to the original time in which the stories were set, accentuating the rich Victorian details separating that more peaceful epoch with a disordered 1939, where war-clouds were already gathering. It has been said that converting *Hound* into a "costume classic" was less a daring than a commercial move, very right for audiences thirsting for escapist entertainment; nonetheless, the idea of a gaslit Holmes was strikingly original, quite set apart from the many modern-dress Sherlocks familiar to thirties moviegoers.

The Hound of the Baskervilles was released in March 1939; it co-starred Richard Greene as Sir Henry Baskerville and Wendy Barrie as Beryl Stapleton. While *The Hound* follows the original story, *The Adventures*, released six months later, is only loosely based on anything Canonical apart from the villainy of Professor Moriarty. The plot has to do with an attempted theft of the Crown Jewels, and ends with a shootout and Moriarty's presumed death at the Tower of London. The heroine, Ann Brandon, was played by Ida Lupino; a bearded Moriarty, by George Zucco.

Two years later, Rathbone began to play Holmes again, grinding out a dozen films for a competing studio, Universal, between the fall of 1942 and the summer of 1946. In these short features (each runs slightly longer than an hour) Holmes was returned to the present day, wearing fedora and trench-coat and jumping onto automobile running-boards. None is based in any significant way on Canonical material; the films frankly attempted to show a Holmes tackling "problems of the present day", which in several cases meant the Nazi evils of World War II. These are the Rathbone films made for Universal Studios:

- *Sherlock Holmes and the Voice of Terror*, 1942, vaguely based on "His Last Bow" but transferred to the World War II era; starring Evelyn Ankers, Reginald Denny, Thomas Gomez.
- *Sherlock Holmes and the Secret Weapon*, 1942, in which Moriarty is hired by the Nazis to steal the new invention; starring Lionel Atwill (as Moriarty), William Post Jr., Kaaren Verne.
- *Sherlock Holmes in Washington*, 1943, about counter-espionage and kidnapping on an American train; starring Marjorie Lord, George Zucco, Henry Daniell.
- *Sherlock Holmes Faces Death*, 1943, vaguely based on "The Musgrave Ritual" but set at an army convalescent home; starring Hillary Brooke, Arthur Margetson, Halliwell Hobbes.

• *The Spider Woman*, 1944, about a series of suicides that turn out to be murders; starring Gale Sondergaard, Vernon Downing, Alec Craig.
• *The Scarlet Claw*, 1944, about a series of killings in a Québec village that are thought to be supernatural but of course prove to be murders; starring Gerald Hamer, Miles Mander, Arthur Hohl. An epilogue to this film, released shortly after the Québec Conference that set the direction for the last year of the war, gives Holmes an opportunity to speak of a golden Anglo-American future.
• *The Pearl of Death*, 1944, more or less based on "The Six Napoleons"; starring Evelyn Ankers, Ian Wolfe, Rondo Hatton.
• *The House of Fear*, 1945, about a group of men living together in a castle who die mysteriously one by one; starring Aubrey Mather, Paul Cavanagh, Holmes Herbert.
• *The Woman in Green*, 1945, about a series of women murdered and mutilated in London; starring Hillary Brooke, Henry Daniell (as Moriarty, who dies again), Paul Cavanagh.
• *Pursuit to Algiers*, 1945, about the attempt to return King Nikolas to Algiers aboard ship; starring Marjorie Riordan, Leslie Vincent, Martin Kosleck.
• *Terror by Night*, 1946, about the transportation of the Star of Rhodesia diamond from London to Edinburgh; starring Alan Mowbray (as Colonel Moran), Renee Godfrey, Mary Forbes.
• *Dressed to Kill*, 1946, in Britain retitled *Sherlock Holmes and the Secret Code*, about the search for stolen engraving plates for Bank of England notes, the clues being concealed in music-boxes; starring Patricia Morrison, Edmond Breon, Frederick Worlock.

Besides Rathbone and Bruce as Holmes and Watson, the films include two continuing characters: Dennis Hoey as Lestrade and Mary Gordon as Mrs. Hudson. Several other actors provided what Steinbrunner and Michaels call "a sort of stock company", appearing in various roles, although the two films that require Moriarty present him through different actors.

But the memorable figure is Basil Rathbone (born June 13, 1892; died July 21, 1967). "The physical resemblance of Rathbone to the Sidney Paget illustrations was quite striking," says one critic, while another maintains that he looked like the Holmes drawn by Frederic Dorr Steele. The energy and arrogance Rathbone shows, at least in his finer scenes, are certainly those of Holmes, although the portrayal cannot be called subtle. Rathbone even snaps, "Elementary, my dear Watson!" now and then, a phrase that never crossed Holmes's lips. He came to the character late in his acting career, having first reached the stage in 1911 and first appeared in film in 1921. In 1930 he played New York detective Philo Vance in *The Bishop Murder Case*. Through the 1930s he was seen in adventure films, and he returned to that genre even after his early appearances as Holmes. In 1940, for example, he made *The Mark of Zorro* (he was the villain, opposite Tyrone Power), and there were other films late in his career, even including *Ghost in the Invisible Bikini*, co-starring Rathbone and Boris Karloff. He also made stage appearances and did much radio work, but never escaped the image of Sherlock Holmes with which he remains associated twenty-five years after his death. He says a few words about Holmes in his autobiography, *In and Out of Character* (1962).

Rathbone's Holmes is complemented in all these films by Nigel Bruce (born February 4, 1895; died October 8, 1953), who plays a decent but dunder-headed Watson. Scene after scene requires Bruce to make a fool of himself with women and children, in awkward physical situations, or simply by lagging hopelessly far behind the insight and energetic action displayed by Holmes. In some of the later films, as Rathbone's enthusiasm was visibly failing, Bruce did get fatter parts to play. "In the climax in at least two of the films," Steinbrunner and Michaels note, "it is he who saves Holmes after the latter has stupidly allowed himself to be trapped by the enemy." But Bruce's Watson is most memorable for the fool he manages to make of himself — quacking like a duck to distract a child in *Dressed to Kill*, for example. Already an experienced actor before he fell in with Rathbone, Bruce is deservedly given much of the credit for the success of their films.

During the years they were making their films together, Rathbone and Bruce also presented Holmes and Watson on radio in more than 200 half-hour episodes.

The era of colour. Holmes was brought to the screen in colour for the first time in *The Hound of the Baskervilles*, a 1959 film starring Peter Cushing, about which few Sherlockians are neutral. It was made by Hammer Film Productions, a British studio previously specializing in horror movies, and it does emphasize the chilling and grotesque aspects of the story. Some liberties are taken, particularly with the character of Cecile (Beryl) Stapleton as played by Marla Landi, and with other aspects of the plot as well. The film also stars André Morell as Watson and, oddly, Christopher Lee as Sir Henry Baskerville. Three years later, Lee appeared as Holmes instead, in *Sherlock Holmes und das Halsband des Todes* (1962), released in English in 1964 as *Sherlock Holmes and the Deadly Necklace*. This German production had Thorley Walters as Watson. Its plot is melodramatic, dealing with attempts by Moriarty (Hans Söhnker) to steal an ancient Egyptian necklace. Then in 1966 came *A Study in Terror*, based on the Ellery Queen novel that pits Holmes against Jack the Ripper. John Neville played Holmes, and Donald Houston was Watson.

The next important Holmes film was *The Private Life of Sherlock Holmes*, a 1970 comedy created by Billy Wilder. The film emphasizes its exploration of the relationship between Holmes (Robert Stephens) and Watson (Colin Blakely) and throws Holmes into a complex relationship with an attractive woman (played by Genevieve Page). The plot takes them to the shores of Loch Ness and gives Holmes an opportunity to meet a grateful Queen Victoria when he has foiled the obligatory enemy scheme. Christopher Lee appears as Mycroft Holmes. The film was considerably cut before release; there are occasional rumours that an uncut version will become available.

They Might Be Giants, released in 1971, is not a Victorian exploit, nor is it conventional in any other way. It stars George C. Scott as a retired judge who becomes convinced that he is Holmes, and Joanne Woodward as his psychiatrist, conveniently named Dr. Watson, who is caught up in increasingly surrealist adventures with him. Steinbrunner and Michaels say this about it:

> In truth, *They Might Be Giants* is every bit as fragile and tender as its cinematic predecessor, and indeed, like *Private Life*, was misunderstood, mutilated, and a box-office failure. . . . The climax is both ambivalent and poignant. Fleeing the police (sent by his brother), Justin [Holmes] and Mildred make their way to Central Park. There, in the dusk, they hear he clatter of horses' hoofs. Justin knows it is the forces of evil — Moriarty — and it may mean their deaths. Mildred Watson by this time has "crossed over," and shares in all of Justin's fancies. Together they will resist the unseen foe hurtling towards them, or die — as the screen is wiped into color.

There are few more touching scenes in all of Holmesian cinematography.

In 1975 Gene Wilder starred as Sigi Holmes in *The Adventure of Sherlock Holmes' Smarter Brother*, a lunatic affair also starring Marty Feldman as Orville Sacker of Scotland Yard and the delicious Madeline Kahn as the music-hall singer whose blackmailing case Sherlock Holmes's brother must handle. (There are brief appearances by Douglas Wilmer as Sherlock and Thorley Walters as Watson.)

The film based on Nicholas Meyer's novel about Holmes and Freud, *The Seven-Per-Cent Solution*, was a popular as well as a Sherlockian success, and did much to stimulate the Sherlockian "boom" that lasted through the late 1970's. Despite its modest budget (reports said it was made in twelve weeks for $4.2 million), it presented a constellation of stars: Nicol Williamson as Holmes, Alan Arkin as Sigmund Freud, Vanessa Redgrave as the chanteuse who must be rescued. The second half of the plot departs considerably from that in Meyer's novel. A review in the *New York Post* was less than complimentary:

> There's only one conceivable suspect in the case, and the story quickly devolves into an extended chase, complete with speeding locomotives and do-or-die sword fights. . . . The film is also dotted with the recurring, inter-cut image of a young boy ascending a staircase — an image that is apparently supposed to whet our appetite for a big psychological revelation.

Other reviewers enjoyed the film more, particularly praising director Herbert Ross. (The screenplay was the work of Meyer himself.) "The Seven-Per-Cent Solution" also starred Robert Duvall as Watson and Laurence Olivier as Moriarty. It opened October 24, 1976.

The other important and successful Holmes film of the modern era is the greatly admired *Murder by Decree*, released in 1979 and starring Christopher Plummer (born December 13, 1927) as Holmes and James Mason as a deliciously doddering Watson. A scene in which Holmes loses patience with Watson's finicky attempt to eat green peas is one of the gems of Sherlockian cinema. The film presents Holmes investigating the Jack the Ripper murders. The solution — based on some of the more improbable speculations of recent Ripperologists — involves Masonic rituals and a government cover-up to protect noted politicians and royalty; the long-drawn-out final scene of the film, in which Holmes confronts the prime minister (played by John Gielgud), is not its high point. More affecting is the role of Geneviève Bujold as a young woman hidden away in an asylum because she knows the guilty secret. A novelization of the film, by Robert Weverka, was published in 1979 (and copyright by "Saucy Jack Inc.").

A few other feature films have appeared in recent years:

- In 1978 Peter Cook (as Holmes) and Dudley Moore (as Watson and other characters) appeared in a comic version of *The Hound of the Baskervilles*.
- Steven Spielberg produced *Young Sherlock Holmes* in 1985, starring Nicholas Rowe as an eighteen-year-old Holmes who solves his first case in the company of schoolmate Watson (Alan Cox). It involves several murders, together with — in one reviewer's contemptuous summary — "an Egyptian cult that pours boiling hot goop over virgins during formal dress ceremonies with a lot of men shaved bald and chanting weird things". The film also uses spectacular special effects to represent drug hallucinations. Sophie Ward appears as the winsome Elizabeth.
- *Without a Clue*, released in 1988, was a comedy based on the premise that Watson (Ben Kingsley) was the brains of the partnership, Holmes (Michael Caine) an actor who bumbles through his role.

Increasingly, Sherlockian films are viewed on videotape rather than in theatres, and collectors excitedly trade information about the appearance of new titles on tape. A few films have also been issued on laser discs.

Radio

The slightly old-fashioned medium of radio seems perfectly suited to the stories of Holmes and Watson. Holmes has been heard over the air in North America, as well as in the Scandinavian countries and elsewhere, but above all, Holmes on radio is a British genre, having begun in 1938 with a single half-hour production of "Silver Blaze". Five years later Arthur Wontner, by then well known as a Holmes in film, starred in "The Boscombe Valley Mystery"; his Watson was Carleton Hobbs, later to be the greatest of radio Holmeses himself. Occasional other British productions followed, notably a 1954 series of twelve episodes starring John Gielgud as Holmes and Ralph Richardson as Watson, produced by the BBC Light Programme.

Carleton Hobbs. Even before the Light Programme gave Gielgud the chance to play the great detective, its BBC rival, the Home Service, had found the definitive radio Holmes. He was Carleton Hobbs (born June 18, 1898; died August 2, 1978), trained at the Royal Academy of Dramatic Arts, who had had a distinguished career on the stage (his debut was in 1924) and in films since 1924, as well as in radio. He was first heard October 15, 1952, in "The Naval Treaty", which was presented as part of "The Children's Hour", like sixteen programmes (including six stories each attempted twice) from 1952 through 1957. Hobbs was then transferred to the Light Programme, where he starred in "The Hound of the Baskervilles" in six episodes in 1958, and in fifty-six further programmes, his last being appropriately "His Last Bow" in July 1969. Most of the performances lasted thirty minutes, but there were ninety-minute interpretations of "A Study in Scarlet", "The Sign of the Four", "The Valley of Fear", and (with a different supporting cast from that of the 1958 series) "The Hound of the Baskervilles". All the stories were based on the Canon; by the end of his radio career Hobbs had presented all but two of the original tales ("The Creeping Man" and "The Veiled Lodger") at least once, eight twice, and five three times. The majority of the Hobbs broadcasts were based on adaptations by Michael Hardwick, prolific writer and broadcaster and well-known Sherlockian. (Hobbs himself became an honorary member of the Sherlock Holmes Society of London.) Hardwick wrote an appreciation of Hobbs on the latter's death in 1978:

> There was some correspondence in *Radio Times* once about the authentic nature of the voice of Holmes. In "The Stock-broker's Clerk" Watson refers to his "high, somewhat strident tones". Carleton Hobbs's tones were not noticeably high, and certainly not strident. Incisive is perhaps the word; the sharp edge which commands, varied with the warmth which endears. Hobbo was passing through his sixties when he recorded those series, which put him a couple of decades beyond Mr. Holmes's prime; but such is radio's deception with voice age, and such Hobbo's art, that he convinced utterly.

Throughout his radio career, Hobbs was complemented by the voice of Norman Shelley as Watson.

The United States. Holmes came to American radio in 1930 in the voice of William Gillette himself, who starred in "The Speckled Band" for half an hour on the evening of October 20. A week later a continuing series began, starring Richard Gordon as Holmes and Leigh Lovell as Watson; it stretched to 100 programmes, the last of them being heard in May 1933. That series was carried (as was Gillette's broacast) on NBC's two networks. It began with Canonical tales and ended with such plausible imitations as "The Case of Vamberry, the Wine Merchant" and "The Singular Affair of the Aluminum Crutch". The scripts were the work of Edith Meiser, a young actress, director, and writer whose work demonstrated her devotion to the Canon. Meiser (born May 9, 1898) was a Vassar graduate whose stage debut in 1921 had been followed by the making of reputations in directing, writing, and (with the firm of McKnight and Jordan) production; she also appeared in several films. Meiser maintained a life-long interest in the Canon, joining the Adventuresses of Sherlock Holmes and becoming, in 1991, one of the first women to be admitted as Baker Street Irregulars. A note by Bill Nadel and Ray Stanich in *Prescott's Press* in 1991 describes

> what would be a truly phenomenal second season of exploits on NBC's two major radio networks (the Red and the Blue) as well as their West Coast pickups. . . . The Holmes cast of Richard Gordon, Leigh Lovell, Lucille Wall, and even Miss Meiser herself would be performing the mystery scripts three times a week, all under the sponsorship of the G. Washington Coffee Company. An avid enthusiast of the Holmes Canon could pick up all three outings of the show each week, if he or she was fortunate enough to live in the Mid-west. Some would even sit by their radios with the Memorial Edition of the tales, checking on the faithfulness of Miss [Meiser's] adaptation.

As the golden age of North American radio continued, a second important series of Holmes exploits was broadcast from Hollywood. Its principal performers: Basil Rathbone and Nigel Bruce, delivering half-hour episodes as Holmes in the intervals of making their films in the same roles. These performances began with "Silver Blaze" on October 2, 1939; by the time they concluded with "The Singular Affair of the Baconian Cipher", on May 27, 1946, a total of 219 episodes had been broadcast. From 1939 through 1942, the Rathbone-Bruce broadcasts were on the NBC "Red" network, thereafter on the Mutual network. To modern listeners, familiar with at least a few of the episodes through scratchy recordings, the commercial sponsors are better known: the Household Finance Corp., Bromo-Quinine, Petri Wine. Edith Meiser was responsible for the scripts until late 1943; Denis Green, a British radio writer, and "Anthony Boucher", by then a recognized Sherlockian, then took over. "Clearly, Green and Boucher were serious about their Sherlockianism," say Robert and William Persing, reviewing the series in the *Baker Street Journal* in 1991. They judge one typical episode "a striking mystery, Canonically inspired, and played intelligently", one strength of the series being the meatier roles given to Watson than Bruce was allowed to play in the Rathbone films of the same era. Audio cassettes of many of the adventures have been produced by a firm calling itself "221A".

Later performers. When Rathbone abandoned the role of Holmes in 1946, it was briefly played for the ABC network by Tom Conway, with Nigel Bruce returning as Watson. Next to try was John Stanley, in a total of 78 programmes for Mutual in 1947-1948. Other actors have taken to the air from time to time, less ambitiously. Clive Merrison (Holmes) and Michael Williams (Watson) starred in *A Study in Scarlet* and *The Sign of the Four* for Britain's BBC Radio Four in 1989, and then embarked on the *Adventures* and *Memoirs* in 1991, with the intent of dramatizing all sixty of the Canonical tales in order, the first time any radio team had done that. The results to date have been congenial to a Sherlockian ear, as Roger Johnson wrote:

> Both actors have what I should call ageless voices, unlike some of their predecessors. Hobbs and Shelley were permanently middle-aged, even when they were young; David Buck sounded too old to be consorting with Barry Foster's energetic young Holmes. Merrison and Williams sound *right* together. They also share with Hobbs and Shelley the helpful fact that their voices contrast, by which I mean that Merrison sounds like Holmes and not like Watson, while Williams sounds like Watson and not like Holmes. . . . Williams as Watson is clearly a normal, intelligent, educated man — a bit of a romantic, but essentially practical and level-headed. Merrison's Holmes has something of the theatrical manner of Jeremy Brett's interpretation . . . the manic-depressive genius that is Sherlock Holmes.

Television

For a contemporary viewer it is hard to see past Jeremy Brett and to remember that before he took to the screen as Holmes in 1984 there had been many other television Holmeses, some of them much admired. A surprisingly detailed history of Holmes in television appears as a long chapter in Peter Haining's *The*

Television Sherlock Holmes (1986), which is chiefly about the Brett productions but which puts them properly in context. The first appearance of the great nineteenth-century detective on the great twentieth-century medium of entertainment came November 27, 1937, in a single broadcast from New York's Radio City. Louis Hector played Sherlock Holmes. The script, "The Three Garridebs", was published three years later as part of a textbook on broadcast production.

There have been other single television shows over the years, including a half-hour programme starring Basil Rathbone in 1953. Among them:

- A 1972 movie of "The Hound of the Baskervilles" starring Stewart Granger (with Bernard Fox as Watson and William Shatner as Stapleton).
- "Sherlock Holmes in New York", made for NBC television in 1976; it starred Roger Moore as Holmes, Patrick Macnee as Watson, Charlotte Rampling as Irene Adler and John Huston as Moriarty, in a plot that brings Holmes to New York to solve a bank robbery with implications for international affairs. A novelization by D. R. Bensen was published the same year.
- "The Return of the World's Greatest Detective", a ninety-minute series pilot in 1976 starring Larry Hagman as "Sherman Holmes".
- "Masks of Death", starring Peter Cushing as Holmes with John Mills as Watson, produced in 1984.
- "The Return of Sherlock Holmes", an improbable confection starring Michael Pennington as Holmes lately thawed out from cryogenic preservation of his body. Margaret Colin is a young Jane Watson who joins him for adventures that include a visit to London Bridge in Lake Havasu City, Arizona. There were speculations that the 1987 film was intended as the pilot for a series.
- "Hands of a Murderer", broadcast in 1990, starring Edward Woodward as Holmes and John Hillerman as an improbably goateed Watson; the plot has to do with Moriarty (rescued from the scaffold), Mycroft Holmes (kidnapped), and international espionage (foiled).
- "Sherlock Holmes, The Golden Years: Incident at Victoria Falls", made in 1991, with Christopher Lee as an aged Holmes investigating a South African jewel theft in the company of Theodore Roosevelt and other prominent figures. Patrick Macnee plays Watson, and Jenny Seagrove is Lillie Langtry.
- "Sherlock Holmes and the Leading Lady", also with Christopher Lee and Patrick Macnee (1992). Morgan Fairchild is a harshly American Irene Adler.

But the characteristic form in television is the series, and several series have brought Sherlock Holmes to the small screen. The first was a set of six programmes in the fall of 1951 on Britain's BBC; they starred Alan Wheatley as Holmes and Raymond Francis as Watson, with Iris Vandeleur as Mrs. Hudson. In the fifth episode, "The Red-Headed League", Sebastian Cabot appeared as Jabez Wilson. A second British series was aired in 1964-65; it consisted of thirteen episodes starring Douglas Wilmer as Holmes and Nigel Stock as Watson. David Burke, later to be a well-known Watson, appeared in one episode, "The Beryl Coronet".

In 1968 came Peter Cushing — nine years after his melodramatic film of "The Hound of the Baskervilles" — with fifteen episodes on the BBC, co-starring Nigel Stock as Watson. Edward Hardwicke, later to be a great Watson, played a minor role in "The Greek Interpreter". Two of the episodes were adapted for television by Michael and Mollie Hardwick, whose hand was behind so much that was Holmesian in Britain for a generation. One enthusiast, Percy Metcalfe, wrote to the *Sherlock Holmes Journal* to protest:

> The series is infinitely inferior to the last one — Douglas Wilmer, to my mind, gave a far more realistic Sherlockian representation than does Peter Cushing, experienced actor though he undoubtedly is.... Not only have the titles been mixed up, but also the text has been tampered with to an extraordinary degree. Take the Dancing Man, for instance.... Why the prolonged love scenes and all that rubbish about Mrs. Cubitt being pregnant? It held up the action of the story.

It is perhaps just as well that such a critic had not seen the 1954-55 television series that appeared in the United States, starring Ronald Howard as Holmes and Howard Marion Crawford as Watson. That the Canon was "tampered with" in these thirty-nine episodes — a full year's series, as television then counted it — is suggested by a mere list of some episode titles:

- "The Case of the Cunningham Heritage", first of the series, broadcast on NBC October 18, 1954.
- "The Case of the Shoeless Engineer".
- "The Case of the Laughing Mummy".
- "The Case of the Baker Street Bachelors".

It is almost a shock to see "The Case of the Red-Headed League" half-way down the list.

But the Ronald Howard shows were much more authentic than their titles suggest. They were the work of Sheldon Reynolds, a young writer-director who was determined to undo what Basil Rathbone had done a decade earlier; he would put Holmes back in Baker Street and back in the 1890's, and present the detective as "not an infallible, eagle-eyed, out-of-the-ordinary personality, but an exceptionally sincere young man trying to get ahead in his profession". Watson, in turn, was no buffoon but, in Crawford's words, "a normal man, solid on his feet, a medical student who gives valuable advice". The shows were filmed at a studio near Paris, with location shots actually in London, and the producers spent much effort to re-create the Baker Street flat and other authentic scenes. Their work was well received both by critics and by Sherlockians. The effusions of Edgar W. Smith, writing in the *Baker Street Journal*, are remarkable, coming as they do from a scholar with a pure devotion to the written Canon:

> The two films which our Committee on Canonicity reviewed last night are authentic in every detail; they capture the full flavor of the times in which Holmes and Watson lived, and they portray faithfully the characteristics and the mood which are, to us, the essence of these tales. ... the conception of the Master, conveyed by Ronald Howard, is the very conception suggested by Sidney Paget in the pages of the old Strand Magazine.

Jeremy Brett. The image of Basil Rathbone as the definitive Holmes was supplanted in the public mind only when Jeremy Brett came to the screen in

1984, in a series of episodes, most of them an hour long, made for Britain's Granada Television. The quality of the early Granada productions is high, and their appeal was tremendous, to the point that a 1991 retrospective in the *Sherlock Holmes Review* was titled "Lifting the Curse of Basil". Jeremy Brett (original surname Huggins; born November 3, 1935) was quickly transformed from a Shakespearean actor, also known for his work in light comedy, into the best-known Sherlock Holmes of the present generation, by far. Brett stars in three dozen hours of drama made for the small screen by Granada, a production company based in Manchester. The enthusiasm with which Sherlockians have greeted Brett's interpretation of Holmes, and the impetus his work has given to the growth of the Sherlockian cult, can hardly be exaggerated, even though not all viewers are equally enthusiastic about his interpretation of the great detective. Speculation about future productions (will the entire Canon be filmed?) has arisen after each new series of episodes; devotees agonized with Brett when he suffered a mental collapse in 1987, rejoiced when he returned to work, and looked cautiously at the two-hour productions of 1992 and 1993 as Granada, after the departure of producer Michael Cox, took greater and greater liberties with the authentic Holmes.

The episodes are as follows:

First series (1984)
"A Scandal in Bohemia", with Gayle Hunnicutt as Irene Adler
"The Dancing Men", with Betsy Brantley as Elsie Cubitt
"The Naval Treaty", with David Gwillim as Percy Phelps
"The Solitary Cyclist", with Barbara Wilshere as Violet Smith
"The Crooked Man", with Norman Jones as Henry Wood
"The Speckled Band", with Jeremy Kemp as Grimesby Roylott
"The Blue Carbuncle", with Frank Middlemass as Henry Baker

Second series (1985)
"The Copper Beeches", with Natasha Richardson as Violet Hunter
"The Greek Interpreter", with Charles Gray as Mycroft Holmes
"The Norwood Builder", with Matthew Solon as John Hector McFarlane
"The Resident Patient", with Nicholas Clay as Percy Trevelyan
"The Red-Headed League", with Roger Hammond as Jabez Wilson
"The Final Problem", with Eric Porter as James Moriarty

Third series (1986)
"The Empty House", with Patrick Allen as Sebastian Moran
"The Abbey Grange", with Anne Louise Lambert as Mary Brackenstall
"The Musgrave Ritual", with Michael Culver as Reginald Musgrave
"The Second Stain", with Patricia Hodge as Hilda Trelawney Hope
"The Man with the Twisted Lip", with Clive Francis as Neville St. Clair
"The Priory School", with Alan Howard as the Duke of Holdernesse
"The Six Napoleons", with Eric Sykes as Horace Harker

Fourth series (1987)
"The Sign of Four", with Jenny Seagrove as Mary Morstan [two hours]
"The Devil's Foot", with Denis Quilley as Leon Sterndale
"Silver Blaze", with Peter Barkworth as Colonel Ross

"The Bruce-Partington Plans", with Geoffrey Bayldon as Valentine Walter
"Wisteria Lodge", with Donald Churchill as John Scott Eccles
"The Hound of the Baskervilles", with Kristoffer Tabori as Henry Baskerville [two hours]

Fifth series (1991-93)
"The Illustrious Client", with Anthony Valentine as Baron Gruner
"The Creeping Man", with Charles Kay as Professor Presbury
"Thor Bridge", with Daniel Massey as Neil Gibson
"The Boscombe Valley Mystery", with Peter Vaughan as John Turner
"Lady Frances Carfax", with Cheryl Campbell in the title role
"The Master Blackmailer" ("Charles Augustus Milverton"), with Robert Hardy as Milverton [two hours]
"The Last Vampyre" ("The Sussex Vampire"), with Richard Dempsey as Jacky Ferguson [two hours]
"The Eligible Bachelor" ("The Noble Bachelor"), with Paris Jefferson as Hatty Doran [two hours]

The episodes were shown first on British television; they had their first North American airing, generally about a year after the British viewing, on the "Mystery!" series of the PBS network.

The greatest strength of the Granada series is its detailed re-creation of the Victorian scene. Success in that respect was no accident, as Cox, the producer until late in the series, wrote in a 1991 memoir:

> We had a wonderful design team who re-created 221-B Baker Street inside and out with absolute devotion. We produced a 70 page document on 221-B and all that went in it, with over a thousand entries. They also made a similar attack on the factual records of the period. If you want to know what offices and restaurants were found in Baker Street in 1890, look at our exterior set.

He went on to talk about the extraordinary fidelity he and his colleagues had maintained to the Canonical text. Long stretches of dialogue are lifted directly from Doyle's page. When the Granada scripts depart from the Canon, therefore, it is of special interest. Cox cites an example in connection with "The Norwood Builder":

> I think that even Inspector Lestrade, who was certainly ahead of his time in the study of fingerprints, had access to the necessary tests of blood and bones. The bones and the blood have to be human bones and blood. Therefore, "enter the tramp," as Holmes says at one point in the story when theorizing over possible solutions. The tramp in our film becomes Oldacre's victim when he needed a corpse to pass off as his own. Holmes of course was familiar with the language of tramps, as he was with all forms of secret writing, noticed the signs left by the doomed man, and began to establish that the remains in the yard were not those of Jonas Oldacre. Why Watson chose to conceal this aspect of the case I simply do not understand.

The Granada scriptwriters and directors can be seen to have taken the Canon seriously, though not always literally. Watson is consistently presented as unmarried; changes were necessary in "The Sign of the Four" to avoid any implication that he marries Mary Morstan at its conclusion. Another feature of interest in the adaptation for television is that each episode begins, not with a Baker Street scene, but with a glimpse of the crime which Holmes will soon be seen investigating.

The productions are rich with detail that a viewer cannot even fully absorb, with Canonical and period allusions, loving touches to the set design and properties, and even carefully chosen music. In "The Illustrious Client", for example, while Baron Gruner leafs through his "lust diary", the music is the "Catalogue Song" aria from Mozart's "Don Giovanni", in which that predecessor of the Baron enumerates his own conquests. The music for the series in general is the responsibility of Patrick Gowers; the violin solo, supposedly by Holmes, that is its theme is played by Kathy Gowers, his daughter. The photography is beautiful, even though, as Brett has said, "I wished we could do it in black and white" to achieve a stark quality. His frequently abrupt physical movement contributes to such an effect; directors (a number of them as the series has progressed) have often posed Brett to duplicate the moments of action captured in Sidney Paget's original drawings.

Brett's Holmes has been complemented by two Watsons. In the first two series, the doctor's part was played by David Burke (born May 25, 1934), who established himself as something better than the stereotypical buffoon. "He is the most ordinary man in the world," Burke told one interviewer. "At the same time he is the best kind of English gentleman." That style of Watson was maintained by Burke's successor, Edward Hardwicke, who first appeared in "The Empty House", looking remarkably like a Burke who had been aged by sorrow and the passage of several years after Holmes's supposed death. In subsequent episodes, and in *The Secret of Sherlock Holmes* on London stages, he has presented a Watson who is sensible, reliable, and moderately intelligent, with experience useful to Holmes from such fields as medicine and military life. Hardwicke (born August 7, 1932, son of the noted actor Sir Cedric Hardwicke) became very close to Brett as the series progressed. In one interview Brett called Hardwicke "the best friend a man's ever had", and in another "England's greatest actor, I believe".

Some of Jeremy Paul's scripts for the series appear in booklet form, accompanied from photographs, by Ian Henry Publications Ltd. *A Centenary Celebration of Sherlock Holmes, 1887-1897*, with text by Kenneth Harris and edited by Michael Cox (of Granada) and Andrew Robinson, includes excellent reproductions of scenes from the series. Also in print, and of interest to the episodes' enthusiasts, is *Jeremy Brett and David Burke: An Adventure in Canonical Fidelity* (1986) by R. Dixon Smith, published by the University of Minnesota Libraries.

Other Media

Music. Apart from the tunes for the musical "Baker Street" and other stage works, and music for film and television, the musical work best known to Sherlockians is "Aunt Clara", a 1940's comic song traced to its source in *We Never Mention Aunt Clara* (1990) by W. T. Rabe. It is sung at the annual dinners of the Baker Street Irregulars and of the Adventuresses of Sherlock Holmes, and on other occasions. Sherlockians also sing other songs, including several written by Harvey Officer and set to familiar tunes. They appear in his *Baker Street Song Book* (1943). Similar ditties, like the "filk songs" beloved of science fiction enthusiasts, are also heard. Jim Ballinger of Toronto is among composers of original Sherlockian melodies. The *Baker Street Song Book* also includes the score for a piece of serious instrumental music, Officer's "Baker Street Suite" for violin and piano; a recording on 78-rpm records was issued in 1943.

Poetry. Vast amounts of mediocre verse are written by Holmes enthusiasts; there have also been some fine poems, most famous of them being the sonnet "221B" by Vincent Starrett. Charles E. Lauterbach (died 1962) was a sensitive poet of the Sherlockian world, his *Baker Street Ballads* (1971) being a collection of his verses. Edgar W. Smith, long-time leader of the Baker Street Irregulars, was among versifiers of the Canonical tales themselves, four of his efforts appearing in 1950 as *A Baker Street Quartette*. Smith may, or may not, have been the reality behind the possibly nonexistent Helene Yuhasova, whose *Lauriston Garden of Verses* appeared in 1946. (Her reality was called into question after she was reported to be an international spy as well as a one-woman society, The Solitary Cyclist of Washington, but the case has not been closed.)

Games. The obvious way to match wits with Sherlock Holmes is through a game. As early as 1904, enthusiasts could do that with a "Sherlock Holmes" card game marketed by Parker Brothers. Writing in the *Baker Street Journal* in 1964, Helen G. Halbach tried to reconstruct it, and reported on the suits in its deck: Robber, Thief, Police, Burglar, Run, Help, Clue, and Stop, and Sherlock Holmes. "Clue", introduced by Parker Brothers forty years later, was originally dubbed "the great new Sherlock Holmes game", but in fact there is nothing Sherlockian about it. However, several board games from other sources do allow players to follow supposed Holmesian adventures. Among the best-known of them:

- "221B Baker Street", produced by Hansen, 1975.
- "Sherlock Holmes", from Whitman, 1980.
- "Sherlock Holmes, Consulting Detective", from Ben Sanders Company, 1981.

Apart from board games, the competitive enthusiast can also tackle Holmes's cases through game books, in which each page offers clues and invites the amateur sleuth to make decisions. A series of these has been published in paperback by Berkley as "Sherlock Holmes Solo Mysteries". *Murder at the Diogenes Club* (1987) is among them. For the less venturesome, there are "murder dossiers" of *A Study in Scarlet* and *The Sign of* [*the*] *Four* — portfolios of reproduced telegrams, letters, newspaper clippings, and photographs, even a sample of blood-stained rope and a gold ring, through which the imaginative follower can join Holmes in examining the minutiae of one of his original cases.

Holmes also appears in games for the personal computer. For example, Icom Simulations Inc. advertises "Sherlock Holmes, Consulting Detective", consisting of three colour video mysteries on a CD-ROM: "Open the private casebook of Holmes to pick the case you intend to solve. . . . Over 90 minutes of interactive video really puts you into the game. . . . When you think you've got a case solved, take it to court." The three cases, none familiar to readers of the Canon, involve the Mystified Murderess, the Tin Soldier, and the Mummy's Curse.

Pornography. Obscenity is in the eye of the beholder, but there have been some clearly pornographic works that use Sherlock Holmes as their central character. He has appeared in the stories offered by sex comics and *Screw* magazine, for example. The most important work in this little genre is *The Sexual Adventures of Sherlock Holmes* (1971), a paperback novel that betrays a deep and sensitive knowledge of the Canon, retelling *A Study in Scarlet* and "The Greek Interpreter" with extensive sexual content. Its orientation is homosexual; it assumes a physical relationship between Holmes and Watson (as other, more mainstream commentators have sometimes suspected) but also, for example, describes the perverted sex life of Enoch Drebber.

Children's books. Although the Sherlockian Canon has sometimes been dismissed as "boys' books", it is not suitable for children; the usual age at which a precocious reader discovers Sherlock Holmes is twelve or thirteen. Even for that age, some passages are strong meat, and there have been some attempts to bowdlerize, for example, *The Sign of the Four* to remove references to cocaine. Such "adaptations" are more possible now that copyright in most of the stories has expired in the United States. New tales with a Baker Street flavour, however, can be written at a child's reading level and with content entirely suitable. The best-known author to have attempted that task is Eve Titus, who created the mouse detective of 221B in *Basil of Baker Street* (1970) and three sequels. Her characters formed the basis for the Walt Disney film *The Great Mouse Detective* (1986), with Vincent Price as the voice of the villainous Professor Ratigan. It included the first tentative Disney venture into computer animation, and although its success was feeble, it was re-released in 1982 (as *The Adventures of the Great Mouse Detective*).

Marjorie Weinman Sharmat's *Nate the Great* (1972) and half a dozen sequels present a boy detective whose working costume is a deerstalker and trench coat:

> I, Nate the Great,
> am a detective.
> I am not afraid of anything.
> Except for one thing.
> Today I am going
> to a birthday party
> for the one thing
> I am afraid of.
> Annie's dog Fang.

Also notable are *The Case of the Baker Street Irregular* (1978) by Robert Newman, a novel about a boy whose life touches that of Holmes, and the absurd and hilarious juvenile novel *The Snarkout Boys and the Avocado of Death* (1982) by Daniel Pinkwater. *Holmes for the Holidays* is a small journal of Sherlockian material for children, such as puzzles, simple stories and pictures to colour, issued by Michael W. McClure of Chester, Illinois.

Comics. Sherlock Holmes has appeared in the comics since before the invention of comic books; "Sherlocko the Monk", drawn by Gus Mager, figured on newspaper comic pages from 1910 to 1913. Mager later created "Hawkshaw the Detective", who appeared in newspapers around 1915, and was collected in magazine format in 1917. There were deerstalkered detectives in conventional comic books from early times, appearing with Mickey Mouse as early as 1945, Bugs Bunny in 1948, Captain Marvel in 1950, Superboy in 1959, Chip 'n Dale also in 1959, Mickey Mouse in 1967, and Little Lulu in 1976. *Mad* magazine published "Shermlock Shomes" in 1953 and "The Hound of the Basketballs" the following year.

Full Sherlockian adventures first saw publication in comic-book form in *Classics Illustrated* in 1944, as part of "Three Famous Mysteries". Four years later the same magazine, now titled *Classic Comics*, presented "The Adventures of Sherlock Holmes" (actually *A Study in Scarlet* and *The Hound of the Baskervilles*). *A Study in Scarlet*, much improved, appeared again in 1953 along with "The Speckled Band". All these were, though abbreviated, plausible adaptations of the original tales. Several other publishers tackled Sherlock Holmes in the next three decades. Finally, *Cases of Sherlock Holmes* was published beginning in 1981 — a series of magazines in which the complete text of the Canonical stories would appear, with exquisite illustrations by Canadian artist Dan Day. Although the series (originally published by Renegade Press in California) staggered and eventually stopped, the dozen volumes that did appear were received with enthusiasm. Day's black-and-white illustrations generally model Holmes and Watson on Basil Rathbone and Nigel Bruce, and convey both Victorian atmosphere and physical energy, even passion, to bring the stories to life. A checklist of such publications is *Sherlock Holmes in the Comic Books* (1985, with updates), privately distributed by Charlotte Erickson of Palo Alto, California. Many classic comics are reproduced in *Sherlock Holmes in America* (1981), by Bill Blackbeard.

Chapter VIII

Fans and Followers

Parodies of the Holmes tales, appearing in England and America at the turn of the century (Doyle's friend Robert Barr wrote one in 1892), indicate how quickly the stories attracted enthusiasts who recognized their distinctive qualities. The preface to *His Last Bow*, published in 1917, is addressed to "the friends of Mr. Sherlock Holmes". But those friends were not yet organized. The first Sherlock Holmes societies were formed in the 1930's, and their successors exist today in more than a dozen countries — embracing, to be sure, only a small number of those who enjoy the stories. To be a "Sherlockian" (in England, a "Holmesian") is to do more than read Sherlock Holmes with delight; it is to enter a world of trivia questions, films, parodies, interlocking societies, little magazines, T-shirts, nostalgia and a dedication bordering on mania. Most Sherlockian activity is conducted face-to-face or through the printed word, but one sign of modernity is the creation of "Sherlocktron", a computerized bulletin board carrying Sherlockian news and databases, which can be reached electronically at (714) 492-0724.

North America

Probably because the stories themselves were more popular in America than in Britain, it was in the United States that the greatest Sherlockian activity developed. Originally limited to a few keen fellows in the New York literary set, the Sherlockian community has grown widely, though in no organized way. No single membership card or initiation rite separates the acknowledged Sherlockian from the private devotee. What distinguishes Sherlockian societies from fan clubs is the frequent presence of genuine literary scholarship, sometimes of the kind favoured by professors of English, sometimes of the humane kind associated with Christopher Morley, founder of the Baker Street Irregulars, and other appreciative readers. He called such companions "kinsprits": kindred spirits.

The beginnings. Christopher Morley (born May 5, 1890; died March 28, 1957) was, circa 1930, an editor of the *Saturday Review of Literature*, a magazine published in New York. A poet and novelist — *Parnassus on Wheels* (1917) was a best-seller, though his most successful book, *Kitty Foyle* (1939), was still ahead — he was also a critic, a mentor, and the most clubbable of men. Writes Robert Keith Leavitt:

> In his early forties, he was stout, lustily active, gregarious, busy, prosperous (in spite of the recent collapse of the Hoboken theater venture) and immensely popular. He rarely lunched with fewer than four people, and often as not, with a group of a dozen or more. Among his countless fascinating traits was the habit of forming clubs on the spur of the moment.

Among these clubs were the Grillparzer Sittenpolizei Verein and the self-explanatory Three Hours for Lunch Club, which gathered often at Christ Cella's restaurant (or speakeasy) on East 45 Street. (*Three Hours for Lunch* is the title of a 1976 biography of Morley by Helen McK. Oakley.) The talk at such lunches and dinners was often of literature and the theatre, and sometimes of Sherlock Holmes. Morley had been commissioned to write a preface for Doubleday's *Complete Sherlock Holmes* in 1930, and actor William Gillette had been making his Farewell Tour in 1929-32; in Britain, three early books of gentle Holmesiana had been published by 1932. The great detective was in the air.

The development of a Sherlockian society from Morley's congenial circle is traced in *Irregular Memories of the 'Thirties* (1990), edited by Jon Lellenberg, who summarizes it thus:

> The GSPV luncheons became more and more Sherlockian — until finally the Baker Street Irregulars spun out of it, centrifugally, and into life on their own, at a cocktail party at the Hotel Duane, on Madison Avenue, on January 6, 1934: called by Christopher Morley (in his column in the *Saturday Review of Literature*) to celebrate Sherlock Holmes's birthday.

Prohibition had ended a month earlier, and Morley was calling for the invention of "a Sherlock Holmes cocktail" at the Duane. Whether or not it was served, the cocktail party did take place, an affair of fifteen or twenty people, according to Leavitt's recollection. They were of both sexes, and he maintains that after drinks and lunch "we played Sardines with the pretty ladies who were our guests", Sardines being a form of hide-and-seek.

Such frivolity was followed by a frivolous constitution for the BSI, published in the *SRL* February 17, 1934:

> ARTICLE I. The name of this society shall be the Baker Street Irregulars.
> ARTICLE II. Its purpose shall be the study of the Sacred Writings. . . .
> ARTICLE IV. The officers shall be a Gasogene, a Tantalus, and a Commissionaire. . . .
> BUY-LAWS. . . . (2) The current round shall be bought by any member who fails to identify, by title of story and context, any quotation from the Sacred Writings submitted by any other member. . . .
> (4) All other business shall be left for the monthly meeting.
> (5) There shall be no monthly meeting.

Then on May 13 Morley's column in the *SRL* presented a crossword puzzle that had been composed by his brother Frank Morley, offering it as an entrance examination for the BSI. About three dozen perfect and near-perfect solutions arrived. Morley soon called "the first formal meeting of the Baker Street Irregulars", for June 5 at Cella's restaurant. "Dress informally of course," his typewritten invitation read. "This first meeting will be stag." That meant that such successful solvers of the puzzle as Emily S. Coit and Katherine McMahon were excluded. Exactly eight people, all male, did attend: Earle Walbridge, Malcolm Johnson, Allan Price, Harvey Officer, R. K. Leavitt, Frank Henry, William S. Hall, and Morley.

A dinner meeting held December 7, 1934, attracted several others who would become legends in the Sherlockian world, including Basil Davenport, Elmer Davis, Gray C. Briggs, Harold W. Bell, and Vincent Starrett. Actor William Gillette and illustrator Frederic Dorr Steele were also among those present — as was Alexander Woollcott, prominent and self-important figure in the New York literary scene. Disagreement has existed ever since about whether Woollcott was invited, how he behaved while he was there, and whether or not he stole Bill Hall's home-made deerstalker hat. The BSI met again in January 1936, but after that not until 1940.

It has been suggested that if the BSI had not been organized in New York when it did, Sherlockian activity in America would have been based on a society founded in the midwest instead, by Vincent Starrett of Chicago (born October 26, 1886; died January 5, 1974). From 1930 to at least 1934, Starrett was in constant, enthusiastic correspondence with Dr. Gray Chandler Briggs (1882-1942), a St. Louis radiologist whose Sherlockian accomplishments included an early identification of the house in Baker Street that might have been 221B. (Their correspondence, edited by Jon Lellenberg, was published in 1989 as *Dear Starrett — Dear Briggs*.) Another important correspondent was Logan Clendening (1884-1945), a Kansas City physician, humorist and writer on literary topics. It was Clendening who gave Starrett some twenty rarities in 1940, to start his second Sherlockian collection after financial difficulties had forced him to sell his first.

Starrett wrote the first, and still perhaps the greatest, book of American Sherlockiana, *The Private Life of Sherlock Holmes* (1933, new edition 1960), in the intervals of his work as a Chicago newspaperman and critic. He was one of the original participants in BSI revels, despite the distance from Chicago to New York, and remained active in Sherlockian affairs. Best-known of his many writings is the sonnet "221B", first published in 1942:

> Here dwell together still two men of note
> Who never lived and so can never die: . . .
> Here, though the world explode, these two survive,
> And it is always eighteen ninety-five.

Starrett's autobiography is *Born in a Bookshop* (1965). A biography with much attention to Sherlockian matters is *The Last Bookman* (1968) by Peter A. Ruber.

An era of growth. The number of acknowledged Sherlockians grew gradually. New societies began to form, starting with The Five Orange Pips of Westchester County, north of New York, which has maintained its traditions of strictly limited (and male-only) membership, eloquent scholarship, and annual black-tie dinners for nearly six decades. Several other societies with similar limitations were formed during the 1940's: the Speckled Band of Boston (founded by James Keddie sr., 1883-1942), the Hounds of the Baskerville [sic] of Chicago (founded by Starrett and a few kindred spirits), the Dancing Men of Providence (founded by Roland Hammond, 1876-1957), the Sons of the Copper Beeches of

Philadelphia, the Six Napoleons of Baltimore, and others. The name "scions" was soon adopted for these cadet or branch societies, the BSI being accepted as the parent.

The BSI originally claimed to have a Gasogene as its president, which was Christopher Morley; a Tantalus as its secretary, which was sporadically Bill Hall; and a Commissionaire, "who shall . . . conduct all negotiations with waiters". That role was soon taken by Edgar W. Smith (born April 1, 1894; died September 17, 1960). He wrote first to Vincent Starrett, who put him in touch with Morley in 1938. By that time he was completing *Appointment in Baker Street*, a biographical dictionary of figures in the Canon, published that year as the first in a series of Sherlockian reference works Smith would develop. By the time the BSI managed to hold a dinner meeting in January 1940, after a four-year hiatus, Smith was in charge of the arrangements and calling himself "Buttons" in allusion to a Victorian page-boy. Soon he was "Buttons-cum-Commissionaire", a title he held to the end of his life as the chief organizer of the Irregulars. Smith, as an executive of General Motors (he loved to call it "the Franco-Midland Hardware Company", and used its secretarial resources freely for Sherlockian purposes), was a modest, efficient organizer. Morley was impressed, though unenthusiastic about the activities he directed:

> Now the scholarly group of Baker Street find themselves swaddled, or saddled, with a publishing business, an annual meeting, and a province of pulp. They have about 30 scionist branches whose letters have to be answered. But not by me.

The "province of pulp" included considerable Sherlockiana from Morley's own pen, articles that have been collected and annotated in *The Standard Doyle Company* (1990), edited by Steven Rothman. It also included several of Smith's works: *Baker Street and Beyond* (1940), a gazetteer, and *Baker Street Inventory* (1945), a bibliography, are the most important. Smith was also represented — along with Morley, Leavitt, and other familiar names — in a hardbound anthology edited by Starrett and published by Macmillan in 1940 under the title *221B: Studies in Sherlock Holmes*. Still more striking was *Profile by Gaslight* (1944), which Smith edited. In this anthology appeared some classic essays of Sherlockian scholarship, from Charles S. Goodman's "The Dental Holmes" to Rex Stout's straight-faced tour-de-force, "Watson Was a Woman". ("That Was No Lady," retorted Dr. Julian Wolff in the next chapter.)

The success of *Profile by Gaslight* made the founding of a Sherlockian magazine inevitable. The first issue of the *Baker Street Journal* appeared in January 1946, with Smith as editor and New York bookseller Ben Abramson as publisher. Leftover essays from the anthology, and similar serious works, shared space with a long pastiche, letters, editorial notes (from Smith, and from Morley as "Clinical Notes by a Resident Patient"), and reports from the scion societies. That remained the pattern of the *BSJ* until Abramson, haemorrhaging money, had to abandon it after the first issue of volume 4 (in 1949). In a much less ambitious format — thinner, and typewritten where the Old Series had been professionally typeset — a New Series of the BSJ was begun in January 1951, and continues to appear quarterly, once again with professional typesetting, as the most important journal for the discussion of Sherlock Holmes. The BSJ was edited until 1960 by Smith; then until 1977 by Julian Wolff; then briefly by John Linsenmeyer, then Peter Blau and then (as "Fred Porlock") George Fletcher; 1985 through 1992 by Philip A. Shreffler; and, from 1993, by William R. Cochran, an English teacher in DuQuoin, Illinois. Publication directly by the BSI, which formed a corporation for such purposes during Smith's era, was succeeded in 1975 by an arrangement with Fordham University Press, which ended in 1992, the BSI becoming directly responsible once more.

Two other prominent Sherlockians of the 1940's were both pseudonymous: Anthony Boucher and Ellery Queen. Boucher, actually William A. P. White (1911-1968), came to Sherlockian notice with the novel *The Case of the Baker Street Irregulars* (1940), a mystery novel about a murder solved by BSI members. He became prominent both in Sherlockian circles (as founder of the Scowrers and Mollie Maguires of San Francisco, the first major Sherlockian society to welcome women as well as men) and among mystery enthusiasts in general; Bouchercon, the leading international convention for mystery-lovers, is named in his memory. Ellery Queen was a partnership of Frederic Dannay and Manfred E. Lee, who wrote novels about a detective (also named Ellery Queen) and edited *Ellery Queen's Mystery Magazine* (founded 1941 and a frequent vehicle for Sherlockian tales for the past five decades). *The Misadventures of Sherlock Holmes* (1940), edited by Queen, was a collection of parodies and pastiches of the Holmes tales.

The early modern era. The BSI was no longer entirely a New York organization, for prominent members included out-of-towners such as James Montgomery (1898-1955) of Philadelphia, James Keddie, Jr. (1907-1983), of Boston, James Bliss Austin (1903-1988) of Pittsburgh, and Clifton R. Andrew (1892-1963) of Akron. The centre of Sherlockian activity began to shift from New York and the BSI to local societies, established in most larger cities and some smaller ones (New Haven, Austin) where one or two enthusiasts managed to light a fire. In the postwar years it became increasingly common for Sherlockians, travelling for business or pleasure, to meet one another and attend the gatherings of one another's "scions". Newsletters sprang up here and there.

Scholarship was flourishing, not only through the *Baker Street Journal* but in privately published pamphlets — many of which, now extremely rare, have been republished in facsimile by Magico Magazine. In a class by itself is the work of Jay Finley Christ (1884-1963) of Chicago, which included many newspaper pieces and pamphlets as well as *An Irregular Guide to Sherlock Holmes* (1947), an idiosyncratic index to names and key references in the Canon. Virtually without exception, Sherlockians were treating Holmes and Watson as real people, the Canon as history, and Doyle as "the Literary Agent". For example, essayists in *The Illustrious Client's Case-Book*, published in 1948 by the Sherlockians of Indianapolis, consider such matters as Watson's middle name and Holmes's prowess at boxing. That was still the fashion in 1962, when *Sherlock Holmes of Baker Street*, a straight-faced "biography" of the great man, appeared to great acclaim. It was the work of William S. Baring-Gould (1913-1967), an executive of Time Inc. and intensely scholarly Irregular whose *magnum opus* was the posthumously published *Annotated Sherlock Holmes* (1967), with hundreds of notes discussing obscurities in the Canon.

An enthusiasm since the early years of Sherlockian activity, both in America and in England, had been "chronology": the attempt to give each case an exact date, in spite of the vague and inconsistent data provided in the stories. The principal chronologists, arriving at conflicting but enthusiastic conclusions, were these:

- William S. Baring-Gould, *The Chronological Holmes* (1955).
- Harold Wilmerding Bell, *Sherlock Holmes and Dr. Watson: The Chronology of Their Adventures* (1932).
- T. S. Blakeney, *Sherlock Holmes: Fact or Fiction?* (1932).
- Gavin Brend, *My Dear Holmes* (1951).
- Jay Finley Christ, *An Irregular Chronology* (1947).
- Henry T. Folsom, *Through the Years at Baker Street* (1963, 1964, 1990).
- Ernest B. Zeisler, *Baker Street Chronology* (1953).

The findings of these chronologists were conflated in *The Date Being?* (1970), a brochure by Andrew Jay Peck.

Julian Wolff (born January 11, 1905; died February 12, 1990) succeeded to the title of Commissionaire of the BSI when Edgar W. Smith died in 1960. Wolff was a physician specializing in industrial medicine (and during World War II an army doctor) and had first come to Sherlockian notice through the maps he had drawn to accompany Smith's *Baker Street and Beyond*. They were later published as *The Sherlockian Atlas* (1952) and have been seen on Christmas cards and in other media over the years. Wolff's later creative works included *A Practical Handbook of Sherlockian Heraldry* (1955) and several brochures. He was a prominent member of the Irregulars through the 1950s, and was acclaimed Smith's successor in a private meeting of leading Irregulars.

The Sherlock Holmes boom. One might say that the Sherlockian world became more organized in the Julian Wolff era. It even briefly boasted a *Who's Who and What's What* (1961 and 1962), edited by Bill Rabe (1921-1992), then of Detroit. Rabe's Sherlockian organization, the Old Soldiers of Baker Street (Old SOB's), moved with him in and out of the United States Army, to Detroit and later to Sault Ste. Marie, Michigan, tossing off publications, audio recordings and other treasures along the way.

More lasting reference works became available: *The Annotated Sherlock Holmes*, edited by William S. Baring-Gould, in 1967; *The World Bibliography of Sherlock Holmes and Dr. Watson*, Ronald DeWaal's first massive volume, in 1974; Jack Tracy's *Encyclopaedia Sherlockiana*, in effect an index to the Canon, in 1977. In 1980 came DeWaal's second bibliography, *The International Sherlock Holmes*. Newsletters and journals proliferated, including *Baker Street*

Miscellanea, founded in 1975 by Bill Goodrich and John Nieminski of Chicago and Donald Pollock, then of Boston. *BSM* took Doyle more seriously, and imposed more consistent standards of originality and quality, than most other Sherlockian publications.

In 1979, Peter Blau of Washington, D.C., introduced a newsletter — originally nameless, now titled *Scuttlebutt from the Spermaceti Press* — offering for cognoscenti a monthly summary, believed to be exhaustive, of Sherlockian news, announcements, and reports of new books, articles and memorabilia. Blau was already known as the nerve and communications centre for Sherlockians everywhere, as well as the organizer of one of the more active local societies, the Red Circle of Washington, D.C. A petroleum geologist originally from Massachusetts, Peter Blau (born 1932) joined the Baker Street Irregulars in 1959, carries on an extensive correspondence across America and beyond, and maintains huge computerized files of Sherlockian addresses, bibliographical information and references. He briefly edited the *Baker Street Journal* (1982-83).

Equally prominent in the Sherlockian world, beginning in the 1960's, was John Bennett Shaw (born 1913), of Tulsa and latterly Santa Fe. An oilman, funeral director and insatiable book collector, Shaw became known as the most fanatical of "completist" collectors, seeking to own every Sherlockian item, every variant, every ephemeral object. His generosity to young enthusiasts, and to scholars in search of obscure material, was recognized in tributes he received in a special issue of the *Baker Street Journal* in 1990. Wrote one friend, Jon Lellenberg:

> He has been behind the founding of more scion societies than anyone else, or anyone likely to come after him. His enthusiasm for the cause is boundless and contagious, and his aphorismic advice, more serious than it seems upon first hearing, is legend today: All it takes to start a BSI scion society is two people and a bottle; in a pinch, you can dispense with one of the people. . . . This is a man who keeps a picture of Moriarty on the seat of his toilet, who keeps a chocolate Sherlockian bunny in a freezer. I know that Shaw has a collection of Sherlockian panties, and don't even want to ask where he keeps them.

Shaw said in a 1991 interview for the *Sherlock Holmes Review* that he had some 10,000 books and pamphlets in his collection: "My particular favorite are four Sherlock Holmes books, printed in Germany and dated 1890 to 1897, which belonged to the Czarina of Russia." Through the 1980's Shaw conducted summer "workshops" once or twice a year with the occasional hiatus — gatherings a few days in length, at which veteran and neophyte Sherlockians could listen to talks, watch films, attempt to answer Shaw's quizzes (famous for their puns), and talk far into the night. The original workshop of that kind was at Notre Dame University, Shaw's alma mater in Indiana, July 31 through August 4, 1977.

The devotees who tried to attend Shaw workshops in the summer, and many others besides, converged on New York each January for what became known as "the birthday weekend". In addition to the BSI's annual dinner, celebrating

Holmes's birthday, a series of other social events came to be expected, including a dinner, at the same hour as that of the BSI, for the members and friends of the Adventuresses of Sherlock Holmes, a women's society that grew to national status because the BSI continued to refuse membership to women.

Involvement in the Sherlockian movement swelled after two 1974 books from mainstream publishers, and the movie made from one of them, attracted widespread attention. The more successful of the two was *The Seven-Per-Cent Solution* by Nicholas Meyer, a Hollywood screen writer, who daringly juxtaposed Holmes and Sigmund Freud in the first modern "pastiche", or imitation of the Canonical stories. In his novel Holmes consults Freud for help in curing the cocaine addiction that has caused him to imagine, and fear, Professor Moriarty. It was made into a successful 1976 film, starring Nicol Williamson as Holmes. The other 1974 comet was *Naked Is the Best Disguise* by Samuel Rosenberg, a New York writer who has identified his book as the first to take Doyle seriously in literary terms. He proposed a "Conan Doyle Syndrome", juxtaposing death, darkness, the written word, and cross-dressing or sexual perversity, finding it in story after story in the Canon. Sherlockians were generally outraged, but interested.

A further influence on the public interest in Holmes was a revival of William Gillette's turn-of-the-century play *Sherlock Holmes*, presented by the Royal Shakespeare Company. It played in England in the summer of 1974, then came to North America for 32 performances in Washington and 219 (between November 1974 and January 1976) in New York, followed by a tour touching Toronto, Detroit, Los Angeles, Denver and Chicago. In 1979 *Baker Street Miscellanea* found it necessary to publish "A Symposium on Collecting Sherlockiana During the Holmes Boom", with comments from several noted figures, including John Bennett Shaw:

> There can be no doubt that there was and still is a Boom, a revival, a resurgence of interest in Sherlock Holmes, a proliferation of books, pamphlets, plays, films, recordings, tapes, articles in periodicals, art and craft objects, and much more. Endlessly! I know this well, probably better than most. I know this as a collector, for I write a dozen or so letters a day to fellow Holmesians, to book-sellers, publishers and so on. I know because I have no space in my library (a room built on to the house in 1970 specifically to house my Holmes collection). I know because I am stretching my avocational budget to the breaking point, buying and housing old and new materials.

The flood of material was acquired not only by the long-time collectors but by a throng of new Sherlockians, for whom new societies were formed, new periodicals optimistically launched.

The Baker Street Irregulars today. By general consent, the BSI remains the parent society of Sherlockian groups in the United States, although its role is limited to approving new groups' names (to avoid duplication) and trying to keep track of them. The BSI itself meets each January, for an annual dinner on a Friday night, and sponsors a "Silver Blaze" race each September at New York's

Belmont racetrack. It also sponsors the *Baker Street Journal*.

The *BSJ* in March 1986, reporting on that year's annual BSI dinner, gave this news:

> The dinner was the occasion for Julian Wolff's announcement that he was retiring from the leadership of The Baker Street Irregulars (having held the job longer than anyone else, Julian said, he decided to be the first to get out alive), and that he had chosen as his successor Thomas L. Stix, Jr.

The June 1986 issue of the *BSJ* was thereupon devoted chiefly to tributes in Wolff's honour. Stix, eschewing Wolff's title of Commissionaire, took the title of "Wiggins", after one of Holmes's original Irregulars. He is the son of Thomas L. Stix, Sr. (born 1896, died July 18, 1974), who was prominent among Sherlockians from about 1950, and founded the "Silver Blaze" event. The younger Stix (born July 11, 1923), a New York stockbroker, became a BSI member in 1961 and followed his father into the Irregulars' inner circle. His mailing address for BSI matters is 34 Pierson Avenue, Norwood, New Jersey 07648.

Other prominent members of the BSI in the 1980s and 1990s include these:

• Jon Lellenberg of Washington, D.C., whose career with the United States Department of Defense somehow leaves time for his editorship of the Baker Street Irregulars history series, most recently *Irregular Memories of the Early 'Forties* (1991). He was formerly an editor of *Baker Street Miscellanea* and is the author of *The Great Alkali Plainsmen of Greater Kansas City: Silver Anniversary History* (1988). He has also served as American representative of Dame Jean Conan Doyle, who holds some remaining copyrights in Doyle's work in the United States and has an interest in "the Doyle Estate".

• Albert M. Rosenblatt of Poughkeepsie, a judge of the New York state supreme court, who has occasionally dropped Sherlockian references into his judgements, and used his authority to conduct weddings for Sherlockian acquaintances. He is a central figure in the Hudson Valley Sciontists, a Sherlockian society in that region, and (with his wife, Julia Carlson Rosenblatt) is the organizer of occasional Sherlockian feasts at the Culinary Institute of America, near Poughkeepsie.

• Bob Thomalen of Eastchester, New York, a central figure in The Three Garridebs of Westchester County, and the organizer of an annual gathering called Autumn in Baker Street, formerly held at the Bear Mountain Resort, more recently at the Hilton Hotel in Tarrytown.

One cannot apply for BSI membership, which is awarded to Sherlockians who have made a mark in published scholarship or in their local societies. Some prominent Sherlockians from overseas have been similarly "investitured". Such honours are awarded on the sole initiative of the BSI's benevolent dictator. The organization has no formal governing body; a group of veterans, known as "the Sacred Six" although they now number considerably more, meet occasionally to discuss BSI business and advise the leader. Membership has since 1944 involved an investiture, or *nom de plume*, which may be a Canonical story title, character or other allusion. Nathan L. Bengis (1906-1979), a New York teacher and book collector, was "The Lion's Mane"; Dean Dickensheet of Los Angeles was "Vamberry, the Wine Merchant". Since 1949 an investiture has been accompanied by a Victorian shilling, the silver coin with which Holmes paid his original assistants their daily wage. As of 1992, 475 people had received BSI investitures over the signature of Morley, Smith, Wolff, or Stix, authorizing them to, in the Canonical phrase, "go everywhere, see everything, overhear everyone". There were 297 Irregulars still living, and there had been 56 recipients of a "Two-Shilling Award" for continued prominent service.

Since Christopher Morley's day, the BSI had admitted only two women, both under exceptional circumstances. (Lee Offord in 1958 may have been accidental, her name being androgynous; Lisa McGaw in 1982 was dubbed "Mrs. Hudson" for her service as organizer of the William Gillette Memorial Luncheon.) Wolff had steadfastly ignored pressure to open BSI membership to successful Sherlockian women, but after his death Stix took that step, extending membership in January 1991 to six prominent women, including Sir Arthur's daughter, Dame Jean Conan Doyle; author Edith Meiser; one of the early solvers of the crossword puzzle, Katherine McMahon; Julia Carlson Rosenblatt, co-author of *Dining with Sherlock Holmes* (1976, 1990) and wife of prominent BSI member Albert M. Rosenblatt; and Evelyn Herzog and Susan Rice, leaders of the Adventuresses of Sherlock Holmes. Further investitures to women came in 1992.

The Adventuresses of Sherlock Holmes. A group of students at Albertus Magnus College in Connecticut, a small Roman Catholic women's institution, discovered a common interest in Sherlock Holmes in the fall of 1965, and two years later had defined themselves as a Sherlockian society under the name of the Adventuresses of Sherlock Holmes (a title said to be have been coined by Julian Wolff). In January 1968 a group of them went to New York to be on the fringes of the BSI celebrations of Sherlock Holmes's birthday, and to meet a few of the prominent Sherlockians with whom they had corresponded. That evening — January 5, 1968 — six of them mounted a brief, cold picket line outside Cavanagh's Restaurant as the Irregulars arrived for a dinner from which, because of their sex, the Adventuresses were barred. John Bennett Shaw and Peter Blau invited them inside for a drink before dinner.

In subsequent years the Adventuresses gradually gained legitimacy and reputation. Four of the original members — Evelyn Herzog, Pat Moran, Mary Ellen Couchon, and Linda Patterson (later Ripley) — continued their Sherlockian interests, and were soon joined by Sherlockian women with no Albertus Magnus connection. By the mid-1980's most Sherlockian women held, or aspired to, ASH membership. The centre of activity was New York, where beginning in 1975 the Adventuresses, or ASH, began holding an annual dinner on the same evening as that of the BSI. At first these dinners were for women only; since 1979 men have also been admitted. The ASH published a newsletter in 1975 and 1976, transforming it into a magazine, *The Serpentine Muse*, in 1977. It was edited by Kate Karlson until 1979, thereafter by Susan Dahlinger, and latterly by Pat Moran.

"Investitures" in the style of the BSI were adopted by the Adventuresses, and available only to women until 1991. An annual "spring meeting" for women only maintained the purity of the group, which is known for its (generally good-natured) teasing of male Sherlockians about sex discrimination, and for its determination not to let the men outdo the women in hearty social activity. After the BSI chose to admit women in 1991, a few men were honoured with ASH investiture. The society has also followed the lead of the BSI in its amorphous form of government. Consensus among an inner circle can be presumed, but the only visible officer is the Principal Unprincipled Adventuress, who has always been, and remains, Evelyn Herzog. A legal secretary for whom Sherlockian activities are a way of life, Herzog can be reached at 360 West 21 Street, New York, New York 10011.

Local societies. More than 350 active Sherlock Holmes societies, the majority of them in the United States, appear on a list maintained by Peter Blau of Washington, D.C. Most local groups take their name from some Canonical reference, and often elaborate it in the titles of their officers. The secretary of the Great Alkali Plainsmen of Greater Kansas City is "Stangerson", after a character in *A Study in Scarlet*, in which the great alkali plain appears. Groups range from the very small to some that draw as many as 100 people to meetings, and from the new and unstable to some that have been in operation for decades. In a few cases, meetings (typically three to ten times a year) have formal programmes of films, lectures, music, and quizzes, but many of the societies devote their meeting time to informal discussion and socializing. Most publish some sort of newsletter. Except for a hidebound few, all welcome women and men on equal terms, and generally there is no admission requirement beyond interest and the payment of modest dues. The smaller scion societies are often built around the enthusiasm of one individual, and can wither when that person leaves or burns out. Larger ones can go on almost indefinitely, and may be governed by clique, consensus, or, in a few cases, elaborate formal procedures. Local Sherlockian societies have all the strengths and weaknesses of other volunteer and hobby organizations, including enthusiasm and camaraderie on the one hand, a field for petty politics and ego display on the other. Some groups have dissolved amid personal rivalries, while others seem little unaffected by dissension.

Following is a list of some well-established local societies in larger American communities, with the name of an official or longstanding member who can provide information.

Baltimore: The Carlton Club (James E. Smith II, 311 St. Dunstan's Road, Baltimore, Maryland 21212).
Chicago: Hugo's Companions (Arnie Matanky, 222 West Ontario Street, Chicago, Illinois 60610).
Cleveland: Mrs. Hudson's Lodgers (Tom Stetak, 15529 Diagonal Road, LaGrange, Ohio 44050).
Detroit: The Amateur Mendicant Society (Peter B. Spivak, 3753 Penobscot Building, Detroit, Michigan 48226).

Hartford: The Men on the Tor (Harold E. Niver, 29 Woodhaven Road, Rocky Hill, Connecticut 06067).

Kansas City: The Great Alkali Plainsmen (Richard R. Reynolds, PO Box 6554, Kansas City, Kansas 66106).

Los Angeles: The Non-Canonical Calabashes (Sean M. Wright, 5542 Romaine Street, Los Angeles, California 90038).

Miami: The Tropical Deerstalkers (Arlyn Austin Katims, 6801 SW 79 Avenue, Miami, Florida 33143).

Minneapolis: The Norwegian Explorers (Pj Doyle, 466 Wilson Library, University of Minnesota, Minneapolis, Minnesota 55455).

Monterey, California: The Diogenes Club (Michael Kean, 3040 Sloat Road, Pebble Beach, California 93953).

New Jersey: Mrs. Hudson's Cliff-Dwellers (Irving H. Kamil, 32 Overlook Avenue, Cliffside Park, New Jersey 07010).

New York: [1] The Priory Scholars (Henry W. Enberg, 250 West 27 Street #3A, New York, New York 10001). [2] The Three Garridebs (Bill Schweickert, 145 Johnson Road, Scarsdale, New York 10583). [3] The Montague Street Lodgers (Thomas D. Utecht, 1676 East 55 Street, Brooklyn, New York 11234).

Philadelphia: The Clients of Sherlock Holmes (Sherry Rose Bond, 519 East Allens Lane, Philadelphia, Pennsylvania 19119).

St. Louis: The Noble Bachelors (Karen Johnson, 11333 Big Bend Boulevard, St. Louis, Missouri 63122).

San Francisco: The Scowrers and Molly Maguires (Ted Schulz, 180 Mount Lassen Drive, San Rafael, California 94903).

Tampa-St. Petersburg: The Pleasant Places of Florida (Ben Wood, PO Box 740, Ellenton, Florida 34222).

Tulsa: The Afghanistan Perceivers (James M. McUsic, 3512 South Joplin Court, Tulsa, Oklahoma 74135).

Washington: The Red Circle (Peter Blau, 3900 Tunlaw Road NW #119, Washington, DC 20007).

The quality and enthusiasm of a scion does not always reflect the size of its home city. Perhaps the most-admired and liveliest local Sherlockian society anywhere is the Occupants of the Empty House of Southern Illinois (William R. Cochran, 517 North Vine, DuQuoin, Illinois 62832).

Canada. Sherlockians in Canada have been closely associated with those in the United States for more than forty years. Among the scion societies of the Baker Street Irregulars in the 1940's was The Canadian Baskervilles, headed by Humfrey Michell of Lennoxville, Québec, and Ron Graham of Hamilton, Ontario. At about the same period, the Baker Street Squires briefly flourished in Toronto.

Both organizations were long extinct by 1971, when the Metropolitan Toronto Central Library began to form a Sherlock Holmes and Arthur Conan Doyle collection in its literature department. A few Canadian Sherlockians, most prominent of them being Toronto judge S. Tupper Bigelow, maintained their attachment to the BSI and the Sherlockian community in the United States. They, and others, were attracted to a "Weekend with Sherlock" conducted by the library December 4 and 5, 1971. When it was over, diehards agreed that a new Sherlockian society in Toronto should be formed. Inevitably, it took its name from the only Canonical reference to Toronto, as the place where Sir Henry

Baskerville acquired his boots, and the first meeting of The Bootmakers of Toronto was held February 4, 1972. The first president — dubbed "Mr. Meyers" — was Derrick Murdoch (born December 7, 1909; died May 21, 1985), a newspaper columnist. His successor was True Davidson, mayor of the Toronto suburb of East York.

The Bootmakers have grown steadily. A newsletter, *Canadian Holmes*, founded early in the society's history, has become a quarterly magazine circulated far beyond the Toronto area. The Bootmakers, with attendance of 80 to 100 people at five to seven meetings each year, and membership of more than 200, can claim to be the largest active Sherlockian society in North America. Its meetings involve formal programs of speakers and other entertainment, with a high degree of organization. It is the only Sherlockian society to be legally incorporated, and is governed by a board of directors elected annually. The Bootmakers' permanent mailing address is 47 Manor Road West, Toronto, Ontario M5P 1E6.

Prominent members of the group since its early days include Cameron Hollyer (born 1926), curator of the Doyle collection at the Metro Toronto Library until his 1991 retirement; Bob Coghill, a young teacher who has made a reputation for speaking to children's groups about Holmes (and collecting stuffed toys and other Sherlockian novelties); Christopher Redmond (born 1949), author of *In Bed with Sherlock Holmes* and other writings; and Maureen Green (born 1939) and Edwin Van der Flaes, a Toronto couple who have constantly held high offices in the society, and who are the best-known Canadian faces in American Sherlockian circles as they travel to events in the United States. Members who have contributed substantially over the years are honoured with the rank of Master Bootmaker (MBt).

The Bootmakers of Toronto came to think of itself as an independent national group — "the Sherlock Holmes Society of Canada" — rather than a scion of the Baker Street Irregulars, although close contact with American Sherlockians continues. It issues charters to its own "scions" elsewhere in Canada, including these groups:

> **Montréal:** The Bi-Metallic Question (Patrick Campbell, 17091 Maher Boulevard, Pierrefonds, Québec H9J 1H7).
> **Vancouver:** The Stormy Petrels of British Columbia (Michael Doyle, PO Box 5174, Vancouver, British Columbia V6B 4B2).
> **Winnipeg:** The Great Herd of Bisons of the Fertile Plains (Mark Hacksley, 167 Carroll Road, Winnipeg, Manitoba R3K 1H1).

Societies exist also in Halifax, Ottawa, Saskatoon and Edmonton.

The Printed Word

Although there are Sherlockians whose chief interest is television or film, most are strongly oriented to the printed word, and large numbers of enthusiasts feel the need to commit their appreciation and insights to paper. They are, in general, avid users of the mail, a service almost abandoned by the rest of the public, both for newsletters and for individual correspondence. Because kinsprits are widely scattered, and because Sherlockians are, whatever else they may be, literate, they write many letters.

Writings. The traditional scholarly article still has a place in Sherlockian publications, although its style is less predictable than it was in the 1940's. A growing number of English professors, purporting to be Sherlockians, have been unable to throw off their professional training completely. (Those who have not thrown it off at all, writing articles about Holmes as a social or cultural phenomenon, or treating the Canon as conventional literature, of course cannot be considered Sherlockians.) The *Baker Street Journal* in the 1980's published articles about "The Semiotic Watson", "Mythological Archetypes in the Sherlockian Canon", and "The Two-Author Theory of 'The Blanched Soldier'", as well as more traditional studies of "Automobiles in 'His Last Bow'" and whether Holmes might have been left-handed. The *BSJ* has even mentioned the name of Doyle from time to time, in sober studies about the Canon's sources and comparisons of the Canonical tales with other Victorian writings.

If, however, there is one thing that distinguishes the contemporary Sherlockian publications (including the *BSJ*) from the *Journals* of earlier decades, it is a widening range of genres in which Sherlockians choose to write. There have always been quizzes, sometimes ingenious and sometimes descending to the level of trivia questions. There have always been pastiches and parodies, of varying qualities. And there has always been poetry, although contemporary Sherlockian verse does not ascend to the art practised in the 1950's by Charles E. Lauterbach; nor does the genre of "tale-in-verse" seem still to exist. But Sherlockian journals now find room for dramatizations, prayers, personal reminiscences, manuscript facsimiles, television reviews, jokes, and even recipes. Sherlockians write more about sex than they used to, and more in simple explanation of the customs and circumstances of the Victorian era, providing information which many readers half a century ago might have been able to remember for themselves. A growing amount of Sherlockian history is also seeing print, as well as straightforward news about the expanding world of Sherlockian societies and activities. Thanks to inexpensive new printing technologies, many of the journals now routinely present photographs, and there has been a flourishing of cartoons, with Scott Bond of Philadelphia perhaps the leading practitioner.

The *BSJ* remains the largest Sherlockian magazine, with a circulation of about 1,800 copies four times a year. (Its business address: PO Box 465, Hanover, Pennsylvania 17331.) Next in prominence is *Baker Street Miscellanea*, privately published, under the editorship of Donald Pollock of Buffalo. It takes a frank interest in Doyle and has not been hesitant to push the boundaries of Sherlockian scholarship. (Its business address: The Sciolist Press, PO Box 225, Winnetka, Illinois 60093.) A third general magazine is *Canadian Holmes*, the publication of the Bootmakers of Toronto, edited from 1979 through 1985 by Christopher Redmond and Kate Karlson; 1986 through 1991 by Christopher Redmond alone; from 1992 by Trevor Raymond. (Business address: The Bootmakers of Toronto, 47 Manor Road West, Toronto, Ontario M5P 1E6.) A number of smaller magazines exist, from *The Serpentine Muse* of the Adventuresses of Sherlock Holmes to *Prescott's Press*, loosely associated with several societies in the New York area, and *Varieties of Ash*, launched in 1990 by Susan Dahlinger of Secaucus, New Jersey. The *Sherlock Holmes Review*, edited by Steven T. Doyle, is another independent magazine of importance (PO Box 583, Zionsville, Indiana 46077). The *BSJ* makes an attempt, at least once a year, to enumerate the newsletters its editor has received lately, some of which are no more than single sheets produced by societies as meeting announcements. Others have reputation and substance: the chatty and substantial monthly *Plugs and Dottles* edited by Robert C. Burr (4010 Devon Lane, Peoria, Illinois 61614) is probably the single publication most representative of what is lively and good-humoured in the Sherlockian world.

The 1980's have seen a number of Sherlockian monographs appear, more in Britain than in North America, the most prominent author being Michael Harrison, whose work in Sherlockiana began as long ago as 1958 with *In the Footsteps of Sherlock Holmes*. Although many of his intervening volumes have been about Victorian London in general more than strictly about Holmes, *A Study in Surmise: The Making of Sherlock Holmes* (1984) returned to the straight and narrow. Following in his footsteps as an interpreter of Holmes's times is another Briton, Kelvin I. Jones, author of such slim monographs as *The Making of Sherlock Holmes* (1984) and *The Sherlock Holmes Murder File* (1985).

Among the many other items that would appear on a bibliography of contemporary Sherlockiana are such volumes as these:

Monographs — *The Elementary Methods of Sherlock Holmes* (1987) and *Sherlock and The Ladies* (1988) by Brad Keefauver; *God and Sherlock Holmes* (1984) by Wayne Wall; *In Bed with Sherlock Holmes* (1985) by Christopher Redmond; *On the Scent with Sherlock Holmes* (1978) by Walter Shepherd.

Anthologies — *A Touch of the Class* (1981), representing work by members of The Master's Class of Philadelphia; *Studies in Scarlet* (1989), edited by David Hammer; *A Singular Set of People* (1990), edited by Marlene Aig and David Galerstein. *Sherlock Holmes by Gas-Lamp* (1989), edited by Philip A. Shreffler, consists of highlights from the first forty years of the *Baker Street Journal*.

Scrapbooks and coffee-table books — *The Sherlock Holmes Scrapbook* (1974) by Peter Haining; *Sherlock Holmes: The Man and His World* (1979) by H. R. F. Keating; *Sherlock Holmes in America* (1981) by Bill Blackbeard; *Sherlock Holmes: A Centenary Celebration* (1986) by Allen Eyles; *Elementary, My Dear Watson* (1986) by Graham Nown; *The Pictorial History of Sherlock Holmes* (1991) by Michael Pointer; *The Life and Times of Sherlock Holmes* (1992) by Philip Weller with Christopher Roden.

Cookbooks — *Sherlock Holmes Cookbook* (1976) by Sean Wright and John Farrell; *Dining with Sherlock Holmes* (1976, 1990) by Julia Carlson Rosenblatt and Frederic H. Sonnenschmidt; *Sherlock Holmes Cookbook* (1989) by Charles A. Mills.

In addition there have been books on such specific topics as film and television, travel (and Victorian London), and chronology, and Sherlockian history.

The Sherlockian writings up to 1980 are fully listed, though without a subject index, in two bibliographies compiled by Ronald B. DeWaal: *The World Bibliography of Sherlock Holmes and Dr. Watson* (1974) and *The International Sherlock Holmes* (1980). A third volume of DeWaal has been often promised, and in 1992 efforts began to produce an electronic listing of the mountains of data he has collected since 1980. Publication of a new edition, with all the entries from the first two volumes as well as new material, was announced for 1994. Although his work is arranged under general subject headings, the only real subject index to Sherlockian scholarship is *Bigelow on Holmes* (1974), edited by Donald Redmond from a card-index originally prepared by S. Tupper Bigelow. The index is now held (and kept up to date by Redmond) at the Metropolitan Toronto Reference Library.

Publishers. Since *Profile by Gaslight* in 1944, from Simon & Schuster, a few important Sherlockian books have been issued by mainstream publishers: Doubleday ventured to publish Jack Tracy's *Encyclopaedia Sherlockiana* in 1977, no doubt feeling some affection for the subject because of its still definitive *Complete Sherlock Holmes*. Many pastiches, which can be expected to have a general readership, have come from general publishers (Scribners, McGraw-Hill, Dutton, Putnam, Doubleday again), and even more have appeared in trade paperback editions, likely to be found on drugstore racks, from Pinnacle, Signet, Warner, Ace, Ballantine and the like.

But these are the exceptions. A good deal of Sherlockian literature is privately published (typeset on someone's personal computer, printed at a local shop, and distributed by the author through the mail, or at best available from a few bookstores specializing in mysteries). Such materials can be frustrating for the would-be collector, to say nothing of the bibliographer. Somewhere in the middle come the products of small presses, themselves little more than hobby activities, specializing in Sherlockian material. Three can be listed:

- Gaslight Publications, 626 North College Avenue, Bloomington, Indiana 47404, which not only publishes its own books but offers Sherlockian books from other presses by mail order. It advertises a toll-free number, (800) 243-1895, because "We can't pretend that it's 1895 any longer." Proprietor: Jack Tracy.
- Gasogene Press Ltd., Box 1041, Dubuque, Iowa 52001, which calls itself "the only solely Sherlockian Press". Proprietor: David Hammer.
- Magico Magazine, PO Box 156, New York, New York 10002, which has specialized in reprints of unavailable Sherlockian classics, as well as some new material. Proprietor: Rabbi Samuel Gringras.

Book dealers. Sherlockian books cannot reliably be found in general bookstores. Current titles are bought, if not from the authors or publishers, then from specialist dealers such as the mystery bookstores that exist in most major cities. Typically such dealers also carry used and rare books, and are as comfortable dealing by mail as selling to their walk-in clientele. Among the best-known such stores are these:

• Murder Ink, 2486 Broadway, New York, New York 10025 (proprietor: Jay Pear-sall).
• The Mysterious Bookshop, 129 West 56 Street, New York, New York 10019 (proprietor: Otto Penzler).
• Sleuth of Baker Street, 1595 Bayview Avenue, Toronto, Ontario M4G 3B5 (pro-prietor: J. D. Singh).

There are also dealers who work only by mail, specializing in used and rare material. The most important:

• Pepper & Stern Rare Books Inc., PO Box 357, Sharon, Massachusetts 02067 (proprietors: James Pepper, Deborah Sanford, Peter L. Stern).
• Gravesend Books, PO Box 235, Pocono Pines, Pennsylvania 18350 (proprietor: Enola Stewart).
• Sherlock in L.A., 1741 Via Allena, Oceanside, California 92056 (proprietor: Vincent Brosnan).

Private collections. Some Sherlockians maintain a short shelf of well-loved volumes. Others are casual collectors of books and other material about Sher-lock Holmes. A few are enthusiasts, and a very few are "completists", keen to acquire a copy of everything, however banal or rare, that touches on Holmes. A collection can become valuable in monetary terms (and a good collection is inevitably expensive to acquire), and is certainly valuable as a resource for a Sherlockian who seeks, as many do, to write about Holmes for publication or to impress fellow members of a society.

Some Sherlockian collectors are chiefly interested in editions of the Canon. First editions can be expensive, but need not be — a copy of the first American edition of *The Hound of the Baskervilles*, in "fair-good" condition, was listed for $60 in one catalogue late in 1991. Later, often obscure and fugitive, editions are also of interest to some collectors, as they were to Nathan L. Bengis of New York, whose unprecedented library of editions of *The Sign of the Four* was col-lected in the 1950's. A striking collection could be formed of paperback editions alone, including some from the middle decades of the twentieth century with lurid cover illustrations by the masters of pulp publishing. Other collectors spe-cialize in the non-Sherlockian works of Arthur Conan Doyle; or pastiches and other derivative works; or classic pamphlets and books of Sherlockian scholar-ship. Some of the latter now fetch breathtaking prices, although the intelligent collector will make careful comparisons between dealers before reaching for the chequebook. An area of growing interest is movies and television programmes on videotape; Jennie C. Paton (206 Loblolly Lane, Statesboro, Georgia 30458) even maintains a "Sherlockian lending library" of such materials.

The greatest Sherlockian collection was probably that of James Bliss Austin of Pittsburgh (whose achievement in that field was paralleled by his collecting and scholarship in Japanese art). After his death his Sherlockiana was offered for sale by the beneficiaries of his will, the generality of the collection fetching $151,000 from Pepper & Stern, who offered most of the material for resale through their catalogues at eye-popping prices. Austin's two greatest treasures were auctioned separately later: the manuscript of *The Valley of Fear* (it sold for $260,000) and a copy of *Beeton's Christmas Annual* containing the first publication of *A Study in Scarlet* ($52,000). Today's leading "completist" collectors are Peter Blau of Washington and John Bennett Shaw of Santa Fe. The latter, amid considerable publicity, has sold his collection to the University of Minnesota, which is receiving it in 1993.

Library collections. Two public institutions, one in Canada and one in the United States, have sizeable collections of Sherlockian material. The Canadian repository is the Metropolitan Toronto Reference Library (789 Yonge Street, Toronto, Ontario M4W 2G8). Its collection was formed in 1971 with the purchase of materials that had belonged to a British mystery enthusiast, Arthur Baillie. The library soon also acquired the collection of S. Tupper Bigelow, a long-time Sherlockian who was a retired Toronto judge, the many variant editions of *The Sign of the Four* that had been part of the collection of Nathan L. Bengis of New York, and a collection assembled by British bookseller Harold Mortlake. Founders of the collection included Cameron Hollyer and Mary McMahon of the library's Literature Department; in an advisory role were the library's director, John Parkhill, and an external friend, Donald A. Redmond of Queen's University. The collection includes the works of Arthur Conan Doyle and associated material (including some Doyle manuscripts) as well as Sherlockiana narrowly defined. There is also the "Bigelow index", a card-index originally created by Judge Bigelow and maintained by Donald A. Redmond, which provides subject access to the whole body of Sherlockian literature; staff at the library will respond to inquiries about what the Bigelow index shows on a specified subject. The whole collection is housed in a comfortable room with Victorian furniture, still called Room 221B although it is on the fifth floor of the library's modern building. Since the 1991 retirement of Cameron Hollyer, the collection has been under the curatorship of Victoria Gill. *A Checklist of the Arthur Conan Doyle Collection*, compiled by Donald A. Redmond, was issued in 1973 (second edition 1977), and *Bigelow on Holmes* in 1974.

The large Sherlockian collection in the United States is at the O. Meredith Wilson Library of the University of Minnesota (Minneapolis, Minnesota 55455). This collection is based on the holdings of a New York Sherlockian, James C. Iraldi, who sold his collection to the university in 1974. It grew tremendously with the acquisition of the treasures, including first and other early editions of the Canon, assembled by Philip S. Hench, a physician at Minnesota's Mayo Clinic and member of the Sherlockian society in the Minneapolis area, the Norwegian Explorers. That collection was was donated to the university by his widow after his 1965 death. The Mary Kahler and Philip S. Hench Collection is under the curatorship of Errett W. McDiarmid, with the frequent assistance of researcher Andrew Malec. The collection will grow enormously with the addition of the John Bennett Shaw collection, being delivered to Minneapolis in 1993.

A number of other libraries have good collections of Sherlockiana and Doyle material, ranging from the Library of Congress in Washington to the Humanities Research Center of the University of Texas at Austin.

Outside North America, a major Holmes collection can be found at what would have been Holmes's neighbourhood library: the Marylebone Library (Marylebone Road, London NW1 5PS, England). That library was a service of the old Borough of St. Marylebone at the time its collection was formed from books and other materials donated for the Sherlock Holmes exhibition that was the Borough's contribution to the Festival of Britain in 1951; with changes in local government, the library is now operated by the Department of Leisure Services, City of Westminster. The collection is under the curatorship of Catherine Cooke, who edited an inventory, *The Contents of a Lumber-Room*, published by the library in 1986.

Sherlockian Life

Sherlockians come from all socioeconomic groups; teachers and librarians are particularly strongly represented. No generalization is possible beyond their common interest in Sherlock Holmes, but certain other interests are widely found: detective fiction (of course), Victorian England, science fiction. Many Sherlockians are also members of groups celebrating such Victorian figures as Charles Dickens, William Morris, and Gilbert and Sullivan. And, by and large, they are friends. While the full range of personalities is, of course, found, the presumption is that Sherlockians will have something in common and enjoy one another's company. Several marriages have grown out of friendships made in Sherlockian organizations; countless other intimate friendships have grown up. One Sherlockian marriage, that of Wayne Swift and Francine Morris Swift, now of Chevy Chase, Maryland, has produced a household that is a focus for good-hearted gossip and support in time of need across the Sherlockian "loop".

Most Sherlockian activity is carried on alone. One reads the Canon (although it is easy to neglect that simple activity in favour of derivative entertainment), keeps up with the scholarship and fantasy being written about it by Sherlockian colleagues, watches what videos are available, corresponds avidly, writes the occasional article for newsletter publication, and looks forward to the monthly or quarterly meeting of a nearby society, at which the same activities can be enjoyed in the company of a few friends. It may even be true that the most important Sherlockian activity takes place not so much on the printed page, but in the theatre of the mind, where for a Sherlockian there is always an immediate escape to 1895:

> When the world closes in with its worries and cares
> And my problems and headaches are coming in pairs
> I just climb in my mind up those seventeen stairs
> And spend a long evening with Holmes.

So writes Bill Schweickert in "A Long Evening with Holmes", first published in *Canadian Holmes* in 1984.

But there are livelier and more sociable activities as well.

A January weekend in New York. Although not all Sherlockians have ever managed to attend, and still fewer make it every year, the chief festival of the Sherlockian world is an annual gathering in New York on the first or second weekend of January. The event of longest standing is the annual dinner of the Baker Street Irregulars, held on the Friday evening of that weekend in supposed celebration of Holmes's birthday. Other events have been added to the schedule in recent years, so that "the January weekend" resembles any convention in its succession of social demands. What it lacks, by and large, is intellectual content: one does not come to New York in January to hear scholarly papers, even of the tongue-in-cheek kind most favoured by Sherlockians.

The centre of the January activity is the Algonquin Hotel on New York's West 44 Street, famous as the home of literary activity since the "Round Table" made its home there in the 1920's. Some Sherlockians are able to stay at the Algonquin, while others choose less expensive hotels nearby. By some time on the Thursday of the week in question, an acute eye will spot the occasional deerstalker at the Algonquin's lobby bar, and that evening parties of Sherlockians are likely to form up there to head out for supper at someone's favourite restaurant. It need not be added that conversation and refreshment will continue far into the night in various participants' hotel rooms.

Friday begins (officially, for the wise will have breakfasted privately first) with the Martha Hudson Breakfast at the Algonquin, an event which used to be conducted without reservations and on the separate-checks principle, but which has had to be more organized as the crowds grew. By the time breakfast is over, the early birds are gathering for another meal, the William Gillette Memorial Luncheon at the Old Homestead Restaurant in the Chelsea neighbourhood. It too is conducted strictly by reservation; those who were too late in applying for tickets, or who decided against a heavy lunch, will be sightseeing instead, or getting a head start on the afternoon's shopping, which may well include visits to the local mystery bookstores. The Mysterious Bookshop often invites Sherlockian authors to be on hand to sign their books and meet their readers.

On the Friday evening BSI members put on their finest (black tie is popular, though not compulsory) and gather for drinks and dinner. The meal has had a series of venues over the years, most recently settling at 24 Fifth Avenue. With the recent advent of women into the Irregulars' ranks, it is no longer true that the cocktail hour will be graced with the presence of only one woman, to be toasted respectfully as "The Woman" and then sent away in a cab as the men go in to dinner. The tradition of The Woman is still maintained — she is usually the wife or widow of a prominent Irregular, and she goes off to dine with previous years' recipients of the same honour. But now a modest number of women remain on hand to dine with the men. There is room for about 175 people altogether at the BSI dinner, and invitations are greatly coveted. Invested Irregulars can expect them in the mail from Wiggins, the BSI's leader, and are allowed to suggest the names of eligible non-Irregulars whom Wiggins will consider inviting if there is room. The wise Sherlockian attending the BSI dinner will bring a folding satchel to carry away the souvenirs and novelties distributed by friends and advertisers. He (or now she) can expect an evening of convivial conversation and long-drawn-out programming, including a series of original presentations and a number of BSI traditions. Someone will read the Constitution and Buy-Laws of the society, someone will recite "Sherlock Holmes's Prayer" as composed by Christopher Morley, there will be a recital of the Musgrave Ritual, a scratchy recording will be played of James Montgomery singing "Aunt Clara".

While these things are going on in a largely male atmosphere, the January dinner of the Adventuresses of Sherlock Holmes is taking place elsewhere in New York. The ASH dinner was for some years held in the historic surroundings of Keen's Chop House, a restaurant where the BSI gathered in its more informal and smaller days, but the ASH too have now outgrown Keen's. This dinner is attended mostly by women, although for more than a decade men have also been welcome — both those who were not able to get invitations to the BSI event, but applied in time for invitations to this one, and men who consciously chose the company of women over the company of men. The program is acknowledged, by those who have tried both events, to be somewhat livelier than that at the BSI dinner, the entertainment more original, and certainly the crowd rowdier and more high-pitched.

The January weekend in New York continues with private parties, visits to bookstores, outings to the theatre if anything Sherlockian is playing, and hours of conversation with friends new and old. The only standing event after Friday evening's dinners is a Saturday afternoon cocktail party. This gathering began as a private party thrown by Julian Wolff each year for "Irregulars and their ladies"; with annually growing crowds, the increasing number of women and men who are not Irregulars attending other parts of the weekend's festivity, and now the arrival of women as Irregulars themselves, the party has become a general-admission event with tickets offered for sale.

Unlike most conventions, the January Sherlockian weekend has no registration desk, no organizing committee and no published agenda. The date is determined by the leadership of the BSI, events are organized by their volunteer sponsors, and the word goes out along the grapevine and through the newsletters: meet in New York on the stated weekend, order lunch and dinner tickets from these sources, prepare for much to drink and little time to sleep, and enough talk to make even a Sherlockian hoarse.

Conventions, workshops, tours. At other times of the year, too, Sherlockians gather. The weekend workshops organized by John Bennett Shaw (first at Notre Dame University in 1977) set the pattern for similar events sponsored by colleges, other institutions, or local Sherlockian societies here and there. A weekend conference is likely to include half a dozen or more formal papers, some films or dramatic presentations, quizzes, music, a banquet allowing the opportunity for participants to show off Victorian costumes if they wish, and many late-night hours of conversation. Events of this sort are usually in the summer, and because of the work involved they generally take place just once, although there are a few repeated events. An annual March workshop is held at Wright State University in Dayton, Ohio. At any such event one can expect to see many Sherlockians from the immediate neighbourhood, particularly members of the sponsoring society if there is one. Out-of-towners will also be there — some who happened to be in the area, others whose passionate enthusiasm for Sherlockian society means that they attend every such event within a thousand-mile radius of home. Finally there will be a few prominent names, mingling with local neophytes who ask them in awed tones about their Irregular friends, their publishing achievements and their deep knowledge of the Canon.

Most notable of the annual events is "Autumn in Baker Street", held each October under the management of Bob Thomalen. Formerly based at the Bear Mountain resort north of New York, it has lately been moved to a hotel in Westchester County. The programme for the 1987 weekend gives some sense of how Sherlockians might choose to spend a little more than twenty-four hours in one another's company:

Saturday Afternoon
Welcome & Introduction — Bob Thomalen, BSI
The Devil's Foot: An Explication — Herb Tinning, BSI
Ground Rules & Dinner Selections
Sherlock Holmes & Switzerland: The 1987 Pilgrimage — Wayne Swift, BSI
Quiz — Professor J. Moriarty
Coffee Break
Slouching towards Baker Street — Dore Nash, ASH
The Friends of Bogie's on Baker Street
Announcements
Retire to Rooms
Cocktails
Dinner
The game is afoot
Thereafter — Ineffable Twaddle and Unmitigated Bleat
Sunday Morning
Breakfast
In Defense of Lestrade, et al — Dave Varrelman
Raffle for Grand Prize
Coffee Break
This Is Holmes? — Charlie Adams
The Man with the Twisted Stethoscope: Some Thoughts on
   the Career of Dr. John H. Watson — Bob Katz, BSI
Closing Remarks — Bob Thomalen, BSI
Farewell Luncheon and Leave Taking

The "1987 Pilgrimage" was a trip to Reichenbach, and other points of interest, led by Sherry Rose Bond and Scott Bond of Philadelphia. Several such ventures have taken place, including trips organized by the Sherlock Holmes Society of London in 1978, 1987, and 1991. That society, unhampered by the expenses of transatlantic travel, has also made journeys in pursuit of Holmes's traces in Oxford, Cambridge, Winchester, and other parts of England. From New York, there have twice been Sherlockian cruises to Bermuda.

An outing to the race track by a group of Sherlockians becomes a "Silver Blaze" event, in honour of the story by that title, if the track authorities will make one of the day's races a special feature and allow the Sherlockians to give a prize to the owner of the winning horse. A Silver Blaze outing to New York's Belmont track takes place each September, organized by the Baker Street Irregulars; in May of each year, the Red Circle of Washington arranges a Silver Blaze at Pimlico, near Baltimore. Other cities have seen such events from time to time, the newest addition to the annual list being a race at Woodbine sponsored by the Bootmakers of Toronto.

Despite what outsiders often assume, Sherlockians do not necessarily frequent "murder mystery weekends" — events in which a house party in a grand hotel, or a chartered railway coach, is disrupted by a murder in which victim, suspects and police are played by actors scattered through the crowd. Some Sherlockians enjoy such activities and seek them out (they are often sponsored by specialist travel agencies) while others do not, but they rarely if ever form part of the entertainment on a strictly Sherlockian occasion.

When a Sherlockian travels, the first hope is to find a special event at the end of the journey; failing that, visitors are always welcome at the regular meetings of local societies. Some such gatherings, such as the annual dinner of the Three Garridebs in May, and the now-defunct dinner of The Master's Class in Philadelphia on the Sunday of the New York "January weekend", are particularly well known. But if nothing is scheduled, a travelling Sherlockian will pick up the telephone anyway to see whether any of the locals are free for dinner. Someone is always happy to greet the visitor, talk about matters of common interest, and raise a glass to the honour of Sherlock Holmes.

Toasts. Especially in some circles in the United States, Sherlockians enjoy a tradition of rowdy drinking, and both in merriment and in imitation of formal Victorian dinners, they often drink toasts. Toasts are proposed chiefly to the health and memory of characters in the Canon, or to their author. (A toast to "the Queen", meaning Victoria rather than Her present Majesty, is also popular, even in the American republic.) This custom may owe something to the one-time vogue for propounding what would now be called trivia questions, with the loser of a challenge buying the next round. Having identified Grimesby Roylott, the company might cheerfully drink to his downfall. Probably from such origins, the traditional toasts of the Baker Street Irregulars are "The Woman"; "Mrs. Hudson"; "Mycroft"; and "Dr. Watson's Second Wife". Enthusiasts have sometimes added Dr. Watson's Third Wife, Dr. Watson's Fourth Wife, *et seq.* Traditionally a toast is a brief sentence, which may however come at the end of a speech of praise, with digressions. Some of the best Sherlockian toasts have been given in verse. A rather formal occasion today might include toasts to the Queen (always the first one); Mr. Sherlock Holmes; Sir Arthur Conan Doyle; Dr. Watson; Mrs.

Watson; and (for example) The Hound. Old-fashioned, non-Sherlockian toasts, such as "The Ladies" and "Absent Friends", are rarely heard.

Overseas

Enthusiasm for Sherlock Holmes is of course not limited to North America. It is particularly intense in Britain, where the earliest readers of the Canon lived, and where it is easy to imagine that Holmes walked these very streets, rode these very railway lines. Although British and American activity developed mostly in isolation, there are growing ties between the Sherlockians of Canada and the United States and the "Holmesians" (their preferred term) of Britain.

Early Holmesians. Sherlockian interest began in Britain before there was anything of the sort in the United States. The father of it all was Ronald Arbuthnot Knox (1888-1957), Roman Catholic priest (later Monsignor), scholar and Bible translator, who chose to make a sectarian point in a satirical way in a paper delivered to an Oxford University student society in 1912. His theme was the merits and limitations of textual "higher criticism" for the understanding of the Bible, and he chose to convey his meaning by trying to apply the Biblical techniques to a more popular Canon. The title he chose was "Studies in the Literature of Sherlock Holmes". Among the students who heard the paper was the young Christopher Morley, later to be founder of the Baker Street Irregulars, who described the impact of Knox's work thus:

> The device of pretending to analyse matters of amusement with full severity is the best way to reproach those who approach the highest subjects with too literal a mind. This new frolic in criticism was welcome at once; those who were students at Oxford in that ancient day remember how Mr. Knox was invited around from college to college to reread his agreeable lampoon.

"Studies in the Literature of Sherlock Holmes" eventually formed a chapter in Knox's book *Essays in Satire* (1928).

The gage was picked up at England's other ancient university, Cambridge, where Sydney (later Sir Sydney) Roberts (1887-1966), an authority on the works of Samuel Johnson, found time to reply to Knox in *A Note on the Watson Problem*, a pamphlet published (1929) by the Cambridge University Press. Other writings by Roberts followed: *Doctor Watson: Prolegomena to the Study of a Biographical Problem* in 1931 (based on an article published in 1930), *Holmes and Watson: A Miscellany* in 1953. Knox had used Sherlock Holmes as a tool in making a theological argument, but Roberts found in Holmes a life-long interest, and established a learned tradition that many British enthusiasts have followed ever since.

In or about 1934, a Sherlock Holmes Society was founded by the pioneer Sherlockians in Britain. It flourished for only a couple of years, having lapsed even before World War II put an end to such frivolities. Any hope of its revival was dashed by the death (in a 1941 air raid) of Archie MacDonell, the Scots novelist who was its secretary and principal moving spirit.

The Sherlock Holmes Society of London. A revival of the society came in 1951. The train of events began with the Festival of Britain, a period of cultural events organized by the government as a way to celebrate the return to peacetime conditions (despite continuing austerity and food rationing). Among the Festival's events was a Sherlock Holmes exhibition sponsored by the Borough of St. Marylebone, the local government in the area of London that included Baker Street. Collectors who lent memorabilia for the exhibition, and others whose interest was stimulated by the exhibition, agreed to form what they called the Sherlock Holmes Society of London. Sydney Roberts became the founding president; R. Ivar Gunn was chairman (his widow, Margaret Gunn, was for many years a central presence in the councils of the SHS); Colin Prestige, a Kent lawyer and expert on the operettas of Gilbert and Sullivan, was among the founders.

Until recently, few British Sherlockians were well known in North America, with the exception of "Don" — Edward A. D. St.G. Hamilton, sixth Marquess of Donegall (1903-1975). A former war correspondent, he was associated in his obituaries with "journalism and jazz", and his career had many other features, from his presence at the coronation of George V in 1911 (he was the youngest person in Westminster Abbey for the occasion) to achievements in boating and skiing. As for his Sherlockian merits, James Edward Holroyd said in the *Sherlock Holmes Journal* that

> It would be difficult to imagine anyone, here or overseas, who more wholeheartedly exemplified Holmes's own dictum of "playing the game for the game's own sake" than Lord Donegall. His favourite adventure was "The Empty House", no doubt in part because it originally appeared in the *Strand Magazine* in October, 1903, the month of his birth. . . . His library, divided between London and Switzerland, was one of the most comprehensive in the field.

Other prominent members of the Sherlock Holmes Society of London have included these:

• Guy Warrack, distinguished orchestral conductor and author of *Sherlock Holmes and Music* (1947).
• James Edward Holroyd (ca. 1902-1985), who first suggested the idea for the 1951 Sherlock Holmes exhibition and then became one of the founders of the SHS. He was author of *Baker Street By-Ways* (1959) and *Seventeen Steps to 221B* (1967), and for many years wrote a column of pithy observations, "The Egg-Spoon", for the society's *Sherlock Holmes Journal*.
• Sir Paul (later Lord) Gore-Booth (1909-1984), for a long period the society's beloved president, in the intervals of his work in a notable diplomatic career.
• Stanley MacKenzie, identified even in 1962 as having a Sherlockian collection that was "probably the largest in Europe", and now even better known for the treasures he delights in showing to friends.
• Philip and Patsy Dalton, a couple who have both been active in the society's councils.
• Anthony (Tony) Howlett, a barrister to whom is attributed the unexceptionable answer "Yes" when he was asked, "Is Sherlock Holmes real or fictional?"

• (Captain) W. R. (Bill) Michell, for some years Honorary Secretary of the society.

The SHS has a highly formal structure including both a President (currently Frank Allen) and a Chairman (Shirley Purves), as well as two Honorary Secretaries (Pamela Bruxner in charge of meetings, and [Commander] Godfrey Stavert in charge of memberships; his address is 3 Outram Road, Southsea, Hampshire PO5 1QP). The society's Council includes such names as Roger Johnson, P. L. Horrocks, and Kathryn White.

Besides its periodic meetings in London, the SHS is known for two series of expeditions. Three times (in 1968, 1978 and 1987) members have travelled to Switzerland in costume, to visit the Reichenbach Falls and other points of interest. Annually, there is a weekend excursion to a British town where the details of one or two Canonical stories can be investigated first-hand. Among other achievements of the society is its involvement in the making of the 43-minute film "Mr. Sherlock Holmes of London", produced in 1971.

Publication of *The Sherlock Holmes Journal* began in May 1952, carrying Sherlockian scholarship and news, originally by SHS members and then by Americans and others as well. The *SHJ*, published twice a year, is now one of the world's finest Sherlockian journals. It is currently edited by Nicholas Utechin and Heather Owen. (Subscriptions for non-members of the society are managed by Derek Hinrich, 11 Lindsay Close, Epsom, Surrey KT19 8JJ.)

Although the Sherlock Holmes Society of London is the national society for British Sherlockians, inevitably its activities are centred in London, so that enthusiasts in other parts of the country have found it worth while to establish local societies. Two of these are of special importance:

• The Northern Musgraves, recently established and with an active programme of publications (David Stuart Davies, 69 Greenhead Road, Huddersfield, West Yorkshire HD1 4ER).
• The Franco-Midland Hardware Company, specializing in correspondence activity for those unable to meet in person ([Squadron Leader] Philip Weller, 6 Bramham Moor, Hill Head, Fareham, Hampshire PO14 3RU).

Distinguished for his scholarship, though not extremely active in social activities, is Richard Lancelyn Green of London, who does find time to manage his business in the intervals of his prodigious work as author, editor, and researcher about Holmes and, in particular, Doyle.

Hardwick and Harrison. Two British Sherlockians, active chiefly outside the circle of the SHS, are in classes of their own. The younger was Michael Hardwick (1924-1991), author of several pastiches — *Prisoner of the Devil* (1979) was particularly admired — and of much other Sherlockian writing as well. He was, for example, responsible for dozens of scripts for the series starring Carleton Hobbs as Holmes on BBC radio. In collaboration with his wife, Mollie, he wrote a minor biography of Arthur Conan Doyle, *The Man Who Was Sherlock Holmes* (1964), and one of the most widely used of Sherlockian reference books, the breezy *Sherlock Holmes Companion* (1962). Alone he produced its successor, *The Complete Guide to Sherlock Holmes* (1986). Michael and Mollie together dramatized several Canonical tales in *Four Sherlock Holmes Plays* (1964), *The Game's Afoot* (1969), and *Four More Sherlock Holmes Plays* (1973). Nor was their work limited to Sherlockian writings; they were associated with "The Duchess of Duke Street" on British television, and with the novelizations of many episodes of "Upstairs, Downstairs". Wrote David Hammer in an obituary notice in the *Baker Street Journal*: "Michael Hardwick was the kindest of men, . . . a masterful teller of tales in print and in person, and a thoroughgoing gentleman. He was the kind of man that one was proud to call a friend and we are all diminished by his loss."

The other unique figure among British Sherlockians was still more remarkable: Michael Harrison (born April 25, 1907; died September 13, 1991). His work was usefully summarized by Roger Johnson in the *Sherlock Holmes Journal*:

> His first important work in the field of Sherlock Holmes resulted from a seven-book contract, and the subject was suggested to him by the publisher. That book was the classic *In the Footsteps of Sherlock Holmes* [1958]. Others were to come, but this painstaking and engagingly discursive investigation of Holmes's England should be on every Sherlockian's bookshelf. Even here, though, Michael's occasional hastiness could be seen. . . . The book was deservedly well-received; a revised edition appeared in 1972, and the author produced a second volume in the same vein, *The London of Sherlock Holmes* [1972], equally invaluable to an understanding of the metropolis in which the detective lived.
>
> *The World of Sherlock Holmes* [1973] followed, and another of the author's quirks became apparent: the tendency to suppose — or even to invent — and then to present the supposition as fact. . . .
>
> Michael Harrison's last books in his field were all published in America. This was a loss for the British reader, as two of them, at least, are among the very best. In 1976, he was invited to compile a *Festschrift* in honour of Dr. Julian Wolff's 70th birthday; the result was *Beyond Baker Street*, which contains not a single dud among its 25 essays. And in 1984 appeared the long-awaited *A Study in Surmise*, in which the author set out what he believed to be the real inspiration for Sherlock Holmes. . . .
>
> Michael Harrison felt that he had been rather snubbed by what he saw as the Sherlockian Establishment in Britain, but he remained on cordial terms with many individuals here.

Particularly striking is *I, Sherlock Holmes*, a purported autobiography of the sleuth, rich like most of Harrison's writing with Victorian detail. His non-Sherlockian books, which were many, ranged from *Fanfare of Strumpets* (1971), about society prostitution, to *Fire from Heaven* (1976), about spontaneous human combustion. There were also a number of novels.

In the United States, he was almost universally beloved among Sherlockians, enjoyed for his great talent at story-telling and knowledge of the Victorian and Edwardian eras. His books sometimes sound rather like transcriptions of the hours he could spend rambling; they are poorly indexed, subjects change on a whim, references are lacking and details sometimes questionable, but the reader who seeks entertainment and the spirit of the age is well rewarded. In old age Harrison made several visits to North America to find appreciative audiences, not only for his talk but for his courtly Edwardian presence, with a gallantry to women and a striking appetite for liquor. At his death there was an outpouring of tribute and anecdote, and Tina Rhea of Greenbelt, Maryland, announced plans to write a biography.

Other lands. In the more distant English-speaking lands, and even outside the English-speaking world, there have been clusters of Sherlockian enthusiasts. Many such groups have been led by a single energetic Sherlockian. Among the best-known, past and present:

> • The Solitary Cyclists of Sweden, led by Ted Bergman of Lidingö; its journal *Baker Street Cab Lantern* was published annually in the 1960's.
> • Sherlock Holmes Klubben i Danmark, led by Henry Lauritzen (1908-1991) of Copenhagen, best known around the Sherlockian world as artist and cartoonist. The society's journal, *Sherlockiana*, was founded as early as 1956.
> • The Sherlock Holmes Society of Australia, led by Alan Olding of Stirling, South Australia.
> • The Crew of the S. S. *Friesland* of Holland, led by Cornelis Helling of Emmeloord; it flourished in the 1950's.

Finally, nowhere in the world does the passion for Sherlock Holmes equal that demonstrated in Japan in recent years. Although Sherlockian activity in that country began with the Baritsu Chapter, founded chiefly by Americans during the postwar occupation, the real father of Sherlockian enthusiasm in Japan is Kouki Naganuma, a deputy minister of finance in the postwar period who wrote several books about Holmes. In 1977, a Japan Sherlock Holmes Club was founded by Tsukasa Kobayashi (born 1929) and his wife, Akana Higashiyama. The two, along with photographer Masaharu Uemura, demonstrated their enthusiasm and knowledge in *Shārokku Hāmuzu no Rondon* (1984), translated into English and published as the sumptuous *Sherlock Holmes's London* (1986). The Japan Sherlock Holmes Club may now be the largest such organization in the world, with more than 1,000 members, including those in eleven branches around the country. The single most active Sherlockian in Japan is Kiyoshi Tanaka (born 1952), an engineer, illustrator, and prolific writer in both Japanese and English. (His address: 8-7 Babacho, Isogo-Ku, Yokohama City, Kanagawa, Japan 235.) Japanese Sherlockians have been responsible for many books, seminars and other activities; the world's first statue of Sherlock Holmes was unveiled in 1988 in Karuizawa Town, Nagano. Attempting to explain the wild popularity of Holmes in his country, Tanaka, as well as citing all the reasons that obtain in English-speaking lands, has added this one: "The stories take place in the Victorian age in England, which corresponds to the dawn of civilization during the Meiji era in Japan — when we modelled our society after those of England and other European nations, and introduced things to Japan such as gas lamps and carriages, etc. Thus, the atmosphere of the stories makes readers feel nostalgic for 'the good old days'."

Chapter IX

A Spreading Influence

Everyone knows who Sherlock Holmes is. "Holmes" is so universally recognized as the name of a detective that when British police created a powerful computer system for cross-referencing the reports and clues associated with complicated cases, they dubbed it HOLMES, for Home Office Large Major Enquiry System. (Other jurisdictions, including Metropolitan Toronto, have now adopted it.) The name is even in the definitive *Oxford English Dictionary*:

> **Sherlock Holmes** *v. trans.*, to make deductions about, to assess, to deduce. . . .

The dictionary also provides evidence for the existence of "sherlocked", "Sherlock-holmesing" and other variations.

To be sure, most of the great unobservant public, who could hardly tell a weaver by his tooth or a compositor by his left thumb, are inclined to identify Sherlock Holmes by his clothes and tools, rather than by his essential traits of principle and brain. The deerstalker hat, the Inverness cape, the magnifying glass, the curved pipe, perhaps the violin: these, in the general estimation, make a detective. But the deerstalker is the invention of illustrator Sidney Paget, the cape its inauthentic if plausible companion; actor William Gillette added the curved pipe, which was enthusiastically adopted by Frederic Dorr Steele for his illustrations. (The "calabash" pipe with its flaring bowl is a still more recent misconception.) Only the magnifying glass, as a tool for observation, and the violin, as a tool for ratiocination, are wholly authentic, although it must be admitted that, in an age before tobacco was understood to be literally poisonous, Sherlock Holmes did smoke. His blue-wreathed image has come down now through a hundred years, and however debased and simplified from the realities of the Canon, it has become a part of England's culture — and of the world's. Holmes and his creator have figured on postage stamps issued by Nicaragua (1972), San Marino (1979), the Comoro Islands (1980), the Turks and Caicos Islands (1984) and Dominica (1991). (Sherlockian connections to "local post" issues and other forms of stamps and coins are summarized in a pamphlet by Benton Wood, *The Philatelic & Numismatic Holmes*, 1990.)

Memorials

Apart from Anne Shirley, whose home "Green Gables" is the chief tourist attraction of Prince Edward Island, there can be few fictional characters whose home is eagerly sought by tourists. But seekers do look for 221B Baker Street, and find no such house. The number 221 is part of an office block occupied by the Abbey National Building Society, a savings and loan institution. Just down the way is the "Sherlock Holmes Museum" at 239 Baker Street, which has not received favourable comment from Sherlockians. Most visitors have been particularly annoyed by the claim of the proprietor, John Aidiniantz, that his building is rightfully 221B and should receive any mail that bears that address. (The post office in fact delivers it to the Abbey National.) The museum, which charges a hefty admission fee, is decorated and furnished in Victorian style and includes a perfunctory reconstruction of the 221B sitting-room, but only a few Holmesian artifacts and souvenirs.

But there are many other places to which Sherlockians can, and do, make pilgrimages.

Museums. The most extensive and reputable of museums devoted to Sherlock Holmes is at Meiringen, Switzerland; it is housed in what was formerly the English church at that village near the Reichenbach Falls. The Sherlock Holmes Museum, on Conan Doyle Place, was opened May 5, 1991, by Dame Jean Conan Doyle, in a ceremony attended by some hundred members of the Sherlock Holmes Society of London during one of that society's pilgrimages to Switzerland. The centrepiece of the museum is a reconstruction of the 221B sitting-room, done by Tony Howlett, a prominent member of the SHS and mastermind of the museum, and architects John and Sylvia Reid. Custodian of the museum is Jürg Musfeld, proprietor of a nearby and longstanding hotel which honours Holmes's name (Park-Hotel Sauvage "Englischer Hof", 3860 Meiringen, Bernese Oberland, Switzerland).

At Crowborough, East Sussex, where Doyle lived in his last years, the "Crowborough Cross" hotel includes a museum and archive, the "Conan Doyle (Crowborough) Establishment", under the management of local historian Malcolm Payne. "All of the old rooms have now been made into one long room," Payne wrote shortly after the Establishment opened in 1989, "and to step inside is to step back into Victorian times. . . . At the present time, we are funded mainly by local businesses which benefit from any tourism which we attract." The Establishment offers to provide some research material about Doyle by mail, on request, for a fee. Doyle's house is now a retirement home, Windlesham Manor. Not far from Crowborough is Minstead, where Sir Arthur and Lady Doyle lie buried in the churchyard; the markers that stood over their former graves, in the grounds at Windlesham, are now in the Minstead church belfry.

Restorations of the 221B sitting-room can be seen in more places than Meiringen alone. The Château de Lucens, also in Switzerland, established by Adrian Conan Doyle, is longer heard of, but enthusiasts as well as casual tourists visit the "Sherlock Holmes" pub in London's Northumberland Street. The cozy replica there, in an upstairs room separated from viewers by a railing and window, includes much of the memorabilia originally assembled for the Festival of Britain exhibition in 1951. A similar, newer reconstruction of the sitting-room is in the "S. Holmes, Esq." pub of the Holiday Inn Union Square, San Francisco.

At the Granada Television studios near Manchester, an exhibition in Holmes's honour includes portions of the sets on which the Jeremy Brett television productions were done. Kathryn White and David Stuart Davies, two prominent British Sherlockians, helped to plan the exhibit, in which one can see not only the sitting-room of 221B Baker Street but part of the "Bar of Gold" opium den, as well as the façade of Bradley's tobacco-shop; there are also exhibits of a more traditional kind, such as *Strand* magazines, film stills, and other artifacts.

The libraries that collect Sherlockian and Doylean material are natural places of pilgrimage, if not strictly museums; the Metropolitan Toronto Reference Library does house its collection in a "Room 221B" with some Victorian ambiance. Gillette Castle in Hadlyme, Connecticut, is a state park and museum celebrating the work of William Gillette, which consisted largely of impersonating Holmes. The visitor to Universal Studios in Hollywood will see a little of Basil Rathbone.

Statues and plaques. The world's first statue of Sherlock Holmes stands in Karuizawa Town, Nagano, Japan, erected there by Japanese Sherlockians to mark the place where the Canon was first translated into Japanese. The second such statue is in Edinburgh; it was unveiled in 1991 by the Federation of Master Builders, close to Arthur Conan Doyle's birthplace. Admirers of Doyle were regretful that it was Holmes, rather than his creator, who was represented, and horrified that Doyle's birthdate was misstated in the inscription on the base.

Plaques associated with Holmes can be seen on two houses where Doyle lived: the little house in Bush Villas, Elm Grove, Southsea, and his house in Tennison Road, South Norwood, London. The home of Holmes himself is not so commemorated, presumably because of the difficulty of finding 221B Baker Street, but in the Baker Street station of the Underground there are tiles and other artworks symbolic of Holmes.

Two sites in London have Sherlockian plaques. One is the Criterion Bar — the building in Piccadilly Circus (no longer a bar) where Watson met his friend Stamford in the incident that led to his acquaintance with Holmes. That plaque was erected by enthusiastic Sherlockians in 1953. The following year, other enthusiasts managed to put a plaque in the room where, according to *A Study in Scarlet*, Holmes and Watson actually set eyes on one another: the old pathology laboratory (now a curator's office) at St. Bartholomew's Hospital. Visiting Sherlockians wanting a look at that plaque generally come away with tales to tell about the difficulty of finding it, as Bart's is far from making it a public attraction — but it does exist and can be seen.

There are several plaques in the area of Switzerland's Reichenbach Falls, where Holmes met Professor Moriarty in mortal combat. The first was erected in 1952 at the supposed Englischer Hof — then the Rossli Inn, now the Sherlock Holmes Sport-Hotel. A pair of plaques was erected in 1957 near the Falls, and yet another in 1992 at the precise spot where Holmes and Moriarty met.

Restaurants and businesses. Holmes's own favourite restaurant appears to have been Simpson's in the Strand, London, but few of the many hostelries named in his honour are at the same gastronomic level as that distinguished establishment. The one clear exception was until recently Sherlock's on Sheppard, in Toronto, which — like Simpson's — specialized in roast beef.

Other Sherlockian restaurants, most with highly collectible menus and beer coasters, include Sherlock's Home in Chicago, Holmes and Watson Ltd. in Troy, New York, Dr. Watson's Pub in Philadelphia, the Sherlock Holmes in Edmonton, Professor Moriarty's in Saratoga Springs, and so on and on. Most of these North American establishments are pubs with a synthetic British atmosphere, with deerstalkers and similar symbols decorating the menus and perhaps the walls. The Sherlock Holmes pub in London's Northumberland Street is by no means the same place as the Sherlock Holmes Hotel, in Baker Street itself; the latter has its own eating-places (including, for a time, the coyly named Ristorante Moriarti). In York Place, Edinburgh, is the Sir Arthur Conan Doyle pub, near the author's birthplace.

Businesses in many cities have borrowed the Holmes name with, perhaps, even less justification — although one can defend Sherlock Security Systems of Baltimore, and certainly Sherlock Bones of Oakland, a detective agency billing itself as "tracer of missing pets". In Toronto, Steve Overbury, a genuine private investigator, is in business as "Sherlock Holmes Canada". Also reported are several tobacconists, including Winston and Holmes Ltd. of Toronto and Sherlock Pipes & Tobaccos of Colorado Springs; a plethora of real estate agencies called Sherlock Homes (Seattle, Miami, Cincinnati and elsewhere); and the Sherlock Holmes Travel Service of Boston.

Souvenirs. The Sherlockian restaurants and bars are lavish sources of coasters, matchbooks, menus, and similar trophies for collectors. So are promotional items from businesses with Sherlockian names (at least one collection boasts a rubber jar-opener bearing the advertisement of Sherlock Homes Real Estate of Wescosville, Pennsylvania). Right in London's Baker Street is the Sherlock Holmes Memorabilia Company, selling souvenirs. Collectibles include many classes of material:

- Stuffed toys, intended more or less for children; there are several deerstalkered dogs on the market, in particular.
- Plastic and cloth figures of Snoopy, the dog from the *Peanuts* comic strip, in the Holmes gear he sometimes also affects in print.
- Pipes, whether intended for actual smoking or only as novelties (a calabash filled with after-shave lotion was available from Avon, the door-to-door sales firm, in the 1970's).
- Clothing, ranging from neckwear (the Baker Street Irregulars has its own tie; the Sherlock Holmes Society of London has both a tie and a ladies' scarf) to lingerie with vaguely Holmesian motifs. There are also many T-shirts, especially those produced by Sherlockian societies for their members and friends.
- Magnifying glasses, including a "Sherlock Hose" model produced in the 1960's by B. F. Goodrich of Canada.
- Busts of Holmes, produced for connoisseurs, including Royal Doulton "toby jugs" in two sizes.

Several small entrepreneurs produce keychains, mugs, letter-openers and other artifacts — not all of the finest quality — for the Sherlockian market. Few of these items have much aesthetic value, although a bust produced by Edgar P.

Smith in the 1960's, as by "Oscar Meunier", is widely admired. For completist collectors they are of course essential, but otherwise their value is in demonstrating how extensively the culture of the English-speaking world has been penetrated by the image, however distorted, of a detective with a magnifying glass and a fore-and-aft cap. Many collectibles are pictured in *The Sherlock Holmes Collection* (1987) by Charles Hall, a Sherlockian in Scotland; the book also reproduces film stills, cartoons and illustrations.

The Common Image

Clearly the customers of businesses that use the name of Sherlock Holmes are not all Sherlockians. The proprietors recognize the appeal of the great detective to every part of the public, and a level of name recognition that few other figures can claim. "Sherlock" stands with Elvis, Marilyn, Romeo, and few if any others as a given name that has become familiar to all. Even toddlers know it, at least in the form of "Sherlock Hemlock", a deerstalkered character on the children's television programme "Sesame Street" and in its spinoff toys, games and books, including *Sherlock Hemlock and the Great Twiddlebug Mystery* (1972). The regular appearance of new made-for-television movies with new challenges for Holmes is an indication that viewers find his figure fascinating even if they are fuzzy about the details.

Allusions. "I hear of Sherlock everywhere," Mycroft Holmes tells Watson in "The Greek Interpreter". The alert reader still hears of Sherlock everywhere a hundred years later, encountering jokes about "amazing deductions" at income tax season and references to unusually perceptive politicians as "the Sherlock Holmes" of the public service. Cartoons, the expression of the contemporary culture in printed form, are full of such references:

> • "Chubb and Chauncey", July 4, 1989: "Must be a fire someplace! . . . The guy is a regular Sherlock!"
> • "Garfield", June 2, 1992: "Somebody ate the piece of cake I was saving. . . . Any suspects, Sherlock?"

Many popular references to Holmes are based on one of two phrases that have become associated with Holmes even though they appear nowhere in the Canon:

> • "Elementary, my dear Watson." Holmes often addresses his companion as "my dear Watson," and several times uses the word "elementary", most strikingly in "The Crooked Man":

> "Excellent!" I cried.
> "Elementary," said he.

But the two are never juxtaposed — save in the mouths of Basil Rathbone and a thousand subsequent actors. Their apocryphal nature does not keep them from being endlessly used and reused:

"Elementary, my dear Watson," said the famous British detective Sherlock Holmes
— a phrase that could also be used to describe the procedure involved in applying
for an award at the [University of Calgary] student awards and financial aid office.

They were even listed, as Doyle's own words, in the 1937 edition of *Bartlett's
Familiar Quotations*, but have been expunged in subsequent editions. Their saving grace is their flexibility in jokes and puns: What school did Sherlock Holmes
attend? (Elementary.) John Bennett Shaw, inveterate punster, wrote about the
detective's eating and drinking habits in the *Baker Street Journal* in 1967 and
titled his article "Alimentary, My Dear Watson".

• "Quick, Watson, the needle!" This phrase is perhaps even more objection-
able than the other, suggesting as it does a desperation in Holmes's use of drugs
by injection. The half-informed public is fascinated by the detective's drug
habit, in the era of "Just say no," and when a Sherlockian gives a talk at a public
library, the first or second question from the audience is bound to be about
cocaine. Whatever Holmes's unhealthy habits, there is no evidence that he relied
on Watson to reach the apparatus for him; indeed, Watson is frequently seen
reproaching his friend for his use of drugs. But as a fragment of folk knowledge
the phrase hangs on.

The best-known case of Sherlock Holmes is certainly *The Hound of the Bask-
ervilles*, which is also the most often mentioned by non-Sherlockian authors.
Cartoonists have had endless fun with it, from Gary Larson's "Parakeet of the
Baskervilles" in "The Far Side" to a Gahan Wilson classic in *Playboy* (1959):
"It strikes me you've made a great deal of bother over very little, Baskerville."
(That was the first cartoon in four pages of drawings by the master of twisted
humour; the last of them is captioned, "Extraordinary thing, Watson — the clues
indicate the killer to have been a man of your exact build and appearance!")

In more literate circles, the Sherlockian words most often alluded to are from
"Silver Blaze":

"Is there any point to which you would wish to draw my attention?"
"To the curious incident of the dog in the night-time."
"The dog did nothing in the night-time."
"That was the curious incident," remarked Sherlock Holmes.

Now this passage has the merit of exactly capturing Holmes's methods and
indeed personality — the almost Zen quality of recognizing that nothing is
something. And it has application far beyond the behaviour of animals around a
horse-barn. Politicians act in some of the same way, newspaper allusions suggest:

The dog-that-did-not-bark aphorism applies almost too closely for comfort to the
universities' reaction to the Government's plan to abolish the long-standing University Grants Committee. (*Times Higher Education Supplement.*)

The report of Mr. Justice William Parker's inquiry effectively ends Mr. Stevens's
political career, but it does not answer a central question about Mr. Mulroney's ini-

tial handling of the Stevens affair and several similar problems. That question, as Sherlock Holmes put it in Silver Blaze, is: why didn't the dog bark? Or at least bark sooner? (*Globe and Mail*, Toronto.)

Well, near enough. Even *Baseball America* used the passage in 1986 to dramatize the reluctance team owners were showing to hire expensive free agents.

In the 1970's a new phrase became popularly associated with Sherlock Holmes: "seven-per-cent solution". It had been in the Canon all along, in *The Sign of the Four*, but it was brought to prominence by Nicholas Meyer's novel *The Seven-Per-Cent Solution* (1974) and the successful movie made from it. Suddenly the phrase was everywhere that a per cent sign might be:

- Andres wanted a wine with a lower alcohol content (seven per cent was the solution). — *Saturday Night*.
- A 5% Solution? — *Time* discusses a scaled reduction of weapons under the Strategic Arms Limitation Treaty.
- The 90 Percent Solution — *Fortune* reports on a federal system of loan guarantees to help American municipalities.

There was a new burst of such constructions in Canada in 1991, when a new national "Goods and Services Tax", with a 7 per cent rate, was introduced; half the editorials about the tax, and advertisements for stores that were offering temporary tax savings, spoke of "the 7-per-cent solution". The per-cent solution has entered the language to the point that many of its users probably no longer think of the Sherlock Holmes connection.

Literature. References to Holmes are not limited to the newspapers, but can be found in every sort of writing. His name may be dropped, or there will be some mention of the Baskerville hound or the Speckled Band, without warning in any novel or memoir. (Not every such reference, however, betrays first-hand acquaintance with the Canon: one sees, for example, the suggestion that looking for a hidden object in plain view is one of Holmes's insights, whereas in fact it was the accomplishment of the Chevalier Dupin in Edgar Allan Poe's "The Purloined Letter".)

Vladimir Nabokov alludes to Holmes here and there in *Pale Fire* (1962), a verse-and-annotations experimental novel that stretches out tentacles into most of western culture. Even more impressive is the Holmesian influence on T. S. Eliot (1888-1965), a poet whose creative roots are in the Edwardian period and who repeatedly writes of London fog and an era that is past. Eliot's best-known allusion to Holmes is in "Macavity", one of the comic poems that make up *Old Possum's Book of Practical Cats* (1939) and were eventually converted into the musical drama "Cats". Macavity is "the mystery cat ... the Napoleon of Crime", with obvious similarities to Professor Moriarty. More important are references here and there in Eliot's more serious verse, including an extract from "The Musgrave Ritual" that is dropped without warning into a tense scene in *Murder in the Cathedral* (1935). Eliot had some scholarly interest in Holmes, corresponding occasionally with American Sherlockians, and did acknowledge the influence of the Canon on his work.

More recently, serious literature has drawn on the Sherlock Holmes tradition in the form of Umberto Eco's *The Name of the Rose* (Italian 1980, English translation 1983). This large and dense novel — on which was based a successful movie starring Sean Connery — is about a mediaeval monk, one William of Baskerville, who turns detective. Eco is himself a scholar and theoretician interested in semiotics, the science of "meaning", and co-editor of *The Sign of Three* (1983), which deals with logic, symbolism and other matters, in a dense and difficult way, including much discussion of Holmes. Naturally, then, similar deep things are readily found in *The Name of the Rose*.

The writers most strongly influenced by Holmes, of course, have been the creators of subsequent detective stories, whose very genre was largely formed by the precedents Doyle set. It can be said that most detective fiction is either a following of Doyle or a rebellion against him, but there are works that explicitly draw on Sherlockian motifs, such as some of the books of Julian Symons (born 1912), a British master of traditional detection. His *A Three Pipe Problem* (1975) is about a young actor whose reputation rests on his role as Sherlock Holmes. *Watson's Choice* (1955) by Gladys Mitchell is in the same category. Most of Ellery Queen can be seen as a tribute to Holmes.

The great detective has even edged his way into science fiction, both overtly (*The Science-Fictional Sherlock Holmes*, a volume of short stories edited by Robert C. Peterson, appeared in 1960) and more subtly. The master of the genre, Robert A. Heinlein, produced *The Moon Is a Harsh Mistress* in 1966; its central figure is a masterful computer called Mycroft. *Earthman's Burden* (1957), by Poul Anderson (himself a Sherlockian) and Gordon R. Dickson, is a delightful collection of episodes about extraterrestrials who adopt one Earthly literary culture after another, including, for a period, that of foggy Baker Street. By a less prominent author, but ingenious and of interest, is *Their Majesties' Bucketeers* (1981) by L. Neil Smith. Away from the printed page, Sherlock Holmes is a recurring background figure in the television and movie series "Star Trek": it is a popular Sherlockian belief that Mr. Spock, played by Leonard Nimoy, is somehow related to Holmes, and a classic is the episode of "Star Trek: The Next Generation" in which Commander Data recreates the Baker Street interior as a holographic environment in which he assumes the role of Holmes.

Advertising. Who has not seen a caricature of a hawk-nosed face, surmounted by a deerstalker hat, in some newspaper or Yellow Pages advertisement? Sherlock Holmes is a commonplace whenever the headline suggests searching, or investigating, or hunting down, some product or service or benefit: "Give us a clue! If you're listed incorrectly in your phone book, please tell us now. . . . Look closer, Watson, a 3 year $1,000 $7\frac{1}{2}$% certificate. . . . You don't have to be a great detective to tell which is the better copy. . . . Looking for the best kitchen value? . . . Why people drive themselves to the airport is a mystery to me." Many such ads are simplistic, with unimaginative drawings of Holmes or, at best, familiar portraits of Basil Rathbone. But a few advertisers, over the years, have done better, creating sympathetic and humorous text as well as elaborately posed photographs. An example of such sophistication is "The case of the disappearing files", a double-page magazine advertisement from Xerox of Canada:

> "My dear fellow, haven't you found that file on 'The Case of the One Armed Man' yet?
> "I know it's here somewhere. What we need is more filing space to organize all our paperwork." . . .
> "But, how did you know this new Xerox 4000 Copier could solve all our filing problems?"
> "Elementary my dear fellow. I spoke to the people at Xerox yesterday."

Then there are the advertisers who have used Holmes as the principal character in a booklet or brochure — such as Boeing Computer Services (*The Great Training Mystery*), State Farm Fire and Casualty Co. (*Surelocked Homes*), and the Ontario Chiropractic Association (*The Discoveries of Inspector Spine*). More substantial and noncommercial, but similar in using Holmes to deliver a message, is *The Life Insurance Conspiracy* (1976) by Peter Spielmann and Aaron Zelman; astonishingly, Holmes has also been used several times as the central character in textbooks of computer programming. In a class by itself is a 1989 campaign from the Canada Post Corporation: "Following Your Mail Closely", involving brochures that explain registered mail and other special services, brochures that were distributed across Canada in counter displays consisting of striking foot-wide cardboard silhouettes of Holmes.

Television commercials starring Holmes have been more ephemeral in a period before the widespread use of video recorders; they have ranged from the seemingly authentic to the absurd. At the latter extreme is a 1992 commercial presenting one baby dressed as Holmes (that is, in a deerstalker) and another as Watson (in a bowler hat) discussing the relative merits of different brands of diaper. The message, as in decades of print ads, is simple: Sherlock Holmes sees the details that others miss, unravels the mysterious, and understands the truth when others, including the viewer and the perennially befuddled Watson, can see nothing.

Academic Scholarship

"Popular culture" is the slightly derisory title under which professors of English classify detective stories, science fiction, romances, and other books that large numbers of people actually and happily read. Such scholars, those who notice Arthur Conan Doyle and Sherlock Holmes at all, usually include the Canon and its study under this rubric, and one Sherlockian book (*Dr. Joe Bell*, by Ely Liebow) was actually published in 1982 by the "Popular Press" of Bowling Green University in Ohio, known as a centre for such study.

Only in very recent years have serious literary presses published works about Sherlock Holmes, or serious literary journals made room for articles about him. Much of the difficulty is of course that Sherlockian "scholars" make playful assumptions about the historic existence of Holmes, Watson, and their associates, pretending to analyse history rather than literature. Even when Fordham University Press was persuaded, in 1975, to take over publication of the *Baker Street Journal*, it was with no pretence that the *BSJ* would be publishing serious literary scholarship. Strikingly, a journal which did sometimes aspire to serious scholarship began publication in the same year: *Baker Street Miscellanea*. Within the year it was acknowledging support from Northeastern Illinois University, not from a department of English but from "the Advisory Committee on Popular Culture". Most of the professors who have written for Sherlockian journals in recent years — anthropologist Donald Pollock, medico Ely Liebow, film historian Frank Hoffman, even literary scholar Robert Fleissner — do so with little hope that Sherlockian articles will be taken seriously in their academic *curricula vitae*. If they manage to introduce Holmes and Doyle into credible scholarly articles in reputable journals, they do so with an effort.

The scholarly disdain for Holmes and Doyle is certainly moderating. A milestone was the 1983 publication by Oxford's Clarendon Press of *A Bibliography of A. Conan Doyle*, by Richard Lancelyn Green and John Michael Gibson, as part of its Soho Bibliographies series. Earlier, the *World Bibliography of Sherlock Holmes and Dr. Watson* (1974), compiled by Ronald B. DeWaal, then humanities librarian at Colorado State University, had received an award as the best work of bibliography published in the United States that year. The lower criticism, at least, was achieving respectability. Then McGill-Queen's University Press published Donald Redmond's *Sherlock Holmes: A Study in Sources* in 1982, and Southern Illinois University Press published *The Quest for Sir Arthur Conan Doyle*, edited by Jon L. Lellenberg, in 1987. With such recognition, Doyle studies, as long as they are firmly rooted in fact, can be said to have become respectable. But why has it taken so long? The simplest answer is snobbery: that academics shy away from discussing literature that ordinary people read and like, in favour of the elite and obscure, which may seem to need more explicating. "Entrance into those rarefied reading lists quite often demands that the writer be either 'dull' or 'difficult' in order to satisfy the critic's sense of hierarchy," writes Kathryn White in *ACD: the Journal of the Arthur Conan Doyle Society*. The neglect of Doyle in the late twentieth century is consistent with the attitude in university English departments, as recently as fifty years ago, that nineteenth- and twentieth-century writings were not deserving of scholarly attention; a century ago, Oxford barely tolerated the study of English literature from any period. Beyond that conservatism, however, there may have been a sense that little in Doyle was important or enduring — most of his books now languish unread, and even Sherlock Holmes is better known as a simplified cliché than from the pages of the works in which he first appeared. White again: "We may, perhaps, agree that Conan Doyle did not write great literature, but his work should not be dismissed without fair trial."

From time to time, non-Sherlockian academics have spoken or written about Doyle with an air of astonished discovery. One example was a 1971 paper by Jay Macpherson, of the University of Toronto's Victoria College, on "Sherlock

Holmes as a Figure of Romance". Another was a 1990 paper by McGill University's Paul Piehler, which included a devastating examination of why so rich a mine as the Canon has been largely ignored by his colleagues in English departments. Papers like these, sounding like announcements that a new continent has just been discovered, can sound patronizing or defensive or merely naïve, and are bound to hit many high points very briefly. They can, of course, report their authors' awareness that the detective story, with its "puritan" virtues and predictability, owes most of its hereditary traits to the genes of Sherlock Holmes. Beyond that, they can reveal that Holmes is a romantic hero or a "mythic" figure; they can tell their unsurprised readers that Doyle was a genius at recording the details of Victorian society; they can note with astonishment that the Canon, like Doyle's other work, draws on the dark side of the psyche, with sexual ambivalences and fears of death. These generalizations are the essential underpinnings of scholarship, but they hardly amount to new scholarly findings. The Canon's readers knew them all along.

A few scholars have done genuinely useful things, both in Sherlockian journals and elsewhere. Absolutely conventional in its method, for example, and enlightening in its results, was a 1972 article in the *Baker Street Journal* by Donald J. Watt: "The Literary Craft of *The Hound of the Baskervilles*". Most important has been a large amount of research about Doyle's life, his methods and the influences on him, published in such books as Donald Redmond's *Sherlock Holmes Among the Pirates*, Owen Dudley Edwards's *The Quest for Sherlock Holmes*, and Kelvin Jones's *Conan Doyle and the Spirits*, as well as in various journals, chiefly *Baker Street Miscellanea* and *ACD*. To date the biographical research has far outpaced the literary study, and a typical step forward involves proof that Doyle saw, knew, or read something, coupled with speculation that some element of his work is the result of that encounter or knowledge.

Professional literary critics have given specific attention to the Canon now and then. The Modern Languages Association's *International Bibliography* now lists about half a dozen articles a year about Doyle and Sherlock Holmes from the dozens of scholarly journals it indexes (apart from numerous articles from the *Baker Street Journal* which it also deems worthy of listing). Tough going, but also illuminating, is a long piece by Audrey Jaffe in a 1990 issue of the Berkeley-based little journal *Representations*. She examined "The Man with the Twisted Lip" using the modern critical technique of "deconstruction", which examines not the author's intent or the reader's subjective reaction, but the actual words of a text, which may be subversive of both. "The Man with the Twisted Lip", Jaffe reports, "both constructs and disables detective fiction's fantasy of social control"; she continues to examine the story in terms of "exchange . . . transformation . . . exposure".

Ordinary readers do not find today's literary criticism entirely congenial or even, always, comprehensible. Semiotics and deconstructionism may be passing out of fashion, but their replacements are likely to be no more easily grasped;

even educated readers are still struggling with the Marxist, Freudian, and feminist approaches that were new in earlier decades. It seems certain that every approach can find something of interest in the Canon, drawing the reader's attention to such matters as Holmes's elitist disdain for physical labour, the infantile breast fixation of Watson, and the constrained role of damsel-in-distress allocated to most of Doyle's heroines. Serious attention to the four novels and fifty-six short stories about Sherlock Holmes has barely begun.

The Appeal of Sherlock Holmes

The constitution of the Baker Street Irregulars defines its purpose as "the study of the Sacred Writings", that is, the Sherlock Holmes tales. Such "study", and publication of elegantly written mock scholarship with the full apparatus of footnotes, is an honoured activity in the Sherlockian world. But it lost some of its novelty as English professors began to trespass on the territory, filling up the *Baker Street Journal* with articles that took the texts seriously and sought not so much to entertain as to bolster their authors' scholarly reputations. The original purpose of Sherlockian activity, after all, was enjoyment — an exaggeration, not an abandonment, of the childish excitement with which the original readers, and succeeding generations, read the Sherlock Holmes tales. There is something compelling about Holmes, something about this figure, or at least about the stories that tell of his adventures, so that they have been continuously in print since their first publication, have been translated into dozens of languages, have made their way onto the screen and into the awareness of billions of people.

Fred Strebeigh addressed the central issue in a 1987 article in *Smithsonian* magazine, describing the phenomenon of Sherlockian enthusiasm, which he did not hesitate to call a "cult".

> What pulls Americans so strongly, 100 years after his literary birth, toward Sherlock Holmes? Isaac Asimov, the well-known science-fiction writer (invested by the Irregulars as "The Remarkable Worm Unknown to Science"), suggests that Holmes may be "the most successful fictional character of all time" because he represents the triumph of the "gifted amateur who could see clearly through a fog." Dr. David Musto ("Dr. Anstruther"), of the Yale Medical School and the Yale Sherlock Holmes Society, says that Holmes appeals to modern readers because he represents a life unencumbered by the petty details of human existence. When you read a Holmes story, says Musto, "you encounter a world in which people have breakfast but never use the toilet." Holmes' world is an "exciting place, but it's also peaceful — a world of modified danger."
>
> Other Sherlockians give different answers. At a meeting of an inner circle of the Irregulars ... I heard a range of explanations of Holmes' appeal: the human scale of 19th-century London, ... the influence of the age of radio that began in the 1930s, ... the mythic vitality of the characters.

More from Asimov, writing in *Newsday* in 1984:

> Sherlock Holmes is the epitome of intelligence and he is always on the side of good. He defeats the villains by his superior brains, but he avoids becoming a villain in his turn by not using shrewdness and trickery. He *is* shrewd and he is not

above using trickery, as in donning a clever disguise. That, however, is not his chief weapon. His chief weapon is a combination of acute observation and keen, logical deduction. . . . Before the end of a story, he is sure to reveal his line of reasoning and all seems plain and clear. . . . The audience, meeting such a rare character, cannot help but be delighted. How wonderful to have intelligence made so plain and straightforward that any reader can feel he might be that intelligent, too, with a bit of luck. (This is especially so when Watson is presented as brave and loyal, but as so dense and misunderstanding that almost any reader feels smart by comparison.)

Thirdly, Karl E. Meyer in *The New York Times* in 1986:

Why Holmes?
     A good tuppence answer is that Doyle knew what he was doing, that Victorian London taken in the right dose is pure tonic and that Holmes as freelance knight errant appeals to American impatience with lumbering institutions. . . . What is distinctive about Holmes is his immutability — the scenes change, but never his personality. He is the first in a line of always-the-same characters reaching one extreme in Superman and Sam Spade, another in the Lone Ranger and John Wayne, and a third (just to be argumentative) in Ronald Reagan.

Some such replies emphasize the person of Sherlock Holmes, others the gaslit era in which he moves; there may even be a few that acknowledge the storytelling skill of Arthur Conan Doyle.

No one could contemplate meeting Sherlock Holmes in the flesh and making friends with him; brusque and insulting rejection would be all too likely. So mercurial and egotistical a figure might be a stimulating acquaintance, but no more. Unless, to be sure, one imagined him as a lover, for it is said that women like dangerous and unpredictable men, and there is not much doubt that some women readers (and women viewers of Jeremy Brett as Holmes, most of all) are half in love with Sherlock Holmes. But a thrilling lover may make a bad husband. Holmes is indeed a heroic figure of the kind Meyer suggests, but in the nature of things heroic figures walk alone. Lois Lane never quite makes contact with Superman, the Lone Ranger is forbidden the community of his former brethren in the Texas Rangers, and even King Arthur is betrayed by the one friend he thought he had. As perceptive writers have been saying for decades, the man to choose for a friend would be Watson rather than Holmes — not so much because of his supposed stupidity (he is not, in the Canon, unusually stupid) but because of his ordinary decency, the comfort with which he moves in normal society. Watson is the man who marries, repeatedly, and Watson stands flat-footed on the ground while Holmes moves eerily through London, in the city but not of it. His hobbies, talents and vices are affectations, his friendships nonexistent, his only relative as improbable a man as he is himself.

It is impossible to imagine Holmes in any activity but detection, the business of establishing justice when the ordinary mechanisms of society fail. Frequently acting around or above or against the law, he is guided by his own principles, and seems as arbitrary as God in his dealings with ordinary mortals. Here, much more than in his personality, lies his appeal to the modern reader, indeed much of the appeal of all detective stories. One can be scared half to death by the Baskerville hound, but it is a healthy kind of fear, with the necessary catharsis coming predictably in Chapter XIV. This experience is in fact a comfort to readers who have to double-lock their doors for fear of real-life burglars, and whose purses can be snatched at any moment on the filthy city street. Vengeance is mine, says Sherlock Holmes within the safe confines of the page. Shortly before what he expects will be his death, in "The Final Problem", he tells Watson that "The air of London is the sweeter for my presence." The police whose deficiencies he supplies are not actually corrupt, as the reader sometimes suspects modern police of being, but they are certainly bumblers, and the reader rejoices at the idea of a powerful, incorruptible, almost superhuman figure bringing murderers to justice and, when necessary, humbling kings.

Superheroes exist in modern literature too, of course, including the ones Meyer mentions, but the appeal of Holmes is greatly increased by his Victorian context. Victorian London is not being met as a new world, like Middle Earth or even the England of Shakespeare. It was the home of our great-grandparents and the immediate source of our own civilization. The streets Watson mentions in his narratives can still be walked by the Sherlockian pilgrim. The people he describes speak intelligible English, bet on horse-races, eat toast and take their fiancées to the theatre — why, once or twice Sherlock Holmes even uses the telephone. But just as London seems familiar, there comes reference to paregoric, a J pen or a governess, and the reader is reminded of a century-wide gulf. Perhaps most important in making Holmes's world different from our own is the absence of the internal combustion engine, with all its implications for urban sounds and smells, rapid movement across the city, and social instability. Hansom cabs — the horse-drawn predecessors of taxis — catch the imagination of modern readers precisely because they emphasize the limited mobility (and, one may imagine, the calm) of a society without cars.

The age of Holmes (say 1880 to 1905) is far enough in the past that today's readers do not know it first-hand, as Christopher Morley and the other early Sherlockians did, but its details are not entirely obscured either. The mind's-eye picture of London, circa 1895, and the scene presented in most movies about the period, is delightfully cozy: swirling fog outside the sitting-room window, trapezoidal gas-lamps casting a yellow glow on the cobblestones while a hansom rattles past. For a middle-class Briton, it must seem, everything was secure, from domestic comfort to economic prospects and the glory of Empire. A little attention to social history makes clear how unrealistic is this picture, summed up by Vincent Starrett as "that age before the world went all awry". The world has always been awry, and so were the 1890's, with as many difficulties of social change, unemployment, malnutrition, alcoholism and rumoured war as any other decade, including the present one. The careful reader of the Canon, indeed, will notice evidences of these problems, for Doyle knew his era well and got the details mostly right. But the average reader of detective fiction hardly wants realism. It is better to imagine one's hero striding through a world in which there were no systematic wrongs, so that the righting of individual wrongs (Grimesby Roylott bitten by his own poisonous serpent, James Windibank horsewhipped) completes the work of justice.

Farewell and hail. Arthur Conan Doyle wrote in the 1927 Preface to *The Case-Book of Sherlock Holmes* that his detective

> must go the way of all flesh, material or imaginary. One likes to think that there is some fantastic limbo for the children of imagination, some strange, impossible place where the beaux of Fielding may still make love to the belles of Richardson, where Scott's heroes still may strut, Dickens's delightful Cockneys still raise a laugh, and Thackeray's worldlings continue to carry on their reprehensible careers. Perhaps in some humble corner of such a Valhalla, Sherlock and his Watson may for a time find a place, while some more astute sleuth with some even less astute comrade may fill the stage which they have vacated.

Doyle was utterly wrong. Famous even by 1927, Sherlock Holmes and his Watson are world-famous now, and if they live in "some fantastic limbo" they live also on the television screen, the advertising billboard, and always the printed page, to say nothing of the never-vacated stage of the active imagination. "So they still live," Vincent Starrett wrote in *The Private Life of Sherlock Holmes*, "for those that love them well." But they live also for those who do not particularly love them but merely know that they existed — that they still exist, like Robin Hood or Cinderella. Meanwhile, who now reads Richardson or Fielding or Thackeray, or even Charles Dickens?

There is no need to imagine a more astute sleuth, for any shortcomings of the original Holmes have long since been supplied by the fancy of generations of readers. Duller and duller Watsons, meanwhile, have been provided to the point of satiation by screen-writers, an injustice that rankles with readers who understand the fine qualities that made the original Watson a worthy companion for Holmes. As for the beaux and belles, the Cockneys and (especially) the reprehensible worldlings, it is easiest to imagine them as clients and witnesses and villains as Holmes continues his brilliant work of detection, ranging across that "fantastic limbo" to right the wrongs and shine light on whatever may be in darkness.

Sherlock Holmes, who was conceived on a page of Arthur Conan Doyle's notebook and brought to birth in a shilling paperback, has escaped his creator's control. Surviving embarrassing distortions by advertisers and film directors, surviving parodies and caricatures, the decay of time and the damage of dog-eared pages, he has earned eternal life. Readers who can never get enough of his dancing grey eyes, his sardonic remarks, his courage and his energy have poured out a hundred years of affection on the stories of Sherlock Holmes, and on the character himself. In response to that passion, he has become for them — for us — a person, a companion, a friend. The Sherlock Holmes whom Arthur Conan Doyle wrote has become the Sherlock Holmes we love.

Appendix

The Sixty Tales

Each story title is listed (with its conventional J. F. Christ **ABBR**eviation in capitals) along with its date of first publication, and the volume and page of *The Annotated Sherlock Holmes* on which it begins.

A **STUD**y in Scarlet[1]	[December] 1887	1:143
The **SIGN** of the Four[1] [2]	February 1890	1:610

The Adventures of Sherlock Holmes

A **SCAN**dal in Bohemia	July 1891	1:346
The **RED**-**H**eaded League	August 1891	1:418
A Case of **IDEN**tity	September 1891	1:404
The **BOSC**ombe Valley Mystery	October 1891	2:134
The **FIVE** Orange Pips	November 1891	1:389
The Man with the **TWIS**ted Lip	December 1891	1:368
[3]The **BLUE** Carbuncle	January 1892	1:451
[3]The **SPECK**led Band	February 1892	1:243
[3]The **ENG**inee**R**'s Thumb	March 1892	2:209
[3]The **NOBL**e Bachelor	April 1892	1:281
[3]The **BERY**l Coronet	May 1892	2:282
[3]The **COPP**er Beeches	June 1892	2:114

The Memoirs of Sherlock Holmes

[3]**SILV**er Blaze	December 1892	2:261
[3]The **YELL**ow Face	February 1893	1:575
[3]The **STOC**k-broker's Clerk	March 1893	2:153
[3]The "**GLOR**ia Scott"	April 1893	1:107
[3]The **MUS**grave Ritual	May 1893	1:123
[3]The **REIG**ate Squires[4]	June 1893	1:331
[3]The **CROO**ked Man	July 1893	2:225
[3]The **RESI**dent Patient	August 1893	1:267
[3]The **GREE**k Interpreter	September 1893	1:590
[3]The **NAVA**l Treaty	October-November 1893	2:167
[3]The **FINA**l Problem	December 1893	2:301

The **HOUN**d of the Baskervilles[1]	August-April 1901-02	2:3

---

[1] Novel length; others are short stories.

[2] In many editions, just *The Sign of Four*.

[3] In the original publication, "The Adventure of" preceded this title.

[4] In its earliest publication, "The Reigate Squire"; in most American editions, "The Reigate Puzzle".

The Return of Sherlock Holmes

[3]The **EMPT**y House	September 1903	2:329
[3]The **NORW**ood Builder	October 1903	2:414
[3]The **DANC**ing Men	December 1903	2:527
[3]The **SOLI**tary Cyclist	December 1903	2:383
[3]The **PRIO**ry School	January 1904	2:607
[3]**BLAC**k Peter	February 1904	2:398
[3]**CHA**rle**S** Augustus Milverton	March 1904	2:558
[3]The **SIX** Napoleons	April 1904	2:572
[3]The Three [3] **STU**dents	June 1904	2:368
[3]The **GOLD**en Pince-Nez	July 1904	2:350
[3]The **MISS**ing Three-Quarter	August 1904	2:475
[3]The **ABBE**y Grange	September 1904	2:491
[3]The **SECO**nd Stain	December 1904	1:301
The VALLey of Fear[1]	September-May 1914-15	1:471

His Last Bow

WISTeria Lodge[5]	August 1908	2:238
[3]The **CARD**board Box[6]	January 1893	2:193
[3]The **RED** Circle[7]	March-April 1911	2:691
[3]The **BRUC**e-Partington Plans	December 1908	2:432
[3]The **DYIN**g Detective	November 1913	1:439
The Disappearance of **LADY** Frances Carfax	December 1911	2:656
[3]The **DEVI**l's Foot	December 1910	2:508
His **LAST** Bow[8]	September 1917	2:792

The Case Book of Sherlock Holmes

[3]The **ILLU**strious Client	November 1924	2:671
[3]The **BLAN**ched Soldier	October 1926	2:707
[3]The **MAZA**rin Stone	October 1921	2:735
[3]The Three [3] **GAB**les	September 1926	2:722
[3]The **SUSS**ex Vampire	January 1924	2:462
[3]The Three [3] **GAR**ridebs	October 1924	2:643
The Problem of **THOR** Bridge	February 1922	2:588
[3]The **CREE**ping Man	March 1923	2:751
[3]The **LION**'s Mane	November 1926	2:776
[3]The **VEIL**ed Lodger	January 1927	2:453
[3]**SHOS**combe Old Place	March 1927	2:630
[3]The **RETI**red Colourman	December 1926	2:546

---

[5] Formally, "The Adventure of Wisteria Lodge". First published as "The Singular Experience of Mr. John Scott Eccles: A Reminiscence of Mr. Sherlock Holmes".

[6] Appeared in the earliest book edition of *The Memoirs*, in its appropriate chronological place, but suppressed thereafter, and introduced into *His Last Bow* twenty years later.

[7] Originally subtitled "A Reminiscence of Sherlock Holmes".

[8] Subtitled "The War Service of Sherlock Holmes" or "An Epilogue of Sherlock Holmes".

Index

"SH" always means "Sherlock Holmes". A page number in **bold** type indicates the page where a term or topic is principally discussed. Titles of major Sherlockian journals are not always indexed where they are mentioned only as the source of a quotation. Definite articles are omitted at the beginning of titles.